EMERGENCY MEN!

The 26th Pennsylvania Volunteer Militia and the Gettysburg Campaign

By Cooper H. Wingert

SCHROEDER PUBLICATIONS

2013

Published by
SCHROEDER PUBLICATIONS
131 Tanglewood Drive
Lynchburg, VA 24502
www.civilwar-books.com
civilwarbooks@yahoo.com

ISBN-1-889246-63-8

ISBN-978-1-889246-63-5

Table of Contents

Photographs, Maps and Illustrations

Acknowledgments

Completing this volume on the 26th Pennsylvania Volunteer Militia of 1863 has been a delightful experience. In the process, I have had the pleasure of working with many knowledgeable persons whom I take this space to thank.

Four people deserve especial and separate recognition based solely upon the sheer volume and multitude of their contributions. First and foremost, Scott L. Mingus Sr. of York, has proved not only a good friend but a key component to this book. Not only did he read over the entire manuscript several times and offer his thoughts, but during the writing process gave me his expert opinion as I tried to decipher the history of this regiment. His assistance is invaluable, and I am ever indebted to him.

Carl Klase, Assistant-Administrator of Pennypacker Mills County Historic Site, has too proved a good friend and has contributed enormous mounds of material from the Pennypacker Mills archives to this work. Carl is undoubtedly one of the world's foremost experts on Governor Samuel Pennypacker, who served in the 26th, and I greatly appreciate his time, help and generosity.

Another person who deserves special recognition is Brian Stuart Kesterson of Lubeck, West Virginia. An expert on the 17th Virginia Cavalry Regiment, which faced off against the 26th Militia, Brian kindly provided me with photos and accounts of members of that unit, along with much-appreciated time out of his busy schedule.

Finally, John Heiser of Gettysburg took time to research and construct several wonderful maps to compliment the text. John also aided me in my research efforts by way of many suggestions and leads, as well as making available the bountiful resources of the Gettysburg National Military Park Library.

Many other people have contributed to the volume; Ken Frew, Librarian, Dauphin County Historical Society; Brian C. Kissler, Archivist, Lebanon County Historical Society; Scott Sagar, Curator of Collections, Lycoming County Historical Society; Carolyn Sautter and the Special Collections staff at Gettysburg College; Dr. Richard J. Sommers, U.S. Army Military History Institute, Carlisle Barracks; Richard Tritt, Photo Curator, Cumberland County Historical Society.

Cooper H. Wingert
Enola, Pennsylvania
December 8, 2012

Introduction

Great Stir and Excitement Among All Classes

For many Pennsylvanians, the news they awoke to on the morning of June 12, 1863, confirmed their worst fears. That Friday morning, the residents of the Keystone State learned through their newspapers and word of mouth of a proclamation issued by their governor, Republican Andrew Gregg Curtin. "Information has been obtained by the War Department that a large rebel force, composed of cavalry, artillery, and mounted-infantry, has been prepared for the purpose of making a raid into Pennsylvania."[1]

The seemingly invincible Robert E. Lee and his Army of Northern Virginia proceeded north down the Shenandoah Valley during the first two weeks of June 1863, signifying the beginning of the Southern general's second expedition north of the Potomac River.

For Lee, there were many and valuable advantages he could garner for his cause by way of an invasion of the Keystone State. The fresh farm fields of Pennsylvania and Maryland could feed Lee's warriors while simultaneously relieving war-torn and pillaged Virginia of the same duty. The invasion also provided ample opportunity for Lee to embarrass Northern war efforts, particularly by capturing Pennsylvania's capital, Harrisburg, or threatening big transportation or business hubs, such as Pittsburgh or Philadelphia.

So far, Pennsylvania had not become a central theatre of the war. The closest encounter was in September 1862, during the Maryland Campaign, when Lee's Southern army was turned back at the Battle of Antietam near Sharpsburg, Maryland. Pennsylvania was aroused by its governor, and hastily raised, equipped and dispatched 25 regiments of infantry along with dozens of independent companies of infantry, cavalry and artillery to her border to defend herself. However, this effort proved fruitless when Rebel forces proved too battered after the bloody clash at Antietam to continue northward. That was the closest the second most-populous state in the Union had come to a large-scale invasion so far, save for a few cavalry raids which had traversed the Mason-Dixon Line.

However, in early June 1863 the Keystone State was vaulted back into the spotlight as Lee's butternut ranks proceeded north once again. Steps to defend the state were first taken as late as June 10, a full week after Lee had begun his march northward, when the War Department formed the Departments of the Monongahela and the Susquehanna. The former, based in Pittsburgh, embraced the part of Pennsylvania west of Johnstown and the Laurel Hill mountain range. Additionally, it would include counties in Ohio and what only a number of days later would became West Virginia. Its counterpart, the Department of the Susquehanna, incorporated the portion of

Pennsylvania east of Johnstown and the Laurel Hill mountain range—including Harrisburg and the Cumberland Valley.[2] The latter was led by Maj. Gen. Darius N. Couch, formerly commander of the Federal Second Army Corps at Fredericksburg and Chancellorsville. Dismayed by the performance of Army of the Potomac commander Joseph Hooker, Couch informed President Abraham Lincoln "that he had served through two disastrous campaigns rendered so by the incompetency of the commanders," and having "no faith in any improvement," he "requested to be separated[.]"[3]

Wartime carte-de-vista of Major General Darius Couch, from Brady's National Portrait Gallery, published by E and H. T. Anthony, New York City. (*Author's Collection*)

The native of Putnam County, New York, had a daunting task ahead of him. When Couch arrived in Harrisburg, he learned that his new department had little to boast of—lest he define a department as sixteen ailing veterans of the War of 1812, the youngest 68 and the oldest 76.[4] Refugees from throughout the Cumberland Valley flocked to the state capital and lands beyond with their livestock and valuables. As every day passed, the vanguard of Lee's army drew nearer to their objective. On June 22, Lee made his intentions clear when he wrote to Second Corps commander, Lieutenant General Richard S. Ewell: "If Harrisburg comes within your means, capture it."[5]

This engraving, titled "Pennsylvania Farmers Removing their Families and Property from Chambersburg Toward the Susquehanna River," was published in the 1885 publication, *The Pictorial Battles of the Civil War*. (*Author's Collection*)

By June 15, the situation had become serious enough to prompt President Abraham Lincoln—urged on by Pennsylvania Governor Andrew Curtin—to call for 100,000 volunteers to defend against the invasion. Half of this burden was laid upon Pennsylvania in a fair manner. Governor Curtin issued a similar proclamation in accordance with Lincoln's, for 50,000 men. "I now appeal to all the citizens of Pennsylvania who love liberty and are mindful of the history and traditions of their revolutionary fathers," Curtin pleaded, "and who feel that it is a sacred duty to guard and maintain the free institutions of our country, who hate treason and its abettors, and who are willing to defend their homes and their firesides, and do invoke them to rise in their might, and rush to the rescue in this hour of imminent peril." The Republican governor made clear that this was no laughing matter—"The issue is one of preservation or destruction. It invokes considerations paramount to all matters of mere expediency; and all questions of local interest, all ties, social and political, all impulses of a personal and partisan character, sink by comparison into insignificance." However, Curtin never raised that figure, or for that matter anywhere even close to it. Remarkably few Pennsylvanians came out to defend their homes—many had doubts as to the seriousness of the situation. The defense of the Keystone state capital would depend largely upon militia and National Guard troops dispatched from New York.[6] However, throughout the commonwealth, numerous pockets of men were buzzing with excitement.

Governor Andrew Gregg Curtin
(From, McClure, *Lincoln and Men of War Times*, 1892)

"In a few of the country towns," explained future Pennsylvania Governor Samuel Whitaker Pennypacker, "there was some little effort to raise men, and in Philadelphia, a meeting was held, the newspaper called on the citizens with glowing words to volunteer but nobody appeared to be willing to shoulder the musket." Pennypacker cites several reasons for this remarkable reluctance to enlist among the male population of the Keystone State—first and foremost, many Democrats believed that the entire invasion was a political scheme hatched by Governor Curtin—a Republican—to save his reelection campaign by keeping them from the polls. Additionally, the previous fall the militia was called out during Lee's Maryland Campaign but did not prove to be of any use. Pennypacker reasoned that it was "the opinion of most persons that it was a mere cavalry raid which would be settled without much difficulty, and there was no necessity for such a great disturbance or interfering with the transaction of business."[7]

Throughout the day of June 16, Pennypacker—then 20 years old and living in the small village of Mont Clare, near Phoenixville, a short distance west of Philadelphia—contemplated joining one of the numerous companies being raised and transported by rail to Harrisburg. He came to the conclusion that if a friend would enlist with him, he would do so. Pennypacker asked his friend, Horace Lloyd, who told young Samuel to return the next day and he would be ready with his decision. "Immediately" after breakfast the following morning, Pennypacker returned to find Lloyd's hometown of nearby Phoenixville in a "perfect furore of excitement." The Phoenixville Iron Works offered to pay their employees one dollar per day to each man that would enlist, and ensured them that their jobs would be reserved for them when they returned.[8]

Young Samuel had spent the winter of 1861-1862 working at a store in Philadelphia which sold iron produced at nearby furnaces. "I assisted Oliver C. Lund, a gouty, white-haired old retainer, perched upon a high stool, to keep the books and also rolled out the kegs of nails and horseshoes, when they needed to be shipped, and did whatever else was to be done," recalled Pennypacker. In the summer of 1862, he learned that Montgomery County would be holding an examination to select teachers for the upcoming winter at its schools. "Without a word to any one, I put a saddle on the bay horse, rode over the Trappe, in company with numerous other applicants took the examination, and in the evening came home with a certificate in my pocket."[9]

At his request, Samuel was given the Mont Clare school, "a little one-story stone building with one room." There Pennypacker taught for eight months, receiving a pay of 30 dollar per month. "The children were of both sexes and ranged from little tots, trying to learn their A, B, C's, to young men and women eighteen years of age, and in all there were from fifty to sixty scholars," later wrote Pennypacker.[10]

This photograph of Samuel Pennypacker was taken only several months before his service in the 26th Militia, while he was employed as a school teacher in Mont Clare. The photo appeared as part of an article in the Philadelphia *Public Ledger* during Pennypacker's term as governor, titled, "Stages in the Life of the Governor." (Philadelphia *Public Ledger*, November 26, 1905)

Carte-de-vista of Samuel Pennypacker, circa 1869.
(*Pennypacker Mills Historic Site*)

But now, in June 1863, Pennypacker was preparing to enlist in the defense of his home state. "Going into Ullman's sitting room where V. N. Shaffer was writing down the names of the recruits rapidly," reminisced Pennypacker, "I was informed that they expected to leave for Harrisburg in the 9½ A.M. train. As it was then 8 o'clock, the time for preparation was exceedingly short, so telling Shaffer to put my name among the rest, I hurried home to get things ready." Samuel later reflected that he believed his mother "would have made more objection to my going than she did, but I was in such a hurry that she had very little opportunity. However, she made considerable opposition, but perceiving that I was decided, assisted me in tying up a red horse blanket with a piece of clothes line so that it could be thrown across the shoulder, prepared some provision consisting of a piece of cheese, several boiled eggs, with sundry slices of bread and butter which were put in one of the boys' school satchels, and a tin cup fastened upon the strap, and thus accoutered, I bade all good-bye, except grandfather who was out in the field, and hastened over to town."

As Pennypacker scrambled into Phoenixville, he found that the departure of the company had been delayed until later that evening. Joseph T. McCord—a member of the company who had formerly seen service in McClellan's 1862 Peninsular Campaign in Company G, 30th Pennsylvania—formed the recruits into ranks and "marched through the borough in the dust to the sound of the fife and drum, and returning to the hotel held an election for officers[.]" John D. Jenkins, a Mexican War veteran and High Constable, was elected captain, McCord first lieutenant, and A. L. Chalfant—another Mexican War Veteran—as second lieutenant. Pennypacker recalled that Jenkins "had the reputation of being very brave and determined, but was entirely unacquainted with the modern drill, and it seems to me, rather slow in thought and action." As for McCord, many in the company thought him "to be of a tyrannical disposition," but Samuel "preferred him to any of the others."[11]

After their lunch, the students of Pennsylvania College in Gettysburg gathered as usual around the soon-to-be infamous town—some at Buehler's book store, while others assembled at Horner's drug store. The group at the book store noted a call for volunteers and wasted no time adding their names to that list. Whether or not the students knew it, one of their own had already called a faculty meeting at the college, where he proposed and received an agreement that, considering the students had but three weeks left before graduation, the college would graduate them early so they could join in the defense of their state. The president of the college, Dr. Henry L. Baugher, approved of the conditions, but cautioned the students as to the grievances of war; the latter which must have been especially very heartfelt to him, considering he had lost his son at the Battle of Shiloh the previous April. "Wise though his counsel may have been," recalled student Edmund W. Meissenhelder, "yet no human agency could have stayed the ardor of the students."[12]

Dr. Henry L. Baugher, President of Pennsylvania College in 1863.
(Special Collections, Gettysburg College)

Student W. E. Parson had just finished a "bountiful dinner" at a nearby club and was "lounging with my old chum [James A. Beeber]" in front of Dr. Horner's Drug Store. Fellow student Luther Jacobs then joined the duo, "contributing his usual share of jollity[.]" About this time someone announced the proclamation from Governor Curtin calling for volunteers to defend the state. Beeber at once proposed to leave on the next train for their homes to join companies there, as many of the young scholars had done in 1862. The jovial Jacobs inquired; "Why can't we get up a company among ourselves, here?" "One remark led to another," explained Parson, "our group enlarged, and became more excited, until to test the matter we went in to Dr. Horner's Drug Store got a sheet of foolscap, put down a single sentence stating the object, and our names following."[13] And so at Buehler's Book Store and Horner's Drug Store in Gettysburg, the "College Guards" were born.

"When the rebels crossed the Potomac and the Gov. issued his second call for the Militia, all the excitement of college was lost in love of country and about sixty of us enlisted," Pennsylvania College student Frank Richards informed his friend.[14] Gettysburg civilian Sarah Broadhead recorded in her diary that "no alarm was felt until Governor Curtin sent a telegram . . . . This made us begin to realize the fact that we were in some danger from the enemy, and some persons, thinking the Rebels were near, became very much frightened . . . ."[15]

The rolls were open to not only college students, but also local citizens. In total, the company consisted of 83 men, composed of 61 current and past collegians—including several from the Lutheran Theological Seminary—21 "boys" from the town, and only one non-Gettysburger—14-year-old drummer-boy Henry Melchior Muhlenberg Richards of Reading, who would join the company in Harrisburg. The company gathered at the college campus, and tendered command to Professor F. A. Muhlenberg, who declined stating that it "would interfere with the discharge of his official duties at the College." The company then formed line in front of Linnaean Hall, where they elected their officers. Frederick Klinefelter, a graduate of the Class of 1860 and a student at the Lutheran Seminary, was elected captain. Unlike many of the collegiate volunteers, Klinefelter had prior military experience as a private in the three-month 16th Pennsylvania Infantry in 1861. William F. Hinkle, a student in the Preparatory Department of Pennsylvania College, was elected first lieutenant, and Luther W. Slater, who had been a student in the Preparatory Department from 1860-1862, was elected second lieutenant. Before long, the company had earned itself several aliases, such as "The Gettysburg Company," "The College Guards," and "The College Company," among others.[16]

On Wednesday morning, June 17, the war-bound collegians gathered in Gettysburg's town square, and were addressed by Professor Muhlenberg who "counseled to a faithful discharge of every duty, that they might prove . . . honor to the State, to Pennsylvania College, and to themselves." Muhlenberg wished them God's blessing, and at 8 a.m., the "College Guards" boarded the train for Harrisburg.[17]

The journey to Harrisburg was hectic to say the least. In what may have been an omen of things to come, about five to six miles east of Gettysburg near Goulden's Station, the train derailed. This minor mishap was enough to send two of the "town boys" who had joined the company without permission of their parents sprinting down the railroad tracks towards home. One of these runaways returned to Gettysburg and reached his home before dinner, leaving his parents completely unaware to his short military excursion until told by another townsperson. No one was injured in the accident, save the pride of the two "town boys." In less than fifteen minutes, the Gettysburgers had transferred to another car, and proceeded to Harrisburg without further incident.[18]

An 1863 view of the Lutheran Seminary. A number of the men in the "College Guards," including Captain Klinefelter, were students at the seminary in 1863. (*Library of Congress*)

In Union Mills, Maryland, near the Pennsylvania border, on June 15, the Shriver homestead was overwhelmed with "flying rumors concerning the approach of the rebels thro' Frederick and at various points were in circulation." News of Governor Curtin's proclamation had not yet reached the home. 26-year-old farmer Henry Wirt Shriver was still tending to his strawberries. Little did he know that in less than 24 hours, he would be off to war.

Word of Curtin's proclamation and definite confirmation of the invasion reached the Shriver homestead about 1 a.m. the following morning, when two friends awoke Henry with shouts that "the rebels were approaching." Further news reached the Shriver homestead when family friend Dave Winebrenner paid a surprise visit, telling them of his intention to go to Harrisburg and enlist. Henry and his brother, Frederick Augustus Shriver, "determined that one of us ought to go with him." Henry drew the lot, "so saying good bye we started about ½ past 9 [p.m.] getting to Hanover at 12 [p.m.]."

"Felt rather blue this morning about leaving," logged Henry in his diary the following morning, "but . . . [gathered] my courage to the sticking point." While in Hanover, Shriver met his father, who, like many skeptics, thought "my going [to Harrisburg] was nonsense but finally agreed." Shriver purchased a shirt and pair of boots, said his final goodbyes, and went to the railroad depot, where, with 52 other enlistees from Hanover, they listened to a patriotic address from some prominent men in the town, prayed, and left en route for the distressed state capital.[19]

The above are three examples of Pennsylvanians—or in Shriver's case, Marylanders—willingly enlisting in the defense of the Keystone State. But looking at the larger picture of the thousands of other Pennsylvanians who remained undeterred in their devotion to defend their state, more questions are raised. Who were these men? Where did they come from, and why did they come? This next section is reserved to examine examples of enlistees from various different militia regiments across the state.

William J. Jones of Lykens, Dauphin County was 36 years old in 1863. During the summer of 1863, Jones would serve as First Lieutenant of Company D in the 26th. Jones certainly had already felt the horrifying effects of war. His younger brother, Benjamin Franklin Jones, a 19-year-old schoolteacher from Pottsville, Schuylkill County, had joined the 25th Pennsylvania Infantry, a three-month unit at Harrisburg in 1861. After being mustered out, Benjamin joined the 52nd Pennsylvania and was killed in action at the Battle of Fair Oaks near Richmond on May 31, 1862, and buried on the field.

His older brother, John J. Jones Jr., was 37 years old and the father of five children. John was a resident of Newton, New Jersey, a small town near Camden. He enlisted as a private in the 15th New Jersey Volunteer Infantry, and was killed in action at Chancellorsville on May 3, 1863. Even more remorse had come previously when the trio's father, John J. Jones, Sr., died four months prior to the outbreak of the war.[20] He had lost his father just prior to the war and two brothers had been killed during the war, yet 36-year-old William still volunteered to defend his state.

17-year-old John F. Curry of Glen Carbon, a small village near Minersville in Schuylkill County, reportedly ran away from his home to join the 39th Pennsylvania Militia. His brother, Daniel F. Curry, 18 years old, was commissioned a first lieutenant in the 53rd Pennsylvania Militia. Perhaps the two younger brothers took inspiration from their common older brother, Michael Curry, who had served in the 5th Pennsylvania Infantry at the outbreak of the war. Yet Michael was not on active duty—he could have volunteered as well, but opted not to.[21] Daniel F. Graham joined Company F of the 26th even after his older brother was also one of the fallen at Fair Oaks.[22] From analysis, it appears many soldiers who had previously served felt they had already done their part, and in-turn failed to reenlist during the "emergency" of June and July 1863.

Benjamin Franklin Jones, 52nd Pennsylvania Volunteer Infantry
(*U.S. Army Military History Institute*)

While the latter statement may be true in general, it certainly does not apply unequivocally. Examples of veterans from earlier in the war enlisting in the "emergency militia," are plentiful. Peter A. Filbert had been a second lieutenant in the "Washington Light Infantry"—Company D, 10th Pennsylvania Volunteer Infantry—at the beginning of the war. Upon his enlistment expiring, he reenlisted in the 96th Pennsylvania Infantry as captain of Company B and was promoted to lieutenant colonel. Home during the time of the invasion, Filbert, a veteran of Antietam, Fredericksburg and many other engagements, became major of the 39th Pennsylvania Militia—one of many cases of seasoned veterans in the Keystone State militia.[23]

Lieutenant Colonel Peter A. Filbert, 96th Pennsylvania Volunteer Infantry
(*U.S. Army Military History Institute*)

Dr. Robert S. Simington had served as the surgeon for the 14th and 93rd Pennsylvania Infantry; he was even slightly wounded at the Battle of Malvern Hill. Simington was forced to resign due to illness, and was therefore home during the invasion. He enlisted in the 41st Pennsylvania Militia and served as that regiment's surgeon.[24]

A new generation of soldiers who had not previously tendered their services came along with the veterans in the 1863 "Emergency Militia." Charles Snell, father of three sons, two of which were already serving in the war, enlisted in Company G of the 26th Militia. One of his sons had been mortally wounded early on in the conflict. Snell was aroused by the Rebel presence in his home state and therefore enlisted. His thirteen year old son, meanwhile "remained at home chafing on the bits because he could not go."[25] Samuel Yorks Thompson of Danville did not enlist upon the outbreak of the war, instead assisting his father in his business and beginning his medical studies. However, when his state was threatened he responded—in September 1862, he enlisted to defend against Lee's Maryland Campaign, though like many others never saw action. When Southern forces came north again in June 1863, Thompson once again readily enlisted in Company E of the 41st Pennsylvania Militia.[26]

Samuel Yorks Thompson
(*U.S. Army Military History Institute*)

Once again, the question to be asked is "Why?" Why did those who had not before enlisted suddenly spring to their feet at the call of their governor? Why did some seasoned veterans enlist while others remained at home? To these questions, there is no one answer. For each man, there were different motives and reasons which either prompted him to or not to enlist. Nicholas Rice was a member of the 50th Pennsylvania Infantry, home due to prior injury in the war. He was therefore a seasoned veteran of the Army of the Potomac. Rice reported his reason as well as the reason of many others for enlisting in the militia: "When the rebels entered our state in the year 1863, I had so far recovered that I felt able to do something towards its defense. There was great stir and excitement among all classes and conditions of people. Men who had excused themselves [from enlisting] up to this time, either from personal interests at home, or a half sympathy with the south, began to wake up and realize that the war was being brought to almost their own door." Perhaps Rice was also reinvigorated by the death of his brother, Captain Edson Rice of the 57th Pennsylvania Infantry, at Chancellorsville less than two months earlier.[27]

There is perhaps no better symbolization of the 1863 "Emergency Militia" than Rice's above remarks. Much frustration among the ranks of Union armies had been expressed as to the remarkable apathy expressed by those in the North who remained at home. John W. Ames, a frustrated U.S. Regular in the Army of the Potomac penned home that he hoped Lee "will get into Pennsylvania or even into New York, for I must say that the North is getting to plethoric with contracts and speculations, that it would be a blessing to have them aroused even by the horrors of war in their own domains."[28] The large majority of men who volunteered during the "Emergency" of 1863 were greatly aroused by the nearness of the war to their doorstep. Some, however were motivated by more selfish intents—a fear for the dreaded draft. After all, those who enlisted in the "Emergency Militia" were thought to be exempt from the draft. William Gautz of Glen Rock in southern York County—a member of the 26th—was in 1863, 25 years old and had been married for two years. He enlisted purely to avoid the draft.[29]

Reflecting on June 29, as the Southern Army was at the outskirts of Harrisburg, an oil operative from Oil City in the northwestern corner of the state observed: "[I]t has been almost three waks [sic] since we first heard that the soil of our noble old state was about to be invaded by the treacherous enemy[.] [A]t first we thought it would not amount to much and that it was merely a scare in consequence of which I felt pretty easy about the matter but time passed by and still they were not checked and this morning we had a Telegram that they were within four miles of Harrisburgh, just to think of our own state Capitol being taken by a Rebel Hoard, and so many strong able bodied men who if had but at once gone forward at the commencement would have prevented such a humiliating occurrence and even now all seem to be holding back[.]"[30]

The 1863 "Emergency Men" were diverse in their own, varying from young, green boys who loved their state to seasoned veterans who reenlisted because they felt they could lend a hand. The young, green men occupied the large majority of the ranks in most of the 35 infantry regiments raised that summer, and the 26th was no different. In Company G of the 26th, the oldest company officer, First Lieutenant Ellis Bryan, was only 24, while Captain Elias C. Rishel was 21, and the second lieutenant was 20. In all, the average age of the entire regiment rests around 24, the youngest member 14 and the oldest 62.[31] The invasion stirred the passions of many Pennsylvanians, old and young, green and veteran, who put their lives on the line in defense of their homes.

Chapter 1

A Regiment is Born:
The Regiment Forms at Camp Curtin

The Hanover Company and Shriver arrived in Harrisburg about 1 p.m. on June 17. They were formed in double file and marched out to Camp Curtin at once. "I expected to find every body in a hurry," Shriver recalled, "and all the bustle naturally attendant upon a beleaguered city; but there was no excitement visible whatever-people regarded us with as much curiosity as if we had marched thro' town during times of peace-we saw nothing of intrenchments [sic] nor in fact anything indicating war except a few carloads of cannon standing on the RR track." When Shriver and the rest of the company reached at Camp Curtin, about an hour after their initial arrival in the city, the Hanoverians "were perfectly astonished to find only about 700 men here in all . . . there seemed to be a poor show for defending the city against a single regiment of Rebels."

At Camp Curtin, 12 tents were allotted to the Hanover Company. "Our rations were served shortly after we had our tent fixed," detailed Shriver. "[W]e had salt boiled beef and army crackers [hardtack]—the beef tasted first rate and it made a hearty meal[.] [W]e had nothing except our fingers and pocket knives for dissecting the beef which was in an old pan. Tin cups were furnished, one to each man[.] We managed during the afternoon to get a camp kettle, and a barrel with both heads out which we laid on its side making a first rate cupboard." In this cupboard, Shriver and his fellow mess placed their ration of hardtack and beef, which was to last them until noon the next day. The company was then called to ranks to elect a captain. Shriver favored 29-year-old John Summerfield Forrest, but 31-year-old Joseph S. Jenkins was generally preferred and "elected by acclamation." Jenkins appointed subordinate officers, which were to serve until the company was mustered in and would elect those posts.

"Hardly anything was said or thought of the rebels," Shriver informed his brother. So much so, that after electing Jenkins as their captain, the majority of the company went into Harrisburg "to make a few purchases." The Maryland native and several Hanoverians journeyed to the capitol grounds, where the Democratic State Convention was in session but no business was going on. Ascending the Capitol Building to the dome, Shriver noted; "The [Susquehanna] river from the dome is the most beautiful I think I ever saw[.] [T]he river studded with Islands covered with rich foliage stretches away as far as the eye can reach above and below the town while the two splendid, bridges [the Cumberland Valley Railroad bridge and the Camelback bridge], almost, or quite a mile long, add very much to the picturesqueness of the scene[.]"[1]

Shriver bought four pewter spoons, a comb, a large spoon, a wisp "to sweep out our tent," as well as an empty box for a table. Returning to camp around 6 p.m., the company enjoyed "first rate coffee and beef with crackers [hardtack] for supper[.]" For the remainder of the evening, the Hanoverians "walked about or sat in our tents[.]" At about 10 p.m., they turned in for the night. "[W]e spread one blanket on the floor," explained Shriver, "[and] folded one and laid it on the pillow foundation [of three stacked wooded boards] and with the other [blanket] covered ourselves."[2]

In the next company "street" behind the Hanoverians was a company from Norristown, who, according to the Marylander, "are great singers[.] [T]he fact is the whole camp is great in singing, all hands were at it nearly all night[.] Some of the songs were new to me and were very good[.] 'Way down in the Louisiana Lowlands low' is a nice thing I wish I could describe . . . . 'Weeping sad and lonely' is absolutely run into the ground already[.]"

About midnight a "Tremendous thunder storm" came over the camp. "I thought the rain would beat our tent to the ground," Shriver recalled, "but it protected us finely[.] The lighting was incessant[.] I never saw anything like it before."[3]

"We could not sleep much[,]" explained the Marylander, "the natural excitement attendant upon our novel situation and the continual singing, hurrahing and general uproar prevented our falling sleepy." Shriver also contributed their lack of sleep to the nearby railroad cars, "which pass within 40 feet of our quarters, every hour all night [and] make the most awful noises as they approach and pass." During this first night in camp, one member of the company awoke frightened and panicked, believing that a train passing nearby was "rushing right among us."[4]

"You would be surprised to see how comfortable we are fixed," detailed the Maryland native. Many Hanoverians re-staked their tents after the down pour of the previous evening, making them "as tight as a drum." Numerous men were annoyed "exceedingly" by "some kind of bugs creeping or flying about[.]" In general, little was done—no drilling or, in Shriver's words no "anything"—save the passing of dozens of rumors. "[T]here is a great deal of disputing about the meaning of [Governor] Curtin's Call and fears are entertained that we will be retained in the U.S. Service after the rebels are cleared out," penned a concerned Shriver. The "most reliable accounts" that the company could get their hands on indicated that the rebels "had already left," but this they would soon learn was not so. In evaluating his dabble into military life after a full 24 hours at Camp Curtin, Shriver observed: "So far, my camp life experience has been really pleasant[.] I expected the worst and have been most agreeably disappointed."[5]

The College Guards were but an hour behind Shriver and the Hanoverians, arriving in the distressed Keystone State capital city about 2 p.m. on June 17. At 5 p.m., they were conducted to Camp Curtin on the northern outskirts of town. Before leaving the city, College Student Mathias H. Richards could not help but notice that the participants of the State

Democratic Convention, who were at this time nominating Judge George Woodward to run against Governor Curtin in the fall, "rather misbehaved themselves."[6]

As the company arrived at Camp Curtin, a lieutenant on General Couch's staff requested they be immediately mustered into service under terms only specified as for the duration of the "emergency" or six months. Many of the Gettysburgers were hesitant to do so, and were certainly not alone in their hesitation. Numerous Pennsylvania militiamen were concerned about the lack of definiteness surrounding the term of service for the "emergency," and feared they would be retained after the invasion was over. Would the "emergency" be adapted to mean the duration of the war? These factors were surely part of an important discussion held by the largely collegiate company shortly after arriving in Camp Curtin. The Gettysburgers "talked the matter over, and determined that there was no time to stand on fine points."[7]

The company was mustered in that evening. Department commander Couch summoned a number of men from the company to serve as clerks at his headquarters and in the Department's Signal Corps. Couch had learned "that the majority of this company were students," and therefore thought highly of the company's men. Several examples among many include Privates George M. Beltzhoover, Theodore L. Seip and Jacob D. Schinale, all of whom were detailed as clerks at General Couch's headquarters on June 20 while the company lay in Camp Curtin.[8]

It was Colonel James A. Beaver of the 148th Pennsylvania Infantry who initially began detailing men from the College Guards. Beaver, recovering from wounds suffered at Chancellorsville, had been temporarily assigned to be commandant of Camp Curtin by General Couch. Beaver recalled:

The militia had been called out and were pouring into Camp Curtin by the thousand. The next morning news was brought to the General that Captain {William} Tarbutton, who had charge of the camp, had unceremoniously left and that pandemonium had broken loose among the crowds of unorganized men who were there assembled. The General in some way discovered that I had been in charge of the outside work of Camp Curtin in 1861, when Colonel Welch of the 45th {Pennsylvania} Regiment had been in command of the camp. He asked me to go out and assume command. I felt utterly unable to do so but, upon his insistent request, I called a carriage and drove out. The scene which met me, as I entered the gate, is indescribable. The entire camp was a mass of unorganized men, without semblance of order. Fortunately, I encountered almost immediately a company from Gettysburg, composed almost entirely of students from Pennsylvania College. The headquarters of the camp were upstairs but I was unable to mount the stairs and seized a vacant building near the gate, called the boys of this company around me, instructed them in a very short time how to make out requisitions for camp equipage, wood and provisions, explained the difference between quartermaster and commissary stores, pointed out the location of each of these departments and sent them around with blank requisitions, directing them to call upon the Captains of companies and fill the requisitions for them for what they were entitled to of camp equipage and also of commissary stores. In a very short time fires began to be kindled all over the camp and, as the companies became supplied with camp kettles, mess pans, plates, knives and forks and with rations to cook, the scene entirely changed and, before night, the camp assumed a military aspect and, in a few days, we were sending organized regiments to the front.[9]

Captain Frederick Klinefelter, Company A
(Special Collections, Gettysburg College)

"Then the thunder clouds that had been threatening a long time burst in all their fury," penned home Corporal Mathias H. Richards, one of the many students within the company. "We had about the distance of a square to go [to our tents], which I covered in about the quickest time I ever made, escaping a severe wetting." Rations were served that evening, consisting of Hardtack, beef that was "rather salty and boiled," and coffee with sugar. "[T]he coffee [was] best of all, the biscuit [hardtack] . . . passable, and the meat not inviting in appearance and by a mental effort able to be forced down," recounted Richards.[10]

"Night came at last," recalled Private Edmund W. Meissenhelder, "And who of that brave company will ever forget the first night in Camp Curtin?

The wild pranks of 'boys let loose from school,' the practical jokes, the college songs, the loud laughter, the genial uproar of hearty good-fellowship, lasting long into the night. And some will perchance recall the coarse song and coarser jest of neighbors less refined. But 'silence came,' at last, 'to heal the blows of sound.' By many the weary night was spent in the board, of all things in the world unlike a bed of down; others, worn out by the fatigue of the day, wooed refreshing sleep, to be broken only by the rushing trains." Corporal Mathias Richards wrote of his experience that first night in camp: "Fortunately I had a gum blanket and kept quite dry, but I was always at the wet side of the tent, six in a tent eight feet square . . . . I kept dry but not cool, perspiring most woefully and slept might little. Then, to add to our distress, every ten minutes a train came thundering along. In the tents were swearing and drunken revelry."[11]

About midnight "came the fierce crash of heaven's artillery, the vivid lighting and the descending torrent," and, as Meissenhelder remarked, the company "had its first brief lesson of war's discomforts, in aching limbs and well-soaked clothing." The night is best summarized by Richards, who quipped that "morning came as a pleasant relief." [12]

The morning of June 18 dawned "bright and clear" as the College Guards arose from their tents, "in vain essaying to make themselves comfortable and presentable after a miserable night." Putting the miseries of the night behind them, the young collegians were glad to be visited by close friends and family. Drills began to be conducted on a regular schedule. "We are now getting down to a regular routine of camp life," logged Corporal William Henry Rupp in his diary.[13]

Samuel Pennypacker and the Phoenixville Company arrived in Harrisburg around 10:30 p.m. on the evening of June 17. "I recall with considerable amusement," later reminisced Pennypacker, "the expectation I had formed of what would be our reception. I had supposed as a matter of course, and I think many of the rest had the same idea, that the Governor would have some officer at the depot ready to receive us, comfortable quarters prepared for us, and treat us as if we were of some consequence. We were, therefore, surprised," continued Pennypacker, "and our feelings somewhat chilled, to find that we were left to provide for ourselves and seek accommodation as best we might. As a company we represented so much strength, but personally we were of no importance whatever."[14]

Because there were no officials present to give any direction to the Phoenixville recruits, "after deliberating a while" the men drifted towards the Capitol grounds. There they found the Democratic State Convention or as Pennypacker termed it, "The Copperhead convention," in session in the State House of Representatives. From outside they heard "shouting, hurrahing and . . . inflammatory speeches, while the pavement, the stone porch, and the floor of the galleries were covered with militia, trying to sleep amidst the din. The thought was enough to anger a saint," wrote an incensed Pennypacker. "[T]he Capital of the State threatened by the rebels . . . and those who respond compelled . . . [to] listen to the disloyal yells of the enemies of the country comfortably quartered within."[15]

This photograph shows the original state capitol building in Harrisburg, constructed in 1822 and burnt in 1897. Samuel Pennypacker, the owner of this photograph, inscribed on the reverse side: "My first night in Harrisburg in 1863 I slept upon its stone steps[.]" (*Photographs and Draughts, Samuel Pennypacker Private Papers, MG 171, Pennsylvania State Archives*)

The future governor's first night in the city from which one day he would govern the commonwealth was not his most pleasant. Pennypacker, friend Horace Lloyd and comrade Andrew R. Whitaker found sleeping quarters on a stone porch near the State House of Representatives that they considered "the most eligible spot, being covered by a roof, more clean, cool and less crowded than inside." It rained that evening, driving the majority of men who had not heeded the growing storm clouds above into the crammed State House chamber. Pennypacker, while not comfortable, unlike many still managed to sleep. "I spread out my horse blanket, put my bread satchel under my head, and endeavored to go to sleep, but the novelty of the position, the solidity of the bed, and the unpleasant practice the man above me had of putting his boots on my head, rendered it almost impossible," evoked Pennypacker. "I finally dozed and dreamed a little, with the shouts of the Copperheads ringing in my ears."[16]

However, Samuel and other militiamen would have their sleep interrupted around 1 a.m. that night, when the "Copperhead convention" adjourned, and its attendants "came out stepping over us, and went to their hotels, all of which they had previously engaged and crowded. The men groaned and cursed them, damned Woodward, McClellan, and traitors generally, and there were several fights in consequence." The wily Pennypacker quickly moved with Whitaker into the chamber, where they "slept the rest of the night in the seats there, very pleasantly[.]" Activity in the chamber did not cease, many of the militiamen tampering with "Copperhead" related items left behind. "A number of our fellow amused themselves in destroying copies of the 'Age' and other papers of like character, which packed up ready for mailing had been left behind. In the morning, we were awake by day-light, with eyes swollen, and feeling very little refreshed by the night's slumber."[17]

Not only did Pennypacker and his Phoenixville comrades awake on the morning of June 18 with swollen eyes and immense discomfort, but also a feeling of discontentment. After all, they had patriotically responded to the governor's call, but were received with little grace. Further, they soon saw dozens of able-bodied men strolling around the city with little concern as to the defense of the state capital. "A feeling of displeasure could not be repressed when thinking that we had come a hundred miles form a sense of duty while those in the immediate vicinity of the Capital, who had every incentive to arouse themselves, were doing nothing," wrote Pennypacker.[18]

A company from Bradford County arrived in Harrisburg "about half past 2 am" on June 18. After a "comfortable time coming down, with [the] exception of a few boys on . . . [the train]," penned home Charles F. Sayles of that company, "[we] marched up to the capitol Grounds and spread our Blankets (those that were fortunate enough to have them) some on the side walks some on the roof of the stats [sic] house and some . . . under the Trees[.] I was one of the latter[.] [W]e stretched out for about 2 hours but [got] little sleep[.]"[19]

"This morning [June 18]," Sayles continued, "[we] opened our sacks and took lunch." After eating, the company called roll, and then marched to Camp Curtin, where Sayles and several others "stretch[ed] . . . down on the ground with a hot sun shining down on my back to write a few things." There the Bradford County boys waited for "rations[,] tents[,] camp dishes &c." Many in this company had doubts if Harrisburg was really in danger. Sayles noted "that [even if] Hooker is defeated by Lee . . . [we still] do not think the city is very much in danger."[20]

The Bradford County soldier then proceeded to complain about camp conditions. "I did not find a Towel when I came to wash . . . this morning, nor a comb to straitin [sic] my hair," he grumbled. Sayles also wrote that there was "no body to give out equipage" and that "the men are coming in fast and all of them complain" about the camp's conditions, a large contrast from Shriver and the Hanover Company's experience.[21]

***

With what historical evidence that is available pertaining to the 26th, it is impossible to pin down specific arrival dates and times for every company of what would become the 26th Pennsylvania Volunteer Militia, save for the above. But shortly after arriving, the companies would all settle down into a similar routine and camp life in Camp Curtin.

"You would be surprised to see how <u>settled</u> we have already become— camp life has entirely lost the ugly aspect it had when our excited imaginations pictured us thrown entirely loose from home comforts among uncongenial companions," Maryland-native Shriver confided to his uncle on June 20.[22] "What rare fun we had lying in camp there," recalled W. E. Parson of the College Guards. "What endless jokes and songs, pulling each other out of the tents, and looking on the matter as a fine picnic."[23]

This circa 1864 photograph taken by Harrisburg photographers Burnite and Weldon shows the Camp Curtin Hospital. (*Historical Society of Dauphin County*)

Throughout the companies which would form the 26th and many of the other companies amassed in Camp Curtin, the College Guards of Gettysburg were commonly envied. "The Gettysburgers sing very well and very often," Shriver described. "I would like to belong to this company—their officers are so much better morally than ours." Perhaps the least envied company assembled in the camp was the Hanover Company to which Shriver belonged. "Our Capt and Lieut keep themselves pretty scarce— 2nd Lieut Pfeiffer is the steadiest of the whole party—the sergeants and corporals have not yet been appointed," Shriver wrote. Along with the frequent absences of the company's two highest ranking officers came consequences that would show themselves roughly a week later. "We've not had a single drill since our arrival—I want to drill as much as possible and I believe so do we (nearly) all, but the Captain [Jenkins] and [First Lieutenant] Forrest are absent all the time except a few minutes in the morning and evening—They don't stay in Camp at night—at least they have very seldom done so."[24]

On a brighter note, one memorable moment shared throughout all the companies was the drawing of uniforms, which took place (for the most part) on June 20. "The drawing of uniforms was a sight never to be forgotten," detailed Private Meissenhelder. Many men had trouble trying to jam a size 13 foot into a size 6 shoe, and "the biggest man in the company in vain essayed to get his huge proportions into the smallest suit." Meissenhelder continued: "How the long, lank, thin student paraded before his armed comrades in the short, stumpy suit made for a man 5 feet 4 inches tall! But by dint of a lively system of exchange, the absurdities of dress were rectified."[25] One Hanoverian held his pants to his chin and the legs touched the ground! "[W]e look pretty well in our uniforms," bragged Shriver. "This morning as we marched to town a soldier asked us if we were regulars? [A]nd he wasn't speaking ironically."[26]

"We get up much earlier here than at home," noted Shriver. "Hardly any one is asleep after 4 oclock [a.m.]—We told [newcomer] Cal [Wirt] that he would be up by that time and he laughed at the idea, but he was up, voluntarily some time before 4 [a.m.] and could hardly believe it when he looked at his watch."[27]

On Saturday, June 20, Rev. Charles Augustus Hay of Harrisburg visited the "College Guards" in camp, supplying them each with a Testament, and invited them to attend his service in Harrisburg's Zion Lutheran Church. Perhaps Hay displayed such interest in the Collegians because he had previously been a student in the Gettysburg's Lutheran Theological Seminary. The following day, Captain Klinefelter and his Gettysburgers accepted Hay's invitation. Reverend Hay "manifested a kindly interest in 'the boys' as Lutheran students entitled to his pastoral care."[28] Gettysburger William H. Rupp remarked that it was an "elegant sermon." After dinner, Hay returned to camp and again preached a sermon; Captain Klinefelter invited several other companies in the surrounding camp to attend.[29]

Reverend Charles Augustus Hays
(*Historical Society of Dauphin County*)

During his time in Camp Curtin, Captain Klinefelter roomed with the son of Pennsylvania College Professor Michael Jacobs, Henry Eyster Jacobs, in the latter's grandmother's home in Harrisburg. The two had formerly been classmates. The 18-year old Jacobs did not enlist in the regiment, but rather accompanied the Collegians as he attempted to convince his grandmother to return home. "I became an expert in casting bullets for his [Klinefelter's] revolver—so primitive were the weapons," young Henry reminisced.[30]

Henry Melchior Muhlenberg Richards
(*Lebanon County Historical Society*)

The drummer of the College Guards was 14-year-old Henry Melchior Muhlenberg Richards of Reading. His brother, Corporal Mathias H. Richards, a student of Pennsylvania College, had joined the College Guards. After Mathias wrote home, informing his mother of his enlistment and providing details of his experiences in Camp Curtin, young Henry pleaded with his mother to be allowed to join his brother. "After a persistent course of teasing I succeeded in getting my mother's reluctant consent to my joining this company," young Richards reminisced.[31] He later recalled of his brief time in Camp Curtin;

> *I cannot recall a single moment that I gave my poor drum a rest during the two days we lay in Camp Curtin at Harrisburg . . . I can recall even now how the surgeon at the hospital near us came to me and begged with tears in his eyes, that I would give his patients what the whole regiment longed for later on, a rest.*[32]

The companies which would make up the 26th were, as far as can be ascertained, all encamped within the limits of Camp Curtin. The Phoenixville Company's location was described by Pennypacker as in "one corner of the camp, very near to the railroad, and by the side of a small tree which stood there." Pennypacker also added that a wheatfield was "within a few rods" which doubled as an outhouse for the men from Phoenixville. Using Pennypacker's description and that of 14-year-old Harrisburg resident Phillip German, it appears that the Phoenixville Company was encamped in the northeastern corner of Camp Curtin. This location is the closest in the camp to the railroad, and nearby young German marks a lone chestnut tree, likely the tree Pennypacker describes. According to Pennypacker, the company closest to them on the camp ground was the College Guards, so the Gettysburgers can also be placed near the lone chestnut tree. On June 22, the Hanover Company, "moved our camp to the upper part of the common near the entrance[.]"[33]

***

Colonel William Wesley Jennings was the fourth-generation descendent of Captain Jesse Jennings, a veteran of the War of 1812. A Harrisburg native, Jennings was born on July 22, 1838, the second son of William and Elmira Jennings. Young William was educated in Harrisburg's public schools until he entered his father's foundry and learned the trade of a moulder at age fifteen. Jennings continued this practice until 1860, when he bought his father's plant, and successfully continued the business for nearly two decades. When President Lincoln called for volunteers at the outbreak of the war, Jennings enlisted as a private, and was soon elected first lieutenant of Company F, 25th Pennsylvania Infantry. This company, predominately raised from Harrisburg, was known as the "Lochiel Greys." After his three-month term of service with the Grays expired, Governor Curtin and Pennsylvania Adjutant General A. L. Russell appointed him Adjutant of Camp Curtin. Jennings soon proved a fast learner and demonstrated his remarkable executive ability. "In this position he developed an executive ability of a high order, and became ambitious to fill a more prominent position."

Jennings remained at Camp Curtin until July 1862. Longing for a more active and "more prominent position," he requested and received permission to recruit a regiment of nine-months' volunteers. The native Harrisburger was assured by both Curtin and Russell that if he were to raise the standard ten companies, he would be commissioned a colonel. Jennings raised what would come to be the 127th Pennsylvania Volunteer Infantry. This nine-month unit, commonly known as the "Dauphin County Regiment" because of its largely Harrisburg roots, would figure prominently in the formation of the 26th Militia in June 1863.[34]

Company A, commanded by Captain F. Asbury Awl, was known as the "First City Zouaves" of Harrisburg. The company had first been organized in the spring of 1861, and had been incorporated into the Keystone state's militia organization, which permitted the company to be armed and equipped by the Commonwealth. Upon being mustered into service in late July, Awl led his company "to the fields north of Camp Curtin," where he established "a camp suitable for the accommodation of troops that were expected to arrive in large numbers," known as Camp Simmons, in honor of Colonel Seneca G. Simmons of the 5th Pennsylvania Reserves, who had been killed during the Peninsular Campaign earlier that same summer. Company A would not join the rest of Jennings' 127th in the field—it was detached for "special duty" "in and about the City of Harrisburg." The company would also establish "Camp Dodge" on Bridgeport Heights, opposite Harrisburg. "This was occupied until cold weather made it necessary to go into winter quarters." This same location later served as the site of fortifications defending the city during the summer of 1863, which would at one point play host to the 26th Militia.[35]

Prominent Harrisburg attorney J. Wesley Awl organized the "Harrisburg Fire Zouaves," which would become Company B of the 127th. Opening a recruiting station at his law office on the west side of North Third Street, "the rolls began to fill up immediately." The company "was composed of a stalwart lot of men, most of them from the city of Harrisburg, and others from the country surrounding Harrisburg." Company C was under the command of Dr. James Henderson of Hummelstown, a short distance east of Harrisburg, from which vicinity the company was raised. Company D was formed from Harrisburg, Hummelstown and Millersburg by Harrisburg attorney Hiram C. Alleman, who had been approached by Colonel Jennings with an offer to become the regiment's lieutenant colonel. Company E— known as the "Greenawalt Guards"—from Lebanon, was headed by Lebanon native Lorenzo L. Greenawalt.[36]

Company F was formed in large part by members of Harrisburg's Hope Engine Company Number 2, as well as "sixteen or eighteen men" from nearby West Fairview, located on the opposite bank of the Susquehanna River from Harrisburg. Captain John J. Ball, Drill Master of Camp Curtin, raised a company at the request of Jennings from Harrisburg. Ball and Lieutenant George Hynicka pitched a tent in Harrisburg's Market Square and "went vigorously to work," recruiting Harrisburgers to form the "Dauphin Guards," which would become Company G. This company was supplemented by a force from Meadville. Company H was raised by Captain—and later major—Jeremiah Rohrer, who recruited "The Susquehanna Rangers," from "Middletown and vicinity," just southeast of Harrisburg. Company I came from Adams County, and was supplemented by "recruits from other localities." Company K "was recruited principally in Schuylkill County," and although "a number" of the company's men were from Lebanon County, it was most often referred to as the "Schuylkill County Company."[37]

Wartime photograph of Colonel William W. Jennings
(*MOLLUS-MASS Collection, U.S. Army Military History Institute*)

By mid-August 1862, all ten companies had assembled at Camp Curtin and vicinity. On the evening before the unit's departure, Hiram Alleman was elected lieutenant colonel, while Jeremiah Rohrer of Company H was elected major. The 127th left Camp Curtin on August 17, 1862, on the flat cars of the Northern Central Railway. They arrived at Baltimore about 5 p.m., and reached Washington early the following morning.[38] For the next several months, the "Dauphin County Regiment" would remain in the general vicinity of the nation's capital. For ten days, the regiment was encamped upon Arlington Heights. Brigaded with the 24th and 28th New Jersey and the 27th Connecticut, the 127th would be assigned to guard Chain Bridge over the Potomac River, connecting Washington to the northeastern counties of Virginia. Colonel Jennings was placed in command of this four regiment brigade. The 127th remained at Chain Bridge "until the opening of winter," when the regiment joined the Third Brigade, Second Division, Second Corps of the Army of the Potomac, and began the march to Fredericksburg, Virginia.[39]

"We soon learned that the Second Corps was the fighting corps of the Army of the Potomac," wrote one member of the 127th, "and that it was invariably in the van, and opened battle; or in a retreat, that it was assigned to cover the retreat." On December 9, 1862, the Army reached Falmouth, Virginia, just north of Fredericksburg. Upon arriving at the former, 127th was designated a camp site on "a scope of ground on a little elevation on the extreme right of the brigade, about a mile north of the hill overlooking Falmouth, and in full view of the city of Fredericksburg and the Rappahannock river." To this location they gave the name Camp Alleman after their lieutenant colonel, Hiram C. Alleman.[40]

When the pontoon bridges spanning the Rappahannock River—the natural barrier between Ambrose Burnside's Yankee Army of the Potomac and the town of Fredericksburg and Robert E. Lee's Army—were finally completed, the 127th charged across, led by Colonel Jennings and Lieutenant Colonel Alleman. During the dash into Fredericksburg, a shell fell directly under Jennings' horse, but miraculously failed to explode, and did not injure either the colonel or his mount. Shortly after entering the town, Jennings was detailed as provost marshal of Fredericksburg. It would not be long before near-suicidal orders found Jennings and his Pennsylvanians charging up the slope of Marye's Heights, beyond the town of Fredericksburg, only to meet with a bloody repulse. Jennings was slightly wounded when a shell splinter entered his boot and scathed his instep. But that was nothing compared to the sacrifice of his regiment and the rest of the army—the 127th suffered a staggering total of 257 casualties.[41]

Writing on January 20, 1863, more than a month after the disastrous assault of Marye's Heights, Hummelstown carpenter Samuel P. Conrad, a private in Company C, detailed preparations taken within the 127th for what would come to be known as Burnside's "Mud March." This futile campaign officially ended Burnside's tenure as commander of the Army of the Potomac, but as far as Conrad's account of the preparations, it provides a great account of Colonel Jennings. "The colonel gave orders just now that we go into a battle now in a day or two," Conrad wrote, "he said no one should run until we see that he runs… he was wounded at the last battle in the foot but … he is nearly good again[.] [H]e is going with the Regt into the battle[.] [T]he colonel wants to go with the colors none wants to go as color corperal [sic] now the colonel wants to go himself as a color guard[.] It is most A Shame to let the colonel go as color guard I would volunteer to go myself if I was right well, I got through safe once perhaps I might go through safe again."[42]

At the Battle of Chancellorsville, in May 1863, the 127th once again fought under Colonel Jennings, suffering 53 casualties. On May 14, the unit's term of service expired, and the regiment was sent back to Harrisburg to be mustered out, "highly complimented in general orders by Gen. [John] Gibbon."[43]

Jennings was only 24 years old when he was authorized to raise the 127th Pennsylvania. In June 1863, when the 26th Militia was forming, he was still 24, but celebrated his 25th birthday on July 22, while in the field with the 26th. "He had a clear head," wrote Lieutenant Colonel Alleman, "displayed excellent judgment, was serene, watchful and undisturbed under fire . . . There was none of the martinet about him, and yet he always commanded respect. He was always courteous to his associate officers, kind and considerate to his subordinates, and was devoted to the regiment, which he made a part and parcel of himself." Alleman summarized: "He grew each day in the respect and affection of his command, and no officer was more popular than he on the muster-out of the regiment."[44]

Chaplain J. Chandler Gregg, 127th Pennsylvania Volunteer Infantry
(U.S. Army Military History Institute)

Chaplain J. Chandler Gregg of the 127th described Jennings as a "model soldier" and further detailed: "While on duty he was *Colonel* Jennings; but off duty he caused all to feel easy and at home in his presence. Recognizing in each a fellow-soldier he never gave evidence that he considered himself a superior. It was this particular feature in his character which rendered him so popular with the men of his command [emphasis original]."[45]

When the 127th's term of enlistment expired, Jennings returned to managing his foundry. However, when news of the Confederate invasion reached Harrisburg, he again responded to the calls of his native state, and received orders to form a regiment from the companies gathered at Camp Curtin.[46] The earliest account of Jennings in Camp Curtin is on Saturday, June 20, when he began courting companies for his regiment.[47]

The task of courting companies for his militia regiment was made significantly easier because of Jennings' welcoming demeanor and his respected reputation. The Harrisburg native soon won over the affections of many of the companies in Camp Curtin. Captain Klinefelter of the College Guards wrote that Jennings was "every inch a 'Colonel,' thoroughly furnished unto his work, and, by his kind and gentlemanly bearing, soon winning the hearts of his entire command."[48] Henry M. M. Richards, the 14-year-old drummer of the College Guards later recalled that Jennings was "thoroughly capable, and brave, he was held in highest esteem by all. He had a high opinion of his own men, and an especial dislike for those regiments which were composed of city chaps, whom he hardly considered worthy the name of soldiers, and only fit for stragglers."[49] "Our Col. is an excellent man," wrote Collegian Frank Richards. "He said he was never in a tighter place."[50]

Samuel Pennypacker was also quick to embrace Jennings. Jennings, Pennypacker related, "an intimate friend of Gov. Curtin, was a fine looking man of about twenty-eight years of age… Every one liked him, because he understood his business, acted toward his men as an officer should, and from former experience know how to take care of them. I never heard a single word of complaint against him, and I think he possessed the respect of every man in the regiment."[51]

In 1894, Jennings' pastor, Reverend C. W. Buoy of the Grace Methodist Church in Harrisburg, eulogized the colonel upon his death;

He early assumed the responsibilities of life, and entered business. He was entrusted with large affairs and his integrity was unimpeachable. His industry and foresight were building up trade, his personality drawing friends and the promise of business success already within his grasp when the awful struggle that imperiled the integrity of the Union took place. He was but a young man attaining his majority when the sad strife began, and at once his business was abandoned and the peaceful pursuit was exchanged for the field of strife. He was heroic, loving his country with ardent devotion, and when the call to arms sounded he was among the first to respond, leaving home and business to save an endangered nation. Brave in battle and obedient, he was soon recognized as a leader and summoned to command. Here the qualities that gave him prominence in after years were already manifest. The soldier grace of the young officer soon won

the hearts of his men, as he shared the fatigues of the march or led them into
battle. High qualities won him distinction.[52]

An 1862 photograph of Colonel Jennings
(From, *History of the 127th Regiment Pennsylvania Volunteers*, 1902)

On Sunday, June 21, Jennings instructed that companies could retain their officers and current organization if they mustered at least 50 men. The Phoenixville Company "made desperate exertions to raise the required number, calling the roll frequently and endeavoring to hunt up recruits through camp." However, the company never numbered more than 48 men. Soon "what little hope was left" ceased to exist when the Phoenixville Iron Company, which had before promised to hold its workers' jobs, instructed its employees to return home or lose their jobs.

Privates Cyrus Nyce and D. W. "Web" Davis of a nearby company raised from Pottstown visited the disheartened Phoenixville Company, and tried to persuade some of the latter's remaining members to join their company; they too being short on numbers, the Pottstown boys feared the possibility of losing their beloved captain, George Rice. As the sun rose on Monday, June 22, the members of the Phoenixville Company contemplated their next move. "As there was no possibility of our raising a company," reasoned Pennypacker, "the only choice left to those of us who still remained was to go home or join some other party and nearly all, disliking the latter alternative, and concluding that having held out as long as there was any chance of effecting an organization they had done all that could be expected of them, determined to return in the first train. I was in a dilemma. I disliked the idea of going home in that manner considering it dishonorable and discreditable in itself and dreading jeers which I knew must be endured and to a certain extent would be merited. I also had a strong inclination to try what a soldier's life was like and to know something of it from experience."

"But in order to do this," Pennypacker realized, "it was necessary to bid farewell to my friends and place myself for an indefinite length of time in a company of strangers, among whom I would be of no importance whatever, with the prospect of having the roughest duties to perform . . . ." Despite such grievances, Pennypacker and several of his Phoenixville comrades joined the Pottstown Company, while Phoenixville soldier Charles H. Combs joined the College Guards.[53]

In this way, the 26th Pennsylvania Volunteer Militia was born. Much of the unit's officers—and a number of enlisted men—had recently served with Jennings' 127th Pennsylvania, or in other units. However, the greater part of the regiment was gravely inexperienced.

The following table shows the companies with their new letter designation[54];

TABLE I: COMPANIES COMPOSING THE 26TH PVM, 1863

Co	Captain	Raised/Recruited	Enrolled	Mustered In
A	Frederick Klinefelter	Gettysburg	June 16	June 17
B	Warner H. Carnochan	Bradford County	June 17	June 19
C	Christopher W. Walker	Clinton County	June 17	June 20
D	James L. Pell	Harrisburg/Lykens (Dauphin County)	June 15	June 19
E	Lorenzo L. Greenawalt	Lebanon	June 17	June 20
F	George Rice	Pottstown/Phoenixville	June 18	June 20
G	Elias C. Rishel	Hughesville, Lycoming Cty.	June 18	June 20

H	John T. Morgan	Harrisburg, Philadelphia, West Fairview (Cumberland County)	June 17	June 21/23
I	Joseph S. Jenkins	Hanover, York County	June 17	June 17
K	Marcius Novinger	Millersburg, Dauphin County	June 18	June 20/22

With 38 officers and 705 enlisted men—a total of 743 men—the 26th Pennsylvania Volunteer Militia became the first newly-raised militia regiment during the 1863 "emergency."[55] During the Maryland Campaign in September 1862, regiments were raised up to the number 25. Only the 20th Regiment returned in 1863, and therefore the 26th received the first new regimental designation. Often a matter of confusion, regimental designation for 1863 "emergency" regiments was determined by what terms the units accepted. As previously stated, the companies of the 26th accepted terms to be mustered in for the duration of the emergency. Therefore, they were frequented as Emergency Militia. These "emergency" units were the 20th, 26th through 31st, as well as the 33rd Regiments—eight regiments in total. These units were officially designated as Pennsylvania Volunteer Militia (abbreviated PVM). All other militia regiments (which by July ranged to the 60th Regiment of Philadelphia), were mustered in for either 60 or 90 days, and were simply referred to as Pennsylvania Militia (abbreviated PM).

The denotation of regiment still did nothing to fix the majority of the men's unfitness for duty, and most of all, inexperience. This was surely proven when the regiment drew arms on June 23. Many of the men had never before handled a gun. Pennypacker recalled: "I took care to reserve for myself a gun which was in first rate order. I was so green, however, concerning the matters of that kind that I had to call upon . . . [assistance] to explain the method of fastening the bayonet[.]"[56] The Pennsylvanians were issued an assortment of weapons, mostly Springfield muskets. The Pottstown Company had "brought with it arms which were not of the regulation pattern," and was forced to exchange these for Springfields. Two men of the company were commissioned to return their irregular arms back to Pottstown.[57]

While a large number of the forming 26th Militia were inexperienced and had no previous exposure to military service—or in the case of Pennypacker and many others, were woefully ignorant of the process of discharging their weapons and fastening their bayonets—the hastily-raised militia unit still could boast of a veteran officer corps as well as a sprinkling of veteran enlisted-men. Favorable and timely circumstances regarding the muster-out of the 127th Pennsylvania and the formation of the 26th Militia permitted a portion of men from the former to once again reunite with their beloved Colonel Jennings in the latter organization. However, only about 50 men of the 127th reenlisted in the 26th—but still a noticeable enough amount to bring some experience to the regiment.[58]

Chapter 2

With A Pie in Each Hand:
The Journey to Camp Wreck

At about 1 a.m. in the predawn hours of June 24, the companies of the 26th read their first order from Colonel Jennings, instructing them "to draw and cook 1 days rations and to be ready to leave at 6 oclock this morning."[1] Private Pennypacker of the Pottstown Company was supplied with a "medium sized piece of meat[.]" When the future Pennsylvania governor inquired how long this mediocre ration was to last, he received the fractious reply; "Until you get some more[.]" "One company after another left their tents," recalled Pennypacker, "and marching out to the [southern] side of the camp toward the town formed in line. First came Co. A. [College Guards] . . . Co. F. [Pottstown Company], next Co. D. [Dauphin County], Captain Pell; and the other seven companies[.]" It was here that the men first learned they were part of the 26th Pennsylvania Volunteer Militia, and for many, first became acquainted with Colonel Jennings. Captain Joseph S. Jenkins of the Hanover Company was elected lieutenant colonel, and Captain Lorenzo L. Greenawalt of the Lebanon Company major. In turn, John C. Brooks became captain of Greenawalt's Lebanon Company while John S. Forrest took over command of Jenkins' Hanover Company.[2]

While remarkably few soldiers—if any—demonstrated any grudge against or dislike of Colonel Jennings, the exact opposite can be said of his second-in-command. "Lieutenant Colonel Jenkins was from Hanover, a man who was said to have obtained his position by some management, and who had in a wonderful degree the faculty of rendering himself particularly disagreeable," related Pennypacker.[3]

Jenkins had originally enlisted upon the outbreak of the war in the three-month 16th Pennsylvania Infantry and quickly rose to the rank of second lieutenant. The unit never saw action, only accompanying the aging General Robert Patterson and the latter's army in the Shenandoah Valley during the summer of 1861. After being mustered out in late-July 1861, Jenkins reenlisted in the 130th Pennsylvania Infantry, a nine-month regiment. Jenkins enrolled as captain of Company C, a troop formed of men from York and Montgomery counties. Before long, the Hanoverian rose to major of the unit. Led by Colonel Henry I. Zinn, the regiment was ordered to Rockville, Maryland, on August 18, to join the Army of the Potomac. Departing on September 7 and arriving on September 12, the regiment became part of the Second Corps, as the 127th later did.

The 130th, however, was unfortunate in the fact that it joined the Second Corps so soon. Because of its earlier arrival, the regiment would take part in the Battle of Antietam near Sharpsburg, Maryland, on September 17, 1862. The 130th advanced on what was known as the "Sunken Road" from which Confederate Infantry poured volley after volley into the ranks of the 130th and other Yankee units. Although the latter were significantly more exposed in the open farm fields of Roulette farm during this musketry duel, the Southern infantrymen were eventually driven out of the "Sunken Road," but only at a heavy cost.[4]

After the battle, the 130th was involved in the dreadful work of burying the dead. Private John S. Weiser of Company G described in a letter home to his siblings that "our Regt was drawn up in line of battle[.] [W]e then stacked arms [and] some were ordered to dig Pits while others were ordered to go out and gather up the dead bodies taking the Union . . . first and placing them . . . on the banks of the Pits[.] When the Pit is . . . deep enough the Bodies are placed crosswise and as many as four by seven in one Grave[.]" Burying their Confederate counterparts was similarly disturbing to Weiser and his comrades. "We buried five Rebs to every one Union Man[.] [W]e seen a many the rebels Boys of fifteen and Sixteen and old Gray headed men[.]"[5]

Afterwards, the unit moved southwest to Harper's Ferry on September 22. With the rest of the Army of the Potomac (including the 127th), the 130th advanced to Falmouth—opposite Fredericksburg—during the waning months of 1862. The 130th was one of the many units engaged in the assault on Marye's Heights at Fredericksburg. "[A]n engagement it was indeed," remarked Private Weiser. The regiment suffered fearfully. Colonel Zinn was killed during the assault the slopes of Marye's Heights on December 13. After participating in the Battle of Chancellorsville, the 130th was mustered out in Harrisburg on May 21.[6] However unpleasant Jenkins may have been, he undeniably possessed valuable experience which could potentially prove extremely crucial for a mostly green militia regiment such as the 26th.

"Major Greenawalt was a large, stout man, with a deep bass voice," recalled Pennypacker. "He had come up to Harrisburg as a captain of a company, and some years previously, I was told, he made two overland trips to California on foot. During all the time we were out, he refused to have a horse, and marched with the men."[7] Born on January 6, 1827, in Lebanon, Lorenzo Leonard Greenawalt was the descendant of Colonel Philip Lorenzo Greenawalt, who commanded Pennsylvania Militia during the Revolution.[8] Greenawalt was 36 years old when he joined the 26th.[9] Prior to and for some time after the war, Greenawalt operated a tannery in his native Lebanon. "There was something about him which drew the admiration of all," Pennypacker noted, "probably his imposing appearance and manly attributes increased by his reputation for great physical strength. It was reported that he was more than a match in a fisticuff for any other two men in Lebanon, his native place."[10]

Similar feelings about their major were quite common throughout the ranks of the 26th. "[A] veteran captain . . . an old campaigner who had crossed the plains to the Pacific Coast in 1852 when the undertaking was a hazardous one," described drummer Henry M. M. Richards. In Richards' words, Greenawalt "was held in special revereuce [sic] by the 'boys' with whom he had always insisted upon marching upon foot; he had a stentorian voice like the roar of a bull, with the heart of a child; he could thrash any two men in the regiment, but never used his strength save for kindly acts."[11]

Wartime carte-de-vista of Major Lorenzo L. Greenawalt
(*Lancaster County Historical Society*)

Greenawalt had formerly commanded Company E in Colonel Jennings' 127th Pennsylvania. Jennings and Greenawalt were close friends—or in the words of Private Cyrus R. Lantz of Company E, there was "at all times" during their service in the 127th a "very noticeable... more than ordinary companionship" between the two. Lantz and his fellow members of Company E of the 127th revered Greenawalt as their captain. "[I]t must be said that he was an ideal soldier," Lantz wrote, "of splendid physique, brave as a lion, gentle and kind as a father to his men. Never on the march or in camp was he known to retire at night until he had first made the rounds among his men to see that they were comfortably situated, or as comfortable as the circumstances would permit." Lantz added that Greenawalt was "a California '49-r, [and] had made the trip overland more than once, and hence knew perfectly the needs of men exposed to the summer and winter exposures of the soldier's life."[12]

Lieutenant Colonel Alleman described Greenawalt as "a quiet, but most determined man. He walked from his home in Central Pennsylvania to California, simply by force of his indomitable will. He was of fine physique, great strength, characteristically mild and gentle, but always firm, and of scrupulous integrity. He acted like a father to his command, and was greatly beloved by every man in his company. He was absolutely without fear, always ready, and performed his official duties with exacting care and punctuality."[13]

Lieutenant Colonel Hiram C. Alleman, 127th Pennsylvania Volunteer Infantry
(From, *History of the 127th Regiment Pennsylvania Volunteers*, 1902)

At the Battle of Fredericksburg, Greenawalt made quite a name for himself. On December 13, as the 127th was preparing to assault Marye's Heights, the Lebanon native was seen coolly leaning "against a low fence between two houses," while the regiment was halted on the outskirts of town. Soon a shell "came screaming, and struck between the two houses, shattering both walls." Private George D. Rise of Company E was particularly struck by Greenawalt's response to the rebel shell—"Captain Greenawalt did not even change his position," Rise wrote, "but calmly turned his head to look at the result."[14] After the charge had boiled down to a bloody repulse, Greenawalt stormed over to General Oliver Otis Howard's headquarters, and brazenly announced to the general "that he did not want his men slaughtered[.]"[15]

Private George D. Rise, Company E, 127th Pennsylvania Volunteer Infantry
(From, *History of the 127th Regiment Pennsylvania Volunteers*, 1902)

Major Jeremiah Rohrer of the 127th recorded of Greenawalt during the month of January 1863, in his detailed wartime diary: "Captain Greenawalt came this morning, as usual, for his breakfast, for he never carries any rations along… Captain Greenawalt was one of four who travelled through to California on foot in 1849. He was a powerfully built man, and feared nothing human. At home, when he drank too much lemonade with a stick in it, he was a terror to all bystanders, and many were the pieces of furniture lying about."[16] One member of the 127th summarized the Lebanon native: "Captain Greenawalt was a very determined man, and when he set himself about to do a thing, he allowed nothing to prevent its accomplishment."[17]

All three field officers in the 26th had had some type of previous experience in field command—Colonel Jennings as colonel of the 127th, Major Greenawalt as a captain in the same and Lieutenant Colonel Jenkins as major of the 130th Pennsylvania.

Additionally, all ten company commanders had seen prior service. Captain Frederick Klinefelter of Company A had served early on in the war, as a private in the three-month 16th Pennsylvania Infantry.[18] Walter Hayden Carnochan, captain of Company B, had served as a captain in Company D of the 132nd Pennsylvania Infantry. A member of an old Scottish family, Carnochan was born on February 8, 1840, in Troy, Bradford County, the son of Nicholas M. and Jemima Carnochan. Early on, Carnochan read law with the Hon. Ulysses Mercur, a judge of the Supreme Court of Pennsylvania. Shortly before the war, around 1858, Carnochan taught at the Troy Academy. It was reportedly through "his influence that the study of United States history was introduced into the schools of Western Bradford, and that he was an authority upon that subject." After the war, in 1868, he would be elected District Attorney of Bradford County, and earned a reputation as "one of the most noted lawyers of Bradford county[.]"[19]

Captain Christopher Wilson Walker of Company C had served in Company I of the 137th Pennsylvania, but was "dishonorably dismissed" in November 1862. Captain James L. Pell of Company D, a peacetime engineer, had served in Company D of Jennings' 127th Pennsylvania as a corporal. Captain John C. Brooks of Company E had served in Company E of the 127th—Greenawalt's Company—as a sergeant. Captain George Rice of Company F had served in the three-month 25th Pennsylvania Infantry at the outbreak of the war, and had responded to the rebel thrust into Maryland in September 1862 by joining the 19th Pennsylvania Militia.[20]

Captain Elias C. Rishel of Company G, a dentist from Catawissa, had served in Company H of the 132nd Pennsylvania Infantry. This unit was involved at the Sunken Road at Antietam, the assault on Marye's Heights at Fredericksburg, and Chancellorsville, where Rishel was wounded.[21] Captain John T. Morgan of Company H was an employee at the McCormick Nail Mill in West Fairview, a small village opposite Harrisburg. He served as a first lieutenant in Company F of the 127th, after leading a squad of "sixteen or eighteen men" to Harrisburg where they joined with "a number of members" of Harrisburg's Hope Engine Company No. 2, to form the company. Morgan was described as "a gentlemanly and courteous officer[.]"[22]

Captain John S. Forrest of Company I had served as a sergeant in the 130th Pennsylvania. Captain Marcius Novinger of Company K served in Company D of the 127th. Therefore, all company commanders had seen prior service, four of them in Jennings' regiment. However raw the large majority of enlisted men may have been, the officer corps was well-rounded, yet still remarkably young—in total, company and field officers in the 26th averaged 28 years old. [23]

This carte-de-vista of Captain John T. Morgan of Company H was taken by Harrisburg photographer D.C. Burnite. (*U.S. Army Military History Institute*)

After forming into column, there was a delay of more than an hour before the railroad cars were ready. "There was a great deal of curiosity to know where we were going," recollected Pennypacker, "but all we could learn from the officers was that there would be a march of about ten miles before we reached our place of destination."[24] Captain Klinefelter of the College Guards later remembered that "we were ordered aboard a train on the Northern Central Railroad, but for what point only the Colonel knew though every member of Company A seemed to think he ought to know—as also in reference to everything else that was done or contemplated. Being of an inquiring turn of mind—perhaps a result of studious habits—they were continually probing their Captain, with 'Why must we do thus and so?' 'Why, and how long do we remain here?' 'Why do we not go at once to meet the enemy?' and a thousand other questions[.]"[25] The Hanover Company had somehow been informed that the train would pass through Hanover, and were quite excited to say a quick hello to their relatives.[26] Members of the Pottstown Company tried to determine the destination by poking their heads out of the cars and trying to identify various notable terrain features.[27]

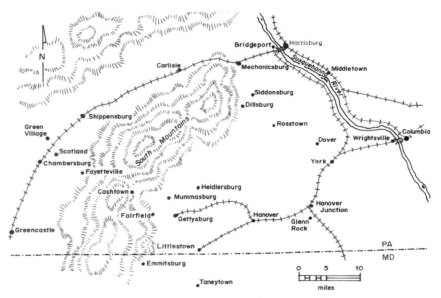

South Central Pennsylvania in 1863 (*Map by John Heiser*)

Pennypacker managed to obtain a few worthy glimpses of the train's path—however, it did little to solve the mystery he and his comrades faced as to their ultimate destination. "I was very desirous of taking a trip down the Cumberland Valley," the future governor later reminisced, "and after getting on the cars, we watched carefully the direction they took." At first, the train "moved slowly to and through Harrisburg, over the railroad bridge across the Susquehanna, then a short distance down the Cumberland Valley road, again up the river, and after thus baffling about finally started off on the road to

York, amid the cheering of all on board." Then began a sluggish ride southward, Pennypacker wrote:

> *We travelled along very slowly, some times stopping for half an hour or more, and then creeping on at such a snail's pace that it was tiresome. I remember very distinctly in what a glorious humor we all were, without any anxiety except to reach the end of our journey. At nearly every house which we passed the women came to the windows and waved their handkerchiefs, and then all set up such a cheering, hurrahing, and tigering that it was enough to deafen one. At several places on the route we passed squads and companies of Colonel W. B. Thomas' twentieth {Pennsylvania Militia} regiment and their camps looked so pleasant upon the green, that the idea passed through my mind of how nice it would be to be stationed in some copse or grove for a few weeks and guard a bridge or something of the kind, then return home and let those Phoenix fellows know what they missed by not remaining.*[28]

Passing through York, where the 26th "waited some time and saw a large number of paroled prisoners from different States who were then going to camp," the regiment continued through Hanover Junction, east of the town of Hanover. At about 3 p.m., the 26th stopped briefly in Hanover, where members of the Hanover Company chatted with family, friends and acquaintances. Here the train was divided, part of the regiment continued west on the cars immediately while the other half "kept several miles in the rear."[29]

The men of the 26th, especially the College Guards, would take special interest in their final destination—Gettysburg, a sizeable town situated at the center of Adams County. In his written instructions to Colonel Jennings, General Couch detailed:

> *Colonel Jennings will use his best efforts to hold the country, harass the enemy,—attacking him at exposed points or falling back in order-and advancing his force or part of it, making flank attacks, etc., doing everything in his power to weaken, {and} mislead the enemy and protect the country.*[30]

Sending the 26th to Gettysburg had been but three days in the making. On June 21, Major Granville O. Haller, commander of the sector of the Department of the Susquehanna comprising Gettysburg and its localities, was contacted by Couch, who inquired if it "would do to send a Regiment of Infantry to Gettysburg?" Haller later wrote that this offer was a pleasant surprise—of course he could use a regiment under his command rather than just a few squads of cavalry roaming the mountains to the west of Gettysburg, though he had believed Couch could not spare any troops from the defenses of Harrisburg. Now with an offer on the table, Haller gleefully replied: "Please send a Regiment, it will restore confidence and rally the people to take arms."[31]

Major Granville O. Haller
(U.S. Army Military History Institute)

Born in York on January 31, 1819, Haller's father died when young Granville was only two years old. After graduating from the York County Academy in 1838, Haller's attempt at an appointment to West Point met with failure when Senator James Buchanan appointed fellow York native William B. Franklin. Undeterred, Haller travelled to Washington where he met with the secretary of war. Haller left enough of a favorable impression to obtain an invitation to appear before a board composed of military officers. This ended favorably for the York native when he was commissioned a Second Lieutenant in the 4th U.S. Infantry in 1839.

Haller spent the next two years fighting Seminoles in Florida before participating in numerous battles during the Mexican War. By the end of the war, Haller had been brevetted a captain for "gallant and meritorious conduct" at the Battle of Chapultepec. In 1852, he was brevetted major of the 7th U.S. Infantry and was transferred to Washington Territory to deal with local Indian insurgencies. When the war broke out in 1861, Haller was remanded back to the east coast, and promoted to major in September 1861. Shortly afterwards he was assigned to Major General George McClellan's staff, and saw service commanding McClellan's headquarter staff during the Peninsular and Maryland Campaigns. Haller continued in that capacity even as the Army of the Potomac's leadership changed hands several times.

"Haller did not have a formal command when the Rebels threatened Pennsylvania," explained historian Scott L. Mingus. "As with dozens of other unassigned officers, he traveled to Harrisburg and offered his services to General Couch. Haller stood out in the crowd of ambitious men eager to resume their service. He was a Regular Army, a career soldier with impressive credentials including years of combat experience against diverse enemies and organization skills enhanced under McClellan." Therefore, Couch detailed him as an aide-de-camp, and selected him to head the defense of Adams and York counties.[32]

Philadelphia Navy Yard Executive Clark H. Wells was a vigorous opponent of Haller after an incident while the two were with the Army of the Potomac shortly after the disastrous battle of Fredericksburg. Wells claimed that Haller uttered the "disloyal sentiment," "Here's to a Northern Confederation and a Southern one while Lincoln is President," as well as pronouncing that he "considered the President responsible for the loss of life at the battle of Fredericksburg." After initially confronting Haller about the alleged comment (which Haller denied), in March 1863, Wells reported Haller to Secretary of War Edwin Stanton "for uttering disloyal sentiments in my presence, on the night of December 16th, or 17th, 1862, in his tent opposite Fredericksburg, Va." Wells claimed that when General Couch appointed Haller to the defense of Adams and York counties, he was "entirely ignorant of the fact, otherwise he would not have conferred upon him an important command."[33]

Despite what Haller wrote, word of the 26th's presence did little to instill confidence in the emotionally-shaken people of Gettysburg. For the past week, small detachments and companies of home guards and mounted militia had roamed the mountainous area west of Gettysburg, scouting and sometimes skirmishing with Confederate forces. "This morning early a despatch [sic] was received," penned Gettysburger Sarah Broadhead in her diary, "that a regiment of infantry was coming from Harrisburg. We do not feel much safer, for they are only raw militia."[34] The Gettysburg *Compiler*, the town's Republican newspaper, had a different, and exaggerated, view of the 26th's ability to defend Gettysburg: "A large number of the men were out in the nine months' service. All look like good fighting material, and will do their whole duty."[35]

After departing Hanover, the forward portion of the train continued onward "without incident" until about six miles from Gettysburg, near Swift Run, where the engine collided with a cow crossing the tracks. Pennypacker reported to a Phoenixville newspaper that that train "kept on its course for some thirty yards," until the cars "completely wrecked and piled together in a heap," which had the effect of "smashing up things in a terrible manner." The College Guards were one of the companies in the front section, and, according to Captain Klinefelter, the incident caused no fatalities, but several, including Private Charles Combs (formerly of the Phoenixville Company) were injured. The tracks were destroyed for some distance, so as to halt any further progress that day. On a positive note, Private Herman S. Cook remarked that the slain cow "furnished tough steaks for many of the boys."[36]

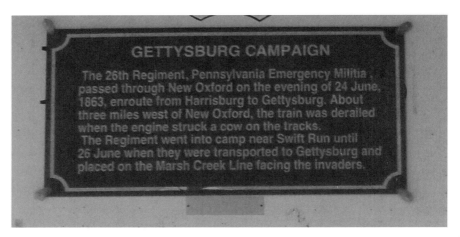

This tablet at the New Oxford Train Station commemorates the 26th's nearby railroad accident. (*Photo by the Author*)

Word of the accident quickly reached the rear train carrying the other half of the regiment. "We slowly approached as near as was safe," Pennypacker reminisced, "and there getting off the cars were marched to a wood on the right of the track where we found the other part of the regiment, and stacked our arms by companies in regular order." Then the Pennsylvanians hastened to the scene of the accident "to see what had happened."[37] After conducting a small-scale investigation, the Pottstown Company concluded;

It appeared that an old woman had been driving a cow along the top of a high embankment where the road crossed a deep gully and small creek. The old woman got out of the way when the cars came up, but the cow ran along the track, was caught about midway and thrown over the bank dead. The cars were forced from the track by the concussion but fortunately kept their course almost parallel with the rails, bumping over the sills until they got beyond the gully, and there all the track was torn up and they badly broken were piled together. . . . the cow . . .

was very old and miserably poor. . . . the old woman . . . was standing there crying, while a number of our fellows among whom was Sergeant {William G.} Meigs, had out their knives and were already busily engaged cutting off steaks wherever any meat could be found. . . . [38]

"We camped about four in the afternoon in a beautiful woods near the place of the accident," reported Captain George Rice of the Pottstown Company, or as they now dubbed themselves, the "Keystone Guards." To this campsite, the company gave the name "Camp Wreck."[39] The encampment was located in a large wood more than two miles west of New Oxford, and immediately north of the railroad.[40] The Hanover Company had a less optimistic name for the bivouac site: "Camp Disaster." "[W]e slept last night in the open air and very soundly too," Maryland-native Henry Wirt Shriver of the Hanover Company penned home concerning the regiment's new campsite. "[W]e spread our tents on the ground, laid on them, rolled ourselves in our woolen blankets and covered our gum covers over the Top[.] [T]his keeps out the damp . . . the dew saturated the wool blankets so as to make them quite wet before morning . . . many complained of cold but [Private] Dave [Winebrenner] and I were very comfortable . . . . The woods looked so pretty by the light of the camp fires . . . all around you could see the sleeping soldiers in all sorts of positions—you cannot imagine how quiet they become I was awake a short time about 1 oclock and had it not been for the extreme <u>snoring</u> going on I could have imagined myself alone in [t]he woods."[41]

The pantries of neighboring farmhouses were soon bare. "The first thing soldiers do after a halt is to scatter all about the neighborhood and hunt up every thing of an edible nature to be found," described Pennypacker in his anonymous correspondence with a Phoenixville newspaper. "The nearer farm houses are soon drained of all the butter, milk and eggs they can furnish."[42]

On the evening of June 24, Colonel Jennings found time to pen the following message to Major Haller of his arrival in the area;

Swift Run Hill, June 24th 1863.
Major G. O. Haller,
Dear Sir: We have met with an accident at this point; the cars having run off the track. We sustained no injury further than damage having been done the track and several cars, I shall camp here and await your orders.
Yours Respectfully,
    W. W. Jennings,
    Colonel Commanding 26th Regiment Pa., Militia[43]

Haller responded by authorizing Jennings "to impress teams to bring up his baggage, and march to Gettysburg, if the railroad was not repaired when he would be ready to move, next morning."[44] Jennings would not move until June 26, when the railroad was repaired. As W. E. Parson the College Guards mused: "We might have marched to Gettysburg in a few hours, but there was no haste; why should we walk when we could ride?"[45]

"Slept well last night in the open air," recorded Shriver in his diary. Breakfast, for Shriver at least, was crackers and sausage with butter, and a little coffee on the side. "We have a very pleasant camp in the woods," added the Maryland-native. Captain Rice wrote to his local newspaper that "[t]he country people [around Swift Run] were kind, furnishing provisions gratuitously or at a reasonable rate . . . ." Pennypacker recalled that "[t]here was a house and a spring very close at hand, but the water had such a bad taste, as to be almost unfit for drinking, and we went nearly a half a mile to a brick house for some which was better. There were also some cherries at the latter place, which did not remain a great while."[46]

Later that morning, Colonel Jennings ordered the regiment to a cleared field immediately south of the railroad. "Drilled about an hour in loading and firing manual of arms, and filing in to line," logged Shriver in his diary.[47] This was the first drill the 26th had undergone as a regiment.

As Company F was drilling, Captain George Rice had his company in the charge stance, when a sudden burst of anger found him throwing his whole weight against Private Samuel Pennypacker's bayonet. The Captain of the "Leap Frogs"—a name which the company had received after an episode with an unusual arrestee in Harrisburg—enviously gazed towards the camp of Company A (the College Guards).[48]

The friends and relatives of Company A had heard of the Gettysburg company's location, and only being several miles away, set out with many edibles intended for their loved ones who now shouldered arms in defense of their state. "As we were on the right of the regiment," recalled drummer Richards, "the first few invoices naturally reached their destination, until the rest of the boys, noticing that all the members of A Company had a pie in each hand, a loaf of bread under the arm and a broad grin on the face, 'caught on' to the thing and quietly walked up to the road a short distance." When the next group of well-wishers arrived, these men—as a disgruntled Captain Klinefelter pointed out, "notably Company F"—claimed to be of Company A, and "cleaned out" the rest of the travelers. From this point on the College Guards would be known within the regiment as the "Pie Company."[49]

The afternoon brought rumors of a Confederate approach to the 26th's peaceful camp. Much of this was sparked by a prisoner being brought into camp who was charged with being a rebel spy. The alleged was taken to Colonel Jennings' tent, and not seen thereafter. Fears were further infused by rumors spread by "the people in the neighborhood," who told the militiamen that the rebels, "in full force," had already occupied Cashtown and were on the move again. Company F was told a similar story by a group of farmers, who "told us . . . that the rebels were advancing in large force, and that considerable numbers of them were in the woods and hills about Cashtown."[50]

"Some of the men were a little uneasy," recalled Pennypacker. Many of the Pennsylvania militiamen stressed that they "came down to fight" but feared being sent off with only the 700 some men in the 26th to face thousands of Confederates. Brightening their attitude somewhat was an issue of that day's Harrisburg *Evening Telegraph*, which had been brought into

Camp Wreck by a passerby. The militiamen were amused and somewhat emboldened to see that they were indirectly mentioned on the front page. "General Couch has thrown a large column of men in the neighborhood of Gettysburg on the enemy's right flank," the paper read. In the middle of the afternoon "a strong wind arose, and then there was every appearance of rain." So the men commenced to pitch their tents and prepared to settle in for the night.[51]

This anxiety prevailed not only among the ranks of the 26th but also among Major Haller and his command in and about Gettysburg. Haller sent stores of ordnance consisting of muskets, ammunition and a small cannon to Jennings, "with orders to make whatever disposition of them I thought proper." Jennings "immediately placed them upon the cars and sent them to Hanover in charge of four men, belonging to a house guard, with orders to report to the Provost Martial [sic] of" Hanover.[52]

Uneasiness also reigned among the civilians of Gettysburg. "To-day passed much as yesterday did," recorded civilian Sarah Broadhead in her diary on June 25. "Every one is asking, Where is our army, that they let the enemy scour the country and do as they please? It is reported that Lee's whole army is this side of the river, and marching on Harrisburg; also, that a large force is coming on here, to destroy the railroad between there and Baltimore. Our militia did not come to town, but remain encamped where they were yesterday."[53]

John C. Wills, son of Charles Wills who was proprietor and landlord of the Globe Hotel in Gettysburg, recalled: "[W]e heard of confederates being seen in South Mountain in considerable number as citizens on Elevated places could see their Camp-Fires burning at night. [C]itizens rode up the Chambersburg pike to the foot of the Mountain and reported having seen confederates. [T]hose trips were made on the morning of several days. [O]n one of the last of those trips they came down the Pike at full speed and reported seeing confederate Bush-Whackers who fired on them." As these reports spread through town, "a general stampeded of the Farmers from that section of the Country" took full effect. "While standing in front of the Globe Hotel," Wills reminisced, "it was a sight, at night in the Moonlight to see them going through the Town with Horses, with Teams[,] A number of the wagons being Loaded with goods[,] A number of them going Southward [towards Baltimore][,] A majority of them going Eastward to York County and into Lancaster County, to places of safety."[54]

The storied First Troop, Philadelphia City Cavalry, in operation since the Revolutionary War when it served as George Washington's body guard, was stationed in town at the McClellan Hotel. With their puffy, novel uniforms, the Philadelphians' appearance provided much needed comical-relief to the distressed Gettysburg civilians. "[I]n the morning they could be seen washing and combing, haveing [sic] fine Soaps . . . and combs wearing white cuffs and collars," Wills mused. "They had fine Horses and Equipments[.] [T]hey were Dandly Looking Soldiers[.] In the morning they would ride up the Chambersburg Pike and return to Headquarters in the Evening."[55] Despite their amusing appearance, the Philadelphians were among the most experienced soldiers Haller had at his disposal, and they frequently skirmished with Confederates in and around South Mountain, west of town.

Haller had also heard these rumors of nearby Southern forces, but the major had the reports of scouts to back up his claims. With this information in hand, he informed General Couch in Harrisburg of the gloomy outlook. Couch replied on June 25: "It would be well if you could find out what the Rebels are doing. Can't you get some Riflemen on their flanks in the mountain?"[56] With this, Haller then contacted Jennings;

> Department of the Susquehanna,   }
> Gettysburg, PA., June 25th, 1863.}
> Col. W. W. Jennings, Commanding 26th Penn. Militia:
>   Colonel: Can you raise a party of reliable riflemen who dare go into the mountain on the flank of the rebels, to discover what they are doing and harass them? Please report quickly how many can be raised.
>   By command of MAJOR GEN. COUCH

Jennings responded;

> Swift Run Hill, June 25th, 1863.
> To Major G. O. Haller:
>   Dear Sir: I will send one hundred (100) men in charge of Capt. {First Lieutenant} Lemuel Moyer—who will march directly and report to you for further orders.

Haller also ordered Jennings to "come up. The cars have been ordered to your camp, at 5:30 o'clock, A.M., to bring your command to this place (Gettysburg). Please be ready and hasten the loading, so as to be here before the hour for the passenger cars to depart. The Regiment will encamp about three miles from town, towards the mountain [west], in supporting distance of the Sharp Shooters [Lieutenant Moyer's Riflemen]."[57]

About 8 p.m. the 100 (one account states 120) men under Lieutenant Moyer of Company E started off down the York Road to Gettysburg. "I thought then it was rather a large picket party," recalled Sam Pennypacker, a member of the group. The future governor continued:

> We started off on the road to Gettysburg, looking into every thicket for a picket station, and imagining that every wood in the distance must form part of the line, but one after another was passed, and still we did not stop. About two miles from camp, we halted at a tavern, but it was only to get some water in the canteens. We there saw some of the outer pickets, among them the 'one-eyed sergeant,' {Third Sergeant William S. Lessig} and after leaving them, we knew that picketing was not the object for which we were sent. It soon commenced to rain, but not very rapidly. That was my first experience in marching, and as the Lieutenant {Moyer} appeared to be in great haste, we moved very quickly, and it was not long before I began to feel exceedingly warm and disagreeable. Those seven miles seemed almost indefinitely prolonged.[58]

The riflemen were not the only ones rather downcast and fearful. "We saw them go with misgivings," recalled W. E. Parson of Company A, "and wondered whether we should ever see them again."[59] As the riflemen came in sight of Gettysburg, Moyer gave a short speech, "saying that he wanted us to go through the streets quietly and in ranks, and that he had been informed, supper and comfortable quarters for the night were already provided for us[.]" "We began to think we were more fortunate than those who were left in camp," wrote Pennypacker.

Moyer marched his detachment into town and halted them before Haller's headquarters at the Eagle Hotel. Moyer directed the squad to remain in column while he entered the hotel to speak with Haller. Apparently, the so-chosen "riflemen" who were supposed to face the Confederates near Cashtown Pass were impatient, and soon dispersed about town. "It was raining," Pennypacker later attributed, "we were tired and anxious to be disencumbered of our loads[.] . . . Quite a number of people collected about us, of whom a large proportion were men and they seemed very slightly discomposed by the state of affairs in the neighborhood." As one Gettysburg school-girl explained: "We were all much interested in the makeup of this company, as many of the boys were from our best families, were still in their teens, and did not have the willing consent of [their] parents." "The lieutenant could not be found," Pennypacker detailed, "and the men began to drop off one after another in search of places to rest . . ."[60]

Moyer, meanwhile, had entered the Eagle Hotel to report to Haller. The major was greatly troubled with what Moyer reported. "Strange to say," Haller grumbled, "the provisions for this Regiment were not, for some reason, brought on with the men, and they were without rations. The one hundred men had no suppers, nor anything to subsist upon in the mountains. Late as the hour was (near midnight) through the assistance of members of the Committee of Safety, some rations were procured." Haller then ordered Moyer to occupy what would in a few days become known infamously as Seminary Ridge, immediately west of the town and containing on it the Lutheran Seminary and nearby Pennsylvania College, the birthplace of Company A. Haller recognized this as a "formidable position," from which to oppose the rebels.

However, Haller was even more upset and stopped the expedition once and for all when Moyer reported that the "old soldiers" who had previously served in the 127th Pennsylvania and other regiments were not chosen for the daring expedition, but rather just a detail of ten men from each company. Moyer also informed Haller that the men he brought with him "knew nothing of deploying or acting as skirmishers: that some did not even know how to load, for the officers had not yet had a chance to drill them."[61] It was about 1 a.m. when Moyer finally returned after his bashing from Haller, aroused his command, and marched them to a restaurant where they were given a piece of bread and hot coffee. From there they marched to the railroad depot, where they were ordered to pass the night.[62]

Samuel Pennypacker, in an anonymous newspaper correspondence to a Phoenixville newspaper, recalled:

{W}e passed the remainder of the night in a filthy depot. To one who left home because the rebels were so near that he could stay there no longer, it was somewhat irritating to see the numbers of men lining the streets apparently as unconcerned as if no danger were near. I thought, however, I could perceive the reason of that when upon asking quite a small boy, 'what a rebel was?' he replied, 'a black abolitionist.' He did not credit me when I told him that I acknowledged that title myself.[63]

Back at Camp Wreck, the remainder of the regiment enjoyed a relatively uneventful night. "Rained all this night," recorded Shriver. "[D]id not get wet much and slept well—The shelter tents are poor protection [a]gainst hard rains[.]"[64] By this time tomorrow, the miseries of the evening of June 25 would seem like small, trifling annoyances. Neither portion of the 26th knew that tomorrow, June 26, 1863, would be the most exciting, dangerous and miserable day of their life.

Chapter 3

Such A Confusion I Never Saw:
The Skirmish of Witmer's Farm and Bayly's Hill

About 6 a.m. on June 26, under a "pouring" rain, the remainder of the regiment departed Camp Wreck, and were "literally packed into [the] house cars," noted Captain Rice of Company F.[1] The regiment traveled down the newly repaired railroad until it reached Gettysburg an hour later, around 7 a.m. As soon as the train reached Gettysburg's station, Colonel Jennings scurried over to Haller's headquarters at the Eagle Hotel. There he shook hands with Haller and got down to business. Jennings reported that he "inquired of him [Haller] the position of the enemy, and whether his scouts were reliable, offering, if they were not, to furnish men from my reg't, who would go forward and discover the position of the enemy, and was assured by Major Haller that they were reliable, and that there was no enemy within ten miles."[2]

The militiamen were permitted to go freely about the town for breakfast, but "shortly afterwards" were called to return to the depot and drawn up in column formation in the street. Marching through the town and mud of the Chambersburg Pike during a light rain, Captain Robert Bell— commanding a company of Adams County cavalry also operating under Haller's command—conducted the regiment to their campsite a short distance east of Marsh Creek, about three miles west of Gettysburg.[3]

Professor Michael Jacobs' son, Henry Eyster Jacobs, who had accompanied the College Guards to Harrisburg and then south to Oxford, at this point departed the unit. Jacobs watched his fellow students march away, noting that they were "in excellent spirit, altho' it was raining lightly." According to Jacobs, the large majority of Gettysburg's civilians "anticipated nothing else than that their presence would divert the Confederate advance from the west, which it was not thought would be attempted in any force." Jacobs and others would soon see their flawed hypothesis play out.[4]

Before departing the town, some of the men of Company A were briefly reunited with friends and family. One boy's mother brought him a pair of rubber boots "to protect his feet from the wet." One observer noted how he "took them . . . to satisfy her motherly solicitude, but they soon found lodgment in a fence corner."[5] Young John Wills heard "talking and noises in front of the [Globe] Hotel." There he found some men of the 26th lying "all over the Pavement and up against the doors taking A rest. Among them I found some of my old acquaintances from Hanover, McSherystown [sic], and Conowago [sic]."[6]

Early twentieth-century photograph of a marker placed at the site of the 26th PVM's Marsh Creek encampment in 1912. (*Photographs and Draughts, Samuel Pennypacker Private Papers, MG 171, Pennsylvania State Archives*)

Nevertheless, about 10 a.m. the regiment arrived at "a wood which stood a short distance to the right [north of the Chambersburg Pike] perhaps seventy-five yards from the road. We filed across the intervening field," recalled Pennypacker, "and were taken to a low spot of ground within the wood, where instead of stacking arms we placed them butts upward, and with the bayonets thrust into the ground in order to keep the powder from becoming wet." The regiment, which according to Pennypacker was stretched out in one long line, then commenced to pitch tents. "It was a very unfavorable place for a camp," commented the future governor, "as the ground in consequence of the heavy rain was almost in the condition of a swamp and the feet sank into the water at every step." Private Shriver and several other militiamen were pleasantly surprised when they were able to floor their tents by raiding a pile of shingles in the woods. Colonel Jennings detached roughly 20 men to serve as pickets on the west side of Marsh Creek, along with a detachment from Bell's cavalry.[7]

On the march to their new quarters, Jennings received the first news that morning of a Confederate advance towards Gettysburg. Jennings related in his report that about a mile and a half out of town, a scout "informed me that the enemy was advancing in force with Artillery, Cavalry, and Infantry, but Capt. Bell . . . assured me this could not be correct, and that this scout was not reliable." Haller, however, gave a different version of events, stating that this encounter not only occurred after Jennings was in camp, but Bell informed Jennings nothing about the scout being unreliable, but instead that he would "go forward and see what it might be." Regardless, Bell went forward and shortly afterward returned, reporting that he saw "a party of Rebels advancing very slowly." Bell wrote to Haller: "I have seen the advance of the Rebels just beyond New Salem [now McKnightstown]—probably 50 or 100." Yet Jennings states Bell reported to him that the enemy, 5000 strong, were "advancing rapidly," and within three-quarters of a mile of his command. Bell, the 26th's Adjutant Harvey W. McKnight and Jennings stood on Knoxlyn Ridge (several hundred yards to the east of Marsh Creek) discussing the situation, and when one member of Company A passed the trio, he never forgot the gloomy, "serious" look clearly illuminated on their faces.[8]

Captain Robert Bell
(U.S. Army Military History Institute)

Haller's recital of the events at this point turns into an intense badgering of Jennings. Colonel Jennings, claimed Haller, had little confidence in his regiment. He supposedly told Captain Bell that "if he only had his old regiment [the 127th Pennsylvania] he would feel safe." Jennings then inquired of Bell for a route of retreat to either Harrisburg or York, and Bell "pointed out the way."[9] When analyzing Haller's account, one must keep in mind that his reputation was somewhat damaged by the rout soon-to-happen—he had to place the blame on somebody. Jennings surely did not have faith in the 26th as much as he had had in the 127th, but his comment (if he actually said it) may be taken out of context—not in that he did not believe in his men, or that he did not think they had the potential to become good soldiers—but that they were simply no match for the highly experienced Southern cavalry galloping down the road ready to kill.

The Confederates west of Gettysburg were part of the division commanded by Maj. Gen. Jubal Early. The feisty divisional commander modified his orders to cross the Susquehanna at Wrightsville (in eastern York County) and advance upon Harrisburg from the rear.

Jennings detached roughly 20 "picked" men from various companies to accompany Bell's company as pickets on the opposite banks of Marsh Creek, under command of Captain John Summerfield Forrest of Company I. Forrest led his little command across Marsh Creek "to discover if the enemy was advancing or not," in accordance with Jennings' orders. Forrest detached Samuel S. Henry and two others "to stay at an old barn on the right hand side of the pike, while he went on with the rest to station them." Henry estimated he had only been at that location for fifteen or 20 minutes when he heard a lone rifle shot, which Captain Forrest alleged had been fired without orders by a soldier "who had been in—or had belonged to the Potomac Army[.]" About ten minutes later, "along came the Rebel Cavalry and gobbled us all up, together with Capt. F[orrest]."[10]

It was shortly after noon, and the picket line west of Marsh Creek suddenly looked down the Chambersburg Pike. In the distance they saw charging rebel cavalrymen. This was Company E, 35th Virginia Cavalry Battalion, commanded by Lieutenant H. M. Strickler, leading the vanguard of Early's Division. The 35th Battalion was at the head of Brig. Gen. John Gordon's Georgia brigade, and was commanded by Lieutenant Colonel Elijah V. White. The Pennsylvanian picket line was organized with roughly 20 men of the 26th behind a fence several hundred yards west of Marsh Creek along with Bell's cavalry in a position to the left and slightly further advanced. One of White's men, Captain Frank N. Myers (commanding Company A of the 35th), observed Strickler's charge towards the militia:

{T}hey came with barbarian yells and smoking pistols, in such a desperate dash, that the blue-coated troopers {Bell's Cavalry} wheeled their horses and departed towards Harrisburg without firing a shot, while the infantry who could do so followed their example, and those who could not threw down their bright, new muskets, and begged frantically for quarter. Of course, 'nobody was hurt,' if we except one fat militia Captain, who, in his exertion to be the first to surrender, *managed to get himself run over by one of Company E's horses, and bruised somewhat.*[11]

Lieutenant Colonel Elijah V. White, 35th Virginia Cavalry Battalion
(Myers, *The Comanches*, 1987)

All of the 26th's pickets were captured.

A short distance away in the camp of the 26th along the soggy eastern banks of Marsh Creek, one of Bell's mounted scouts arrived with a warning for Colonel Jennings as White's Southern Cavaliers approached to within a mile of the pickets. Jennings immediately gave the order to "strike tent[s] and fall in line." This order served as an annoyance to many, especially the Pottstown Company, the members of which were just about to eat lunch. Not only did it interrupt their lunch—they had just gotten there. Scarcely had the Pennsylvanians pitched their tents when they heard the order to "strike tents immediately." Frank Richards of the College Company wrote to a friend that the Collegians "had just had our tents struck, and were beginning to breathe a little free, when the order came to stake tents and fall into line as quickly as possible. We marched away on quick time." Drummer Richards explained that many "did not understand this movement, and were grumbling considerably." Private Rudolph M. Schick of Company A remarked that he "never saw anything done so quickly in my life." In about five minutes, the 26th was marching away "on quick time"—all during a steady rain.[12]

Edmund W. Meissenhelder of Company A had gone into the woods near the regiment's camp to find "some of those coveted shingles" and when he came back, he "found the camp silent and deserted, with here and there a musket or a discarded haversack." Realizing the camp had been abandoned, Meissenhelder managed to overtake the 26th, which he credited to "a good pair of legs and a wholesome dread of Libby [Prison]."[13] Not all were as fortunate as Meissenhelder. Several men had gone to get straw, and upon returning found themselves behind rebel lines and prisoners of war.[14] Private Thomas Ruddy of Company F had gone "foraging after chickens" shortly after the regiment had gone into bivouac, and returned to be captured by White's cavalrymen.[15]

The retreat continued as the 26th hustled eastward through several fields until it reached Belmont School Road (then a dirt-road), which it turned onto, and continued north. Colonel Jennings reported his belief that this "was the only course by which I could save my command, avoiding the main roads."[16] Samuel Pennypacker wrote of the march:

> *It is scarcely necessary to state, that in consequence of its muddy and slippery condition, travelling was laborious and tiresome. At first, we chose our path as much as possible, and avoided the mud puddles, but we had not gone a great way before we came to a running stream about knee deep. There was nothing to do but ford, and through we went. . . . The route pursued was an exceedingly crooked one, turning at nearly every corner. We had not marched many hours before a number began to flag, and a rest being absolutely necessary, we halted for a few minutes, but soon started on again.[17]*

The effect of what Pennypacker describes was that the stronger men of the regiment led in the front while the weaker fell back to the rear. Company organization was "scattered and confused." Private Frederick W. Baugher of

Company A was familiar with the terrain, and for that reason guided the regiment from the head of the disorganized and panting column. "[W]e were loaded with our Tents[,] haversacks[,] blankets and ammunition and the roads were so muddy that we staggered at every step," lamented the Maryland-native Shriver, who added in a letter home: "you must bear in mind that it was raining all this time[.]"[18]

Drummer Richards of Company A further described what the men felt during the march (besides being exhausted);

> I need hardly say to those who have been through the experience that the private soldier knows at the time very little, indeed, of what is going on about him, of the plans that have been laid, of the movements of troops, or of the storm about to burst on his own devoted head. It will therefore be a matter of no surprise when I say that the occurrences of the moment certainly indicated an alarming condition of affairs to us, but otherwise we were in blissful ignorance, the principal feeling moving many of us to say 'cuss words' because the Colonel would not halt long enough for us to get our traps in good condition and reach our places in line.[19]

Captain Klinefelter of the Collegians recalled his thoughts;

> Here was an 'emergency' indeed! A regiment of raw recruits, deserted by him {Major Haller} who had forced them into the face of an enemy with whom we bore no comparison in numbers or discipline, and cut off from the railroad and all hope of reinforcement. Fortunately our leader {Colonel Jennings} was no 'tenderfoot,' but fully equal to the situation. With him at our head, we started off in good order, over by-roads and through muddy fields, Company A taking down the fences, and the rear company replacing them {to cover their trail}. Burdened with wet shelter tents and blankets, water and gravel in our shoes, and no time to dump them out, made this first march a rough initiation.[20]

"After some hours' tramping[,] the tremendous pace and strain," wrote drummer Richards, "coupled with the miserable condition of the roads, for it continued raining the whole of that day . . . began to tell on the men, but rest was out of the question, and 'Onward!' was still the command . . . ." As Corporal William Henry Rupp of Company A reasoned with himself, "nothing but fast marching could save us from capture." The regiment had marched about four miles from Marsh Creek at this hurried pace. They had crossed the Mummasburg and Middletown Roads, and were at this time continuing northeast towards Hunterstown and the town's namesake thoroughfare.[21]

While at the intersection of the Goldenville and Tablerock Roads, on what was then called Bayly's Hill, Colonel Jennings left the head of the column and looked out with his field glasses from the crest of the hill. "I had a view of the country, for a considerable distance," reported Jennings, "and by the assistance of my glasses, I discovered a body of the enemy (Infantry) numbering about 800 or 1000, moving in a direction which would bring them in contact with my command." In all probability, this infantry force was a two-regiment detachment from the storied "Louisiana Tigers" brigade of General Jubal Early's Confederate division. It was here that Jennings, Jenkins and Greenawalt realized just how close the Confederate pursuit was to the 26th. Jennings continued the retreat, with the knowledge that he would have to find a defensive position and make a stand soon.[22]

Meanwhile, Maj. Gen. Jubal Early was leading his rebel division after the 26th Militia. Earlier, General Early had split his column at Cashtown Gap, about a mile and a half west of Cashtown, taking three of the four brigades in his division plus most of his cavalry and artillery north along the Hilltown Road, through Hilltown and to Mummasburg. Meanwhile, his fourth brigade, Brig. Gen. John B. Gordon's brigade of Georgia Infantry and Lieutenant Colonel Elijah White's 35th Virginia Cavalry Battalion continued directly east to Gettysburg along the Chambersburg Pike. White forced the 26th to retreat from their Marsh Creek campsite. Behind White was Gordon's brigade, the former and latter both entering the town of Gettysburg after White drove the 26th away.[23]

View from Cashtown Gap, just west of Cashtown, facing northeast. Here General Early split his column, taking the majority of his division along with French's 17th Virginia Cavalry northeast on the Hilltown Road, while Gordon's brigade continued east via the Chambersburg Pike to Gettysburg with White's battalion. (*Photo by the Author*)

"I had heard on the road that there was probably a force at Gettysburg," reported Early, "though I could get no definite information as to its size, and the object of this movement was for Gordon to amuse and skirmish with the enemy while I should get on his flank and rear, so as to capture his whole force." This flanking column consisted of the 17th Virginia Cavalry, commanded by Colonel William H. French, Brig. Gen. Harry Hays' "Louisiana Tigers" brigade, Colonel Isaac Avery's (Hoke's) North Carolina brigade and Brig. Gen. William "Extra Billy" Smith's brigade of Virginians—all told nearly 4,000 men. Through an incessant rain, Early reached Mummasburg, where he "was informed that there was but a comparatively small force at Gettysburg, and I halted to wait for the infantry, whose march was impeded by the mud, sending out one of French's companies towards the latter place to reconnoiter."[24]

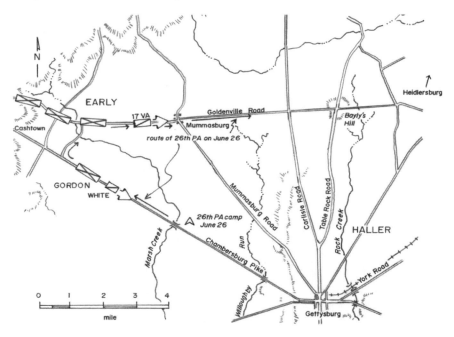

Troop Movements Near Gettysburg, June 26, 1863 (*Map by John Heiser*)

At the outbreak of the war, Colonel William Henderson French was nearly 50 years old. Born in Giles County, Virginia, in 1812, French later moved to Mercer County (now West Virginia). In 1842, 1843 and 1845, he served as the representative for Mercer County to the Virginia State legislature. In 1861, French lost a "bitter" campaign against his brother, Napoleon, an "ardent abolitionist." In July 1861, French recruited a company principally from Mercer County. This company would become Company A in the 17th. "Colonel French thought it was the best company he had," boasted Private Lewis P. Campbell of Company A. "They were all very respectable men, always ready to obey their officers and do their duties as good soldiers should."

French's company initially was mustered in as Company D of the 8th Virginia Cavalry Regiment. During the fall of 1862, French was ordered to organize a battalion of cavalry. The company was transferred from the

8th and formed part of the 33rd Virginia Cavalry Battalion (also known as "French's Battalion") in December 1862. With the arrival of more companies, the 33rd Battalion became part of the 17th Regiment in late January 1863. French was generally well-liked within the 17th. "[A] perfect gentleman," French "was good and kind to his men and his men all liked him." One lieutenant wrote that French "was a good hearted man but not much for emergencies." Throughout the war, French suffered from ongoing illness and poor health. He ultimately resigned due to his health concerns in June 1864.[25]

Colonel William Henderson French, 17th Virginia Cavalry (Redrawing of a painting in "The Story of Mercer County, WV," reprinted in John Harper Dawson, *Wildcat Cavalry*, 1982)

The 17th Virginia Cavalry was not among the elite clique of the well-equipped "black horse cavalry" of Jeb Stuart. In fact, Captain James S. A. Crawford's Company F (known as the "Night Hawk Rangers") was the only company in the 17th which was fully equipped as cavalry. Crawford's men carried revolvers, sabers and carbines (most of which were Richmond sharps or captured Federal carbines). Many of the other companies in the 17th were armed with Enfields, Mississippi rifles, short Enfield rifles and a whole assortment of diverse weaponry. Prior to the campaign, many men only had a single revolver or saber. One account even states that prior to the campaign "a number" of men had no mounts and followed the unit dismounted. However, by the time the 17th crossed into Pennsylvania, they had already countered many of these problems with massive captures of Federal Army stores and private property along the way north.[26]

From Mummasburg, General Early had dispatched Company A of the 17th to reconnoiter the surrounding country. The Virginia Cavaliers had galloped off in the direction of Gettysburg, capturing "some prisoners, from whom it was ascertained that the advance of Gordon's force [White's cavalry]... had encountered a regiment of militia, which fled at the first approach[.]" Furthermore, the company brought word that this militia regiment was only four miles away. "I immediately sent forward Colonel French with his cavalry to pursue this militia force," reported Early.[27]

Following French's cavalry were two regiments of Brig. Gen. Harry Hays' brigade, known as the "Louisiana Tigers." After arriving near Mummasburg, the Louisianans were preparing their dinners when word came of the nearby presence of Pennsylvania militia. Two regiments of the brigade were detached and sent eastward from Mummasburg to assist French; however they only neared to within a distant glimpse of the affair about to transpire between French and Jennings.[28]

With Early unleashing French's cavaliers to catch the 26th, it was now a mere race—they were now on the same road (the Goldenville Road north of Gettysburg) but the Pennsylvanians, or at least the enlisted men, did not know it yet. It was *inevitable* that French's *mounted* rebels would overtake the swollen-feet of the enlisted men of the 26th. And so they did.

The first sign of danger that Sam Pennypacker, who was in the middle of the column, observed, was when Lieutenant Colonel Jenkins rode past him, muttering under his breath, "We'll go up here a little way, get a good position, and give 'em hell before they *do* take us [emphasis original]." After hearing this, Pennypacker pondered whether Colonel Jennings really believed in him and the rest of the regiment. An hour later, Pennypacker would be sure that his colonel's judgment was woefully correct—they had no chance against the seasoned Southern cavalrymen.[29]

Meanwhile, William Hamilton Bayly, a young boy of thirteen years of age, whose father owned a nearby farm and blacksmith shop near the intersection of the Goldenville and Tablerock Roads (hence the name Bayly's Hill), happened to spot the column of the 26th as it moved eastward. Bayly, mounted on his beautiful chestnut mare Nellie, saw "soldiers moving in an easterly direction . . . . The afternoon being cloudy and dark, with rain still falling, made it impossible to distinguish uniforms."[30]

It was now nearly 4 p.m., and after roughly four miles of a hurried march, a halt was ordered about two miles west of Hunterstown, at the brick farmhouse of Henry Witmer, situated on the brow of a ridge. "Most of the command threw themselves down by the wayside to rest," recalled drummer Richards, "whilst others visited the house in search of food, and the balance climbed a row of cherry trees along the fence to eat fruit." Other Pennsylvanians formed a line at the well in front of the Witmer farmhouse. This 1860 farmstead boasted a two-story brick home, complimented by a barn and log storage house. Jennings later reported that he ordered this halt so he could again reconnoiter, as he had done on Bayly's Hill.[31]

The Witmer Farmhouse (*Photo by the Author*)

Only the front of the column had ample time to enjoy this respite. "There they are," shouted one Pennsylvanian, "and sure enough," recalled W. E. Parson of Company A, "on looking back, we saw the cavalry coming up on the brow of a hill an eighth of a mile away." Lieutenant Colonel Jenkins rode up and down the line, instructing the men "to fix up our guns [and] that the rebs were only ¾ of a mile from us." Many did not believe their lieutenant colonel, but soon turned their heads only to find themselves gaping at enemy cavalrymen. Colonel Jennings was heard to bellow: "[F]all in boys and load the Rebels are upon us."[32]

Captain Warner Carnochan's Company B, which had been designated the rear guard, was near a small stream at the eastern base of Bayly's Hill. Carnochan's soldiers came under attack first. Few of the Bradford County boys eluded capture that day, including Captain Carnochan. 16-year-old Hiram Gifford of the company managed to escape, though his three older brothers did not.[33]

Approximate view obtained by French's 17th Virginia Cavalry from Bayly's Hill. In the center of the photograph is the ridge on which Jennings' main line was positioned. *(Photo by the Author)*

The majority of the regiment was still in column, and had not even learned of the halt at Witmer's yet. "I noticed a sudden movement in front," wrote Shriver, "and all hands commenced scrambling over the fence and the Colonel ordered us to form in line of battle behind a fence." Different commands circulated, men rushed to get away from the rebels, all organization was thrown away, and the picture of Rebel cavalry men and the horrid tales of Richmond's Libby prison flashed into the minds of every Pennsylvanian. Events went too fast for many to think. "It was an occasion when veteran soldiers . . . would have been 'rattled,'" lamented drummer Richards. Many men had trouble comprehending what happened to their deathbed. "I heard the sound of bugles, saw a body of horsemen charging down on us, our own men leaping over the fence, rushing across one field and forming behind a fence in the next," Richards detailed all he understood, "and then I put my best foot forward and joined my company." [34]

"Such a confusion I never saw," later penned Shriver. "[E]verybody gave orders and nobody obeyed[.] [W]e were all green and knew nothing about regular forming and half the reg't were skedaddling already[.]" "At first there was a great deal of confusion and all jumped over the fences into the fields," Sam Pennypacker penned home to his mother. "Some of the men ran across two or three fields before they stopped." Captain Klinefelter of Company A recalled that the orders given to him were "to fall in as best we could along the fence at right angles to the road. We obeyed, amid a good deal of shouting and yelling, each fighting according to his own discretion." To add even further to the confusion, some of the rebel troopers were dressed in blue overcoats, causing many militiamen to hold their fire for fear of firing on friendly troops. [35]

View along the site of Jennings' line (*Photo by the Author*)

Little to no semblance of organization could be found on the line Jennings was attempting to form in the fields south of the Witmer farmhouse. Dennis B. Shuey of Company A found himself entangled with the Lebanon boys of Company E. Samuel Pennypacker, near the middle of the column, was unaware of the approaching enemy, and like Shriver, upon "seeing all of our men jumping over the fences on the right, I followed suit, and found myself in a corn field." Pennypacker soon saw the main line in sight, and crossed through the corn field to a nearby Wheatfield, along which was the "stake and rider" fence where the 26th's chaotic line of battle was situated. This fence extended south of the Goldenville Road, opposite the Witmer farmhouse and outbuildings which were north of the road. A cornfield sat directly in front of the fence, and at its southern end laid an adjacent wood, the latter about 150 yards distant from the road. Bayly's Hill, heavily wooded in 1863, was situated half a mile to the west.[36]

Company H, which was apparently near the front of the column, was one of the most efficient companies at Witmer's farm that day. Rallied quickly by First Lieutenant David Reese and Second Lieutenant George H. Manson, they were formed "in line of Battle two fields south from Ballys [sic] [Witmer's] house." From their position, Company H was one of the first Companies to organize and open fire on the approaching rebels. When one man of Company H was taken prisoner, Hiram J. Dunbar and several other men fired at the Southern captor and hit him near his breast, felling him from his horse.[37]

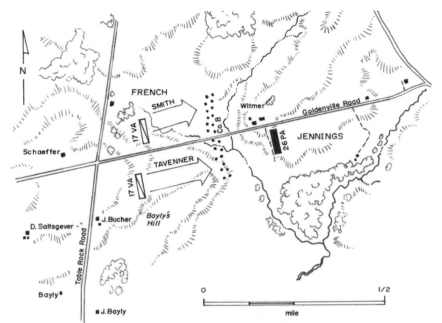

Engagement at Witmer's Farm, June 26, 1863 (*Map by John Heiser*)

"[A]s soon as I got over the fence," recalled Henry Wirt Shriver of Company I, "I called Dave [Winebrenner] and got with part of our company, prepared my gun-(I had to blow it out first- 'twas wet) and loaded[.] [M]ost of the fellows were firing already[.] I saw about <u>six</u> mounted rebels crossing the field about ¼ of a mile distant—our boys were firing at them—the road was lined with stragglers form our reg't who were in as much danger as the Rebs from our shots[.] The rebs fired too and I heard two bullets whistle over our heads—I fired one shot, more to try whether my gun would go off than anything else." Shriver describes a key problem—many of the guns were wet, and would not fire. "Our pieces were in a bad condition," remarked Frank Richards of Company A. "Half of them did not go off at first firing, they being so wet and still raining. I only got to fire three rounds, as my gun did not go off at first."[38]

That was not the only problem—Sam Pennypacker observed one of his comrades who was either "so excited or ignorant that he rammed down the first ball, and poured the powder on top, thus rendering his musket useless."[39]

The Confederate small-arms fire soon provided for some exciting experiences for many of the Pennsylvania militiamen. Dennis B. Shuey of Company A came uncomfortably close to death when two bullets struck the rail directly in front of his face.[40]

Private Rudolph M. Schick of Company A related his experiences in a letter written just several days after the affair:

I had gone into a neighboring yard to fill my canteen. I heard our Colonel cry 'fall in boys and load the Rebels are upon us.' I struck my tin cup into my knapsack and ran out in the road and saw the Rebels charging along the road in our rear{.} Here a new difficulty arose. I could not get the stopper out of my gun. I twisted in vain. At last a happy idea struck me. I stuck the stopper between my teeth and after some effort succeeded in getting it out. I loaded my gun, primed it carefully and took deliberate aim at the foremost Rebel and pulled the trigger. But alas! the Rebel did not fall. The gun absolutely refused to go off after being treated so badly as being carried in the rain all morning. This was the case with many others but fortunately not all as some half dozen Rebels felt to their sorrow.[41]

Private Rudolph M. Schick, Company A
(U.S. Army Military History Institute)

French's Virginians had now formed straddling the Goldenville Road which ran through the center of the battlefield. "As the ground was too rough and steep for horseman," recalled trooper James Hodam of the 17th Virginia Cavalry, six companies of the cavalry regiment were dismounted. Companies D, E and G, led by Lieutenant Colonel William C. Tavenner were dismounted and advanced on the south side of the road, facing Jennings' line behind the "stake and rider" fence. Major Fredrick F. Smith and Companies A, B and C were deployed north of the road, and advanced on the Witmer farmhouse.[42]

About fifteen to 20 Pennsylvanians were inside the Witmer farmhouse, and from there fired at the Southern cavalrymen as they approached. Outnumbered and eventually surrounded, they were forced to surrender even as the fighting continued on the opposite side of the road. The Pennsylvanians would be held within the house until the engagement ceased. Some of the more innovative soldiers within the Witmer home managed to avoid capture. One militiaman eluded capture when he borrowed some of the Witmers' clothes to appear as an innocent farmer, while another hid himself in a meat tub. In a more inglorious fashion, a surgeon was captured hiding in an oven. "He made a fit subject of the boys fun with his fine uniform all covered with soot and ash," recalled Virginian James Hodam. Hodam and his fellow rebels even found "a soldier lying on his face as if shot dead. Some thought he was dead sure, but when Charley Hyson tickled him a little with his sabre he jumped up all right." About a dozen Pennsylvanians hid in the bushes near the house.[43]

There was a third party of Pennsylvanians, who had not made it to the farmhouse and were cut off from the main body. Drummer Richards recalled:

> {T}hose who had been cut off from the main body of our regiment formed in squads, fighting where they stood and, in some instances, driving off their assailants, thus enabling them to rejoin their comrades; but the poor fellows in the cherry trees had reserved for them the worst fate, for as the cavalrymen rode up they pricked them with their sabers in that part of the body where a trooper generally half-soled his trousers, and pleasantly invited the Yanks to 'get down out of that,' and they could only reply in the words of the bear who saw that Davy Crockett had a 'dead bead' on him, 'Don't shoot, I'll come down!' Worst of all, they had not even a good start on the cherries, but my recollection is that, as I looked at those trees before the fight and saw there was no room on any of the limbs for more, I noticed that the cherries were 'sour,' so perhaps it was best that they did not eat too many.[44]

"[T]he ... rebel cavalry had formed in line of battle on the pike and opened fire on us with their carbines," Richards summarized, "whilst our own men from their line at the fence were in turn firing on them, and I quietly sat on my drum behind my company taking it all in."[45] In the eyes of James H. Hodam of the 17th Virginia Cavalry, he and his comrades had come to the end of "an exciting chase of several miles." Hodam recalled that "but few shots were fired by either side but the yelling on our side would have done credit to a band of Comancha [sic] Indians."[46]

Drummer Richards continued from behind the main line:

Whilst sitting on my drum behind my company, with nothing to do but much to engage my attention I was especially interested in watching a Rebel color-bearer who sat calmly beside his commanding officer in front of the regiment bearing his guidon. Unfortunately others seemed to be equally interested in him, for in a short time I saw him go down and his flag with him , the latter only to be grasped in a moment by a comrade and again displayed.[47]

Samuel Pennypacker had a memorable journey through the cornfield in front of the "stake and rider" fence, which held the 26th's main position. The future governor recalled:

Every one knows the disadvantage of going through a wet corn field, and how the mud clinging to the feet, impedes every moment. If in addition, they remember that I carried a pretty heavy load upon my back, was wearied with the previous fast tramping, and the 'rebs' not far behind, they can form a pretty good idea of an unpleasant situation. I thought to myself, 'Well, I wouldn't run across this field if the devil himself were after me,' and I do really believe, that if the whole rebel army had been within a few paces, I would have turned around to fight in a kind of determined desperation. So I walked slowly toward the rest. In this field {the cornfield}, there was the greatest imaginable confusion. The officer were running around waving their swords, shouting and swearing, but no one dreamed of obeying them; the men having been previously all mingled together, were separated from their companies, and each fellow did as he thought proper. In fact they were compelled to do so, for the commands from half crazy Captains and Lieutenants were often unintelligible, and perfectly contradictory. Collected tighter in little knots, or standing alone, they commenced firing off their pieces as rapidly as possible. Some were falling in behind the fences, and others were streaking off over the fields. I believe every man was shouting or yelling. I did not see any of the regimental officers, and think they must have been further ahead. After firing off one load and ramming down another, I began to look around for Co. F., but could not see any one of them. About half a company were drawn up behind the next fence, and thinking I might find some of them there, I went over to them. The great bulk of the regiment were much farther off, and the balls from their muskets and the rebel carbines whistled over our heads very rapidly. We were rather between the two there, and had the benefit of all the firing. . . Here I met Sergeant {George} Scheetz and . . . proposed . . . {that he} take charge of the squad, and post them where he thought proper. He suggested that it would be better to take a position on the edge of the wood, as the cavalry could not come through without being broken up, and giving us good opportunity to pick them off. . . . {W}e joined the small party who had already stationed themselves there. . . . Our regiment were now nearly all collected together, and were drawn up in line . . . we concluded we had better go over and join them, which we did.[48]

In 1863, Samuel Pennypacker recorded that this wood-line south of the Witmer farmhouse and the Goldenville Road extended to within 150 yards of the roadway, several hundred yards closer than it reaches today. Major Greenawalt's contingent of the regiment entered this wood as they retired from the line at Witmer's. (*Photo by the Author*)

Colonel Jennings rode along the line giving orders, which, in the words of one member of Company A, "seemed to be misunderstood" and as a result the regiment split in three. Major Greenawalt took about half of the regiment and entered the woods at the southern end of the battlefield, while Colonel Jennings and the other half "started [in] an almost directly opposite direction." The design, recalled Captain Klinefelter, was to change "our base to higher ground, and waiting for a short time the renewal of the rebel column." In his report, Jennings explained his belief that French's cavalry had fallen "back on the infantry following them, taking with them a number of prisoners of the rear guard and men who were not able to endure the march. Believing that [the] Infantry which I had previously seen moving to my right, would cut off my retreat, should I remain there any length of time." Jennings—who had most likely spied the Louisiana Tigers during his brief survey from Bayly's Hill shortly before the engagement at Witmer's broke out—knew that this moment was his best chance to disengage.[49]

Most of the militiamen were rejoiced to be relieved from the line, though some felt they could have held longer and were reluctant in doing so. Jennings' portion of the regiment retired to a ridge roughly a mile east of Witmer's, on the northern end of which sat the farm of William Wert. Here the two halves reunited and formed line of battle behind a fence and awaited another assault. Private Hiram J. Dunbar of Company H later claimed that his company remained in line in the fields south of Witmer's while the rest of the regiment retired to the Wert farm, and that "we would not [have] left the field but [for] our Lieutenant Seen thare [sic] [the Confederates] we are [sic] going to Right flank us and the number to[o] great for us he ordered us of[f] the field[.]" Dunbar also wrote that the company was forced "to double quick it for the Best part of a mile to get to the Balance of the Regiment" at Wert's. The third portion of the regiment, the part of Jennings' plan that went awry, was left aimlessly wandering the ground near the "stake and rider" fence "and consequently found themselves in a very few minutes as stragglers between the two portions of the Regiment. The cavalry dashed in upon these men with sword and carbine drawn, taking these stragglers prisoners." "And to the end of my days it will be one of the regrets of my life that I was not one of those stragglers," later reflected W. E. Parson of Company A. "They suffered no harm, [and] escaped the hardships of the march that followed . . . ."[50]

The renewal of the assault never came. After several minutes, Jennings interpreted that French was pausing to bring up reinforcements, and quickly withdrew his regiment eastward. The fight had lasted a mere 30 minutes, it now being close to 5 p.m. Casualties were slight. Only one member of the 26th was seriously wounded, but on the other hand, they had lost a staggering number—nearly 200—men captured. However, Captain Rice of Company F claimed that the regiment was able to unhorse at least six Rebel horsemen.[51] Casualties will be discussed in more detail in the next chapter.

Meanwhile, French's cavalry were indulging themselves on the battlefield. Trooper James Hodam blamed the lack of pursuit on the fact that Jennings' men had taken "advantage of our scattered advance to tear up a bridge delaying us a short time and a hard rain setting in[.]" This bridge Hodam refers to is likely what bridged the small stream at the eastern base of Bayly's Hill, where Captain Carnochan's Company B was nearly all captured. However, these factors were only trifles to many of the advancing Confederates, who sought to loot the battlefield of the many straggling militiamen and items dropped by Jennings' men in hasty retreat. Lieutenant Robert Gore and his Company D single-handedly captured nearly 100 Pennsylvanians, and for his remarkable feat Gore was promoted to captain on the field of battle. "The main body of the enemy," wrote James Hodam of French's Cavalry, "kept fleeing in the highway, but many, as they became exhausted[,] Sought refuge in the fields, orchards and farm buildings by the way, and many laughable incidents occurred as we gathered them in."[52] Hodam continued:

> Six were found hid among the branches of a large apple tree. One portly lieutenant in attempting to crawl under a corn crib, had stuck fast by the head and shoulders, leaving the rest of his person exposed. Comrades Charley Hyson and Morgan Feather had hard work to drag him out by the heels. But the most fun came when we dragged from a family bake oven a regimental officer, who in his gold laced uniform was covered with soot and ashes. . . . During my whole army life I never came across as fine equipped a body of men, especially with the

luxuries of home and for a few days our regiment wore a white boiled Shirt and blowed it nose and with clean pocket handkerchiefs. I found in a knapsack that I appropriated a fine black wool hat, two white shirts, a box of paper collars (the first I ever saw) and too small for me. There was several fine towels and handkerchefs {sic} bearing the name of 'Jack' worked in a neat manner with red thread. It was too bad that Jack never had time that hot June day to mop his forehead with one of these nice gifts but I can assure the donor that a young fellow called 'Jim' appreciated those little tokens of kindness very much. The brass band was the first prisoners taken, big drum and all. While returning from escorting a lot of prisoners to the rear I met a large body of prisoners hurrying by, while at a short distance behind them a little drummer boy was trying to keep up. He was bare headed, wet, and muddy but still retained his drum. 'Hello, my Little Yank. Where are you going?', I said. 'Oh I am a prisoner and am going to Richmond', he replied. 'Look here', I said, 'You are too little to be a prisoner, so pitch the drum into that fence corner, throw off your coat, get behind those bushes, and go home as fast as you can.' "Mister don't you want me for a prisoner?' 'No' 'Can I go where I please?' 'Yes'. 'Then you bet I'm going home to mother.' Saying this as he threw his drum one way and his coat another, he disappeared behind a fence and some bushes.[53]

One member of the 26th was fortunate enough to obtain a buggy ride to Hanover, perhaps his place of residence. When within a mile of Hanover, he borrowed a saddle and "rode up [the] other edge of town and seeing the Rebs. [he] put spurs to his horse and made [for] the Susquehanna[.]"[54]

While Hodam and his comrades of the 17th Virginia Cavalry were rounding up the Pennsylvanians by the dozen at Witmer's farm, a detachment made up from various companies still remained in town, completely oblivious to the fate of their comrades. Captain Christopher W. Walker of Company C commanded this detachment. Private Augustine W. Shick of Company F related his experiences in town in a previously unpublished letter;

I was detailed, with others, to guard {the} baggage-car at Gettysburg. When word came that the rebels were coming, all but five jumped on the baggage car. The brakes were taken off the car, and the car ran down the grade till near the toll-gate. They then left the car and retreated down the railroad-the woods about a mile below the toll-gate covering their retreat. We stragglers marched down the {Baltimore} Pike and when about half a mile east of the toll gate, an orderly of the Provost Marshal came riding along, and said the rebels were not near and ordered us to go back and take care of the baggage-car. Just then, a Captain, a member of General Hooker's staff, visiting in Gettysburg, came riding along getting out to f the way of the rebels. He halted—a council of war was held—he said we must take care of the baggage we about faced—were on our way back to {the} baggage car when we saw the orderly dismounting at the toll-gate. We could see two others on horse-back. The Captain said, 'Boys, they are rebels. We must make the most of it.' He detailed two along the railroad, two along the fence, I took the middle of the pike covering the Captain. The Rebs came riding down on us. *The Captain ordered us to fire, (which was not a very prudent act). One rebel rode past me and fired twice with his revolver. Another came riding down on me swearing and saying 'Why did you fire at us?' I judge that the bullets went near their heads. This Reb fired twice at me. I dodged around under his horse's head to escape his bullets. The Captain said, 'Stop firing. We surrender.'*[55]

Corporal Charles Macdonald of Company F, who was attempting to overtake the regiment gave his account as to what took place;

While we were at lunch, a gentleman came in hurriedly; and, barely showing his face in the dining room, said "The Rebels are in town": and then disappeared in the rear of the building. His sister, our kind hostess, smiled sweetly and said, "Oh! never mind that. It is an old story, which I have heard repeated every day for the past week." Accordingly, we proceeded "not to mind it" and finished, in blissful ignorance, the generous meal which had been provided. Then, taking leave, we shouldered muskets and walked down to the Square; and asked the way to the Chambersburg Pike, and took up our line of march.

When we had about reached the spot selected for the Monument {immediately west of the town square}, we were met by a man in civilian dress, on horseback, who ordered us back to the {railroad} station. He informed us that he was Major Granville O'Haller, Staff Officer of General Crouch {sic}; that our regiment had been scattered by the Rebels 'all over York County'.

We, accordingly, returned to the station and found . . . {Captain Walker's detachment} in great anxiety as to what was best to do. {Private John R.} Rollie Caswell {of Company F} had telegraphed for an engine but it did not come; and the general sentiment appeared to be that, as we could not ride, we had better walk as lively as circumstances would permit. The cars were started down the grade; and the boys got on board, with the exception of George Steele and myself. We had not seen any Rebels, and did not know enough to take other people's word for it; so we stood and cursed our luck for a little while, until the air got blue; and then we moved down the track towards the cars.

They had halted at the foot of the grade, about a third of a mile from the station; but, when we reached there, the escort, with the exception of the Commissary, had retired. We three held a council of War and decided that, next to opposition, destruction was the proper duty of the soldier; and that the cars should be burned. We had not matches, however, and walked on to the toll-gate house, some 200 yards beyond, for the purpose of getting some. About 300 yards beyond this point, we saw four of our men holding another Council of War. We joined them, and were about to return towards the cars, when an officer in uniform, followed by an orderly, came up on horseback. He had an Army of the Potomac badge on his hat, and I believe his name was Roberts; but, of this I am uncertain. We stated out case to him; found that he was on leave of absence, to visit some friends in Gettysburg; was entirely ignorant of the condition of affairs; and would have ridden unwittingly into the enemy's hands.

We asked him if he would take charge of us, which he did at once. Throwing his horse's rein over a rail in the fence, he formed us in line across the {Baltimore} turnpike and gave the command to 'double quick' towards the car.

We had scarcely started, however, when a number of suspicious looking horseman made their appearance at the toll gate which we had just left. He halted us and sent the orderly forward, to reconoitre {sic}. The orderly stopped half way and shook his head ominously; but the Captain motioned him forward, and the next minute he was covered by the pistols of the unknown horseman and taken prisoner.

We did not require any further explanation as to who they were, and were entirely satisfied that the rebels were in town. However, our little Captain did not propose to run way from a paltry squadron or two; so quickly gave the order 'Two men on the right, behind the railroad bank', 'Two men on the left in the fence corners', 'Two men, stand here to catch the horses; and do not be afraid boys, not one shot in a thousand hits'. Before he had completed the order, every man was at his post. It did not take me long to get to mine, as I was one of the two left in the road to 'catch the horses'.

I saw the horses coming down the road all right, but the thing that troubled me, and has caused me a good deal of uneasiness ever since, was, How was I expected to catch those horses? My companion evidently made up his mind that it was too much of a contract for him to undertake, and, not wishing to stop any bullets, he lay down flat in the road.

I was attracted by a peculiar pattering sound behind me, at every shot which was fired. Glancing back, I saw my young friend striking the hard road-bed spasmodically two or three times with his open hand, as the sound of each shot reached him. . . .

The horseman came down upon us with a rush; our Springfields fired off their little shots, and then we were powerless. By this time, the enemy were on top of us; discharging revolvers in a most promiscuous manner. One of our Pottstown boys {Company F} . . . distinguished himself by going for a horseman with his bayonet, dodging meanwhile the Rebel bullets which were meant to put a stop to his efforts.

Seeing that the contest was unequal on our part, I assumed the offensive by taking command of the troops on both sides. I called a halt, in as martial a tone as I could effect, and brought he fight to a close; whereupon, we all, without regard to previous condition of servitude, proceeded to congratulate ourselves that nobody was hurt.[56]

Captain Walker and most of his men, however, did escape from Gettysburg, and "footed it to Hanover, and from there were carried on the cars." They eventually arrived at Wrightsville, where they assisted

Major Haller in the defense of the covered bridge that spanned the Susquehanna there. Haller detailed in his official report that "immediately around the bridge . . . A few hopper cars (iron), loaded with iron ore, were retained to barricade the main street leading from York to the bridge. The side streets were obstructed by boards piled together so as to make complete breastworks for defense." This area near the bridgehead was garrisoned by Walker's detachment of about 50 men, which Haller described as "very much worn down by their retreat from Gettysburg[.]"[57]

One member of Walker's squad, Private John R. "Rolly" Caswell of Company F, did not think highly of Haller. "Rolly curses Major Haller for an arrant coward," recorded Pennypacker, a close friend of Caswell's, "and says, that when the 'rebs' were coming, he drew them up, told them if they wanted him to send for him, and scampered over the bridge as fast as he could travel."[58] After the skirmish near Wrightsville on June 28, Walker retired with the rest of Haller's troops across the Susquehanna eastward to Columbia. Captain Walker rejoined the regiment on July 1.[59]

When the 26th arrived in Gettysburg on the morning of June 26, a detachment of "8 to 12 men" was left in the town under command of Captain John T. Morgan of Company H. Their duty was to follow the regiment "with two wagon loads of provisions." The group had reached the western edge of the town, on Seminary Ridge, when several troopers of the lavish Philadelphia City Troop "came dashing towards us, saying, get back get back, the rebels are coming." Private J. Howard Jacobs of Company F, a member of this group, recalled that the "troopers flew back to Gettysburg, and did not show up even to guard our train."

Without protection, the small group hastened back into town. "We turned our wagons back and landed them in town," Jacobs wrote, "but lacked sufficient experience to burn them, or perhaps, we feared a conflagration might induce the rebels to burn the town. Our little squad, then under the command of Captain Morgan, retreated [east] towards Oxford." Jacobs noted the general commotion which had overtaken the area. "The citizens from all directions were fleeing with their stock—the wives and children seemed to have but secondary thought—horses and cattle first." Jacobs met up with a "little Irishman" whom he convinced to join him in an endeavor to meet up with the rest of the regiment. "After riding into the night without getting any word from the regiment," Jacobs returned to Morgan's squad at New Oxford. The following morning, Morgan's group "followed the railroad back to Hanover Junction, where we got an engine and cars" which took them through York and eventually to Wrightsville. At the latter, the 26th partook in the engagement and subsequent burning of the bridge. During the engagement, Jacobs reported that the squad was "standing guard" by the bridge, likely near Walker's detachment. Morgan rejoined the regiment by July 1.[60]

Chapter 4

Discretion as the Better Part of Valor:
Analyzing the Skirmish of Witmer's Farm

1. The Legacy

The 26th has received much negative feedback from historians and fellow combatants alike for its poor performance in the actions around Gettysburg on June 26. Before criticizing the regiment, one should analyze in more detail their performance during the battle, and consider the odds against them. "I could not help notice the difference in action between the two bodies of troops," recollected drummer Henry M. M. Richards. "[B]oth thoroughly brave, but one also thoroughly disciplined by years of service, whilst the other was entirely undisciplined for lack of them. The rebels, who were losing more heavily than we, sat firm and steady on their horses, in straight and compact lines, whilst our men were full of excitement, most of them yelling at the top of their voices, some loading and firing without any pretense as to aim . . . ."[1]

Continuing on Richards' theme, a number of men within the 26th were later struck by how seemingly nerveless they were in combat at Witmer's. "I always thought that if I should be brought into an engagement, I would tremble like a leaf as you know I am naturally nervous," Sam Pennypacker confided to his mother, "but I never was more cool in my life and have trembled more handling a cup of coffee at home. The balls whistled around rapidly but did not disturb me any, except once when I ducked my head at one that came particularly close."[2]

After several decades, what could be termed a "historical stereotype" formed against the 26th, principally regarding their actions at Marsh Creek and Witmer's farm on June 26. This label fabricates that the 26th fled at the first sight of the approaching Confederates, scarcely making a stand.

The roots of such criticism can be traced back to the 26th's Confederate opponents. William J. Seymour, the adjutant of Hay's "Louisiana Tigers" Brigade of Early's Division, logged in his journal on June 26: "While preparing to cook rations, news came of a large force of Pennsylvania Militia being six miles distant, skirmishing with our cavalry. Two of our regiments were despatched [sic] to attend to them; the militia, who, no doubt, had previously resolved to die, if need be, in the defence [sic] of their homes and friends, changed their minds when they caught a glimpse of our two little regiments in the distance, and most precipitately and ingloriously fled from the field."[3] Seymour's exaggeration contains several errors; while Colonel

Jennings likely spotted the two Louisianan regiments during his survey from Bayly's Hill immediately prior to the affair at Witmer's, it is doubtful any of the rank-and-file of Jennings' regiment ever laid eyes on the Tigers' approach.

It did not take long for many rebels to formulate witticisms and puns to throw at the Pennsylvanians they captured. Sue King Black, a resident of nearby Bayly's Hill, recognized some of the collegians of Company A. She may not have been so proud to know them, considering what happened shortly thereafter. "One of the boys hid under a bed where a Reb found him and asked if his mother knew he was out," she recalled.[4]

Major General Jubal Anderson Early
(Library of Congress)

General Early took a parallel tone in his criticism of the 26th. "[They] seemed to belong to that class of men who regard 'discretion as the better part of valor,'" critiqued the Southern general. "It was well that the regiment took to its heels so quickly, or some of its members might have been hurt." To add insult to injury, Early dubbed them "frightened militia," and wrote that the prisoners he had taken were "rejoicing at this termination of their campaign."[5] Another report circulating throughout the townspeople of Gettysburg (doubtless spread by Early's Confederates) was that "about forty of them had tried to hide in one bake oven at a farm house[.]"[6]

There were many factors against the militiamen on June 26. As previously stated, many of these Pennsylvanians had not yet mastered the concept of loading and firing their weapons. Few had spent more than an hour drilling, and thusly had a colonel who understandably had little confidence in them. Further, when the French's cavalry arrived, the majority of the regiment was still in column, and completely oblivious to the threat approaching. These factors and many more all led to the defeat at Witmer's farm and the ultimate demise of the reputation of the 26th Pennsylvania Volunteer Militia.

First and foremost, inexperience plagued the militiamen in their first engagement. As previously stated, many of the men had little training, and while some companies had drilled at Camp Curtin, they had really only spent one day together as a regiment (June 25 at Camp Wreck), and in that day a mere one hour of drill. Colonel Jennings had little confidence in them, and rightly so. But more importantly, they could not have braced themselves for the fears of combat. A mere ten days ago, they were simple country farmers, students or businessmen. The large majority had never been in battle, had never felt the sensation of killing which overcomes a man when he is invested in the hot rage of battle. It should be applauded that these men even left the safety of their homes, firesides and sweethearts *voluntarily* to come to the defense of their state. They were proud of their state, and intended to defend it. Samuel Pennypacker later reflected;

It is certainly remarkable that a boy should leave his quiet country home and within a few days' march, as it were, direct to Gettysburg, not only the pivotal point of that tremendous conflict, but the scene of the most important events in all American history.[7]

Secondly, when French's cavalrymen arrived within sight, the 26th was in about the worst possible position to defend itself. Colonel Jennings and Lieutenant Colonel Jenkins both knew the rebels were near when they had reached Bayly's Hill, and determined to halt at Witmer's farm. French was closer than Jennings and Jenkins had thought, and therefore the 26th was caught out of position with the majority of its' members either up in the cherry trees or still in column. This was one of the biggest fears for any infantry commander—to be attacked by any enemy force, especially cavalry, while in column formation. It was difficult enough to respond in column, and much easier for the attacker to multiply the effects of the attack. This factor combined with the first aspect of inexperience, began the skirmish of Witmer's Farm about as bad as an engagement can begin.

This sketch by Alfred Waud depicts a generic Civil War infantry column. (*Library of Congress*)

2. Colonel Jennings vs. Major Haller

According to Pennsylvania College Professor Michael Jacobs, Haller's order for Jennings to move out west on the Chambersburg Pike was met with the "earnest remonstrances of Jennings." The professor termed it "a suicidal movement of a handful [of] chiefly inexperienced men, in the face of a large body of experienced troops." Jacobs additionally lamented that "the rebels afterward laughed at the folly of the order."[8]

If the above is true, it should be expected that Jennings, in his report to General Couch, would make at least some reference to his dissatisfaction with Haller's orders—especially considering the disastrous rout which followed. Jennings, however, reported that after conferring with and receiving Haller's orders in Gettysburg shortly after his arrival, he "*immediately* proceeded to exicute [sic] [emphasis added]."[9] The word *immediately* certainly does not imply a prolonged or brief argument or disagreement with Haller. If Jennings disagreed with the order, and by Jacobs' account, offered Haller his "earnest remonstrances," why did he not mention such in his report to Couch? The end result of the order eventually cost him nearly 200 men, which is certainly reason enough to complain or express his dissatisfaction. He could have attempted to shift much of the blame for the embarrassing debacle onto Haller's shoulders.

However, in Colonel Jennings' presence in 1892, Adjutant Harvey McKnight, who was at Jennings' side as the events unfolded on the morning of June 26, praised the colonel for his *"prompt obedience* to the order to advance to Marsh Creek, when he knew that a mistake was being made and after *courteously remonstrating* with his superior officer [Haller]; his quick comprehension of the situation when the enemy was reported to be in force within three-fourths of a mile of our position [emphasis added][.]"[10] Judging from McKnight's reliable account, Jennings may have expressed to Haller his reluctance to advance to Marsh Creek, but likely did not do so by way of "earnest remonstrances," as Professor Jacobs indicated.

This study is the first to incorporate Jennings' previously unpublished report, which gives an essential view towards the controversy. Jennings' report serves as his only known written testimony to the events which occurred on June 26. In Jennings' words, he describes his arrival at Gettysburg and the controversial events which occurred afterward between himself, Haller and Captain Bell;

Next morning {June 26} we embarked upon the cars and arrived at Gettysburg at about 7 A.M. I immediately reported to Major Haller, and inquired of him the position of the enemy, and whether his scouts were reliable, offering, if they were not, to furnish men from my reg't, who would go forward and discover the position of the enemy, and was assured by Major Haller that they were reliable, and that there was no enemy within ten miles. Major Haller then ordered me to move my command to a place three miles above {west of} Gettysburg, which order I immediately proceeded to exicute {sic} and after having advanced about one mile and a half, was met by one of Major Haller's scouts, who informed me that the enemy was advancing in force with Artillery, Cavalry, and Infantry, but Capt. Bell, who was in command of the scouts assured me that this could not be correct, and that this scout was not reliable. I continued my march and encamped at the place designated by Major Haller and immediately sent out a reliable Lieut. {Captain Forrest} with twenty picked men to discover if the enemy were advancing or not, which party was captured about one mile from that point. The Camp had not been formed when Capt. Bell rode up to me in great haste and informed me that the enemy was three fourths of a mile from my encampment, and were advancing rapidly. I then asked him if he considered scouts who allowed the enemy in as large force as his representative (which was five thousand) within three fourths of a mile of my command without giving me information reliable. The only excuse that he could give was that the heavy rain, which had set in on the night of the 25th of June, and which still continued, prevented them from discovering the enemy at a great distance. . . . Believing the enemy to be to{o}strong for my command and having orders from you {Couch} in such case to fall back. I ordered my men to fall in, {and} started for the direction Hunterstown, feeling assured that this was the only course by which I could save my command, avoiding the main roads.[11]

In his report, Jennings seems more inclined to criticize Bell's apparent lacking performance in providing him timely intelligence as to the enemy's whereabouts than Haller's disposition of his regiment. Jennings states that both Bell and Haller led him to believe that the nearest enemy forces were several miles away, when Confederate forces were actually approaching close by and in considerable force. According to Jennings, Haller informed him "that there was no enemy within ten miles."[12]

However, it was not Jacobs who picked the fight. Jacobs' narrative was published in 1864, and Haller's Memoir, reputing his dismissal from the service, was published in the fall of 1863. In his memoir, Haller placed the blame for all parts of the fiasco on Jennings. The major claimed that Jennings "expressed a want of confidence in his men, saying if he only had his old regiment he would feel safe: then asked how he could get away from his position. Captain Bell replied that the road to Gettysburg was open: the Colonel answered that the enemy would overtake him before he got there. Captain Bell then inquired which way he wanted to go: the Colonel answered Harrisburg or York, when Captain Bell pointed out the way."[13]

Bust portrait of Captain Robert Bell
(*U.S. Army Military History Institute*)

Haller further criticized Jennings' performance: "[I]f I had been in Command of that Regiment, I should have considered it my first duty to ride to the front with Captain Bell, and see that the scouts took positions to ascertain the possible number approaching, with a view to make proper disposition of my Regiment, to meet them, or retire, as the case required." Jennings, Haller maintained, "hurried off without informing me of his unexpected movement, and without giving any orders to his detachment which he had left in Gettysburg to guard the cars . . . [T]he slow and cautious advance of the Enemy, would have allowed the Regiment ample time to reach Gettysburg unmolested," contended the major.[14]

Haller attempts to paint the picture that Colonel Jennings ran off without orders at the first sight of the enemy, was negligent with scouts and left his detachment in the town deprived of instructions. The only accusation in this list that Jennings could fairly be held accountable for is the latter, leaving his detachment in town without orders. Perhaps Jennings was at the time more concerned about the well-being of the majority of his regiment; however the veteran colonel can certainly be found at fault for this mishap. Jennings also should have informed Haller of his retreat.

Haller's first accusation, that Jennings had no faith in his militiamen may be partially true, but is probably exaggerated to some extent for his own defense. The second, that he ran off without orders is, according to Jennings, not true, who reported that he believed "the enemy to be to[o] strong for my command," and additionally that he had *orders from you {General Couch} in such case to fall back* [emphasis added]." Within Haller's own pamphlet are Couch's orders to Jennings; "Colonel Jennings will use his best efforts to hold the country, harass the enemy,—attacking him at exposed points *or falling back in order*—and advancing his force or part of it, making flank attacks, etc., doing everything in his power to weaken, [and] mislead the enemy and protect the country [emphasis added]."[15] Couch's orders do state that Jennings had the authority to fall back "in order[.]" Additionally, the general phraseology of Couch's instructions seems to intend for Jennings to operate for the most part under his own command. However, Jennings certainly had trouble with falling back "*in order* [emphasis added]"—the 26th's retreat to Witmer's farm and beyond was certainly chaotic and disorderly at the least.

Haller went on to criticize Jennings' colonelship, stating that as colonel of a regiment he would have personally tended to the scouts. However, Jennings even took this step. As he states in his report, he offered Haller upon his arrival in town that morning to fill scouting positions from his own ranks, which Haller declined. Instead, the major informed Jennings that his scouts were "reliable[.]" Even despite Haller's assurances, Jennings would send out on picket 20 men under Captain Forrest of Company I, largely due to Bell's conflicting and confusing reports.[16]

The rout was the fault of a combined failure of Haller and Bell. The former should not have sent the 26th west on the pike without more positive information as to the whereabouts of the approaching Confederates, and the latter's confusing and conflicting reports befuddled and delayed the veteran colonel. Jennings is unquestionably at fault for his abandonment of

Captain Walker's detachment of the 26th guarding baggage in town, and his leaving Haller uninformed of his decision. But otherwise, Bell and Haller are to blame. Jennings was hastily placed in a chaotic situation with conflicting scouting reports and an enemy of undetermined size which was closing fast. In what he truly felt, and arguably what was, the only way to save his regiment, he quickly hustled his men several miles to the northeast, where they engaged French's cavalry at Witmer's. In a frenzied and disordered situation, with superior enemy forces quickly approaching, Jennings managed to withdraw his regiment to safety. "His coolness and bravery were remarkable," an 1894 circular distributed by the Pennsylvania Commandery of the Military Order of the Loyal Legion (MOLLUS) wrote of Jennings, "and great praise was awarded him for the skilful [sic] manner in which he conducted his regiment and saved the regiment from capture."[17]

3. The Casualties

While the skirmish at Witmer's farm may have permanently destroyed the reputation of the 26th, it did equal damage to its ranks. According to General Couch's official report, 176 officers and men were captured or missing from the engagements at Witmer's Farm and Marsh Creek.[18] Since only the picket detachment of roughly 20 men was captured at Marsh Creek and a number captured in Gettysburg, more than 120 men were captured at or on the retreat to Witmer's farm.

But more specifically, where were the men who constituted this staggering number captured? First, many stragglers that dropped out of the column on its way to Witmer's farm were of the captured. Company B was almost entirely captured while serving as the regiment's rear guard during the initial stages of the affair at Witmer's. Furthermore, the men left behind aimless and confused with Jennings' retreat plan, when the regiment mistakenly split in three, were quickly feasted upon by Lieutenant Robert Gore's Company D of French's 17th Virginia Cavalry. But this was not all. Samuel Pennypacker revisited the battlefield nearly 20 years later, in August 1881, and wrote that "a number of our men were captured" at the William Wert farm, a mile east of Witmer's, where Jennings had formed his second line of battle. Likely many of these men were too fatigued to follow the regiment in retreat.[19]

The one man seriously injured within the 26th was 20-year-old Private Thomas H. Dailey of Company C, who was wounded in the face. Second Lieutenant Edward S. McCormick of Company C recalled that Dailey "was struck in the face by a ball, which glanced from a rail of the fence, but did not injure Daly [sic] enough to require the services of the surgeon[.]"[20]

Confederate casualties, however, are more extensive and difficult to document, considering no official tally survives. Confederate Cavalry commander Jeb Stuart stated that he mislaid French's report. As narrated in the previous chapter, several Confederate cavalrymen were seen to fall from their horses during the engagement. William Few of Company E, who was among those captured at Witmer's farm, wrote after the war that he "saw a number of confederate horses running . . . riderless." Private George B. Lessig of Company F, who was in the Witmer farmhouse, related similar observations: "I saw some dozen or more cavalry horses running about without riders." As stated in the previous chapter, Private Hiram J. Dunbar of Company H along with several others recollected felling a rebel that had taken one of their own prisoner with a shot to the breast. Frank Muhlenberg of the College Guards "took deliberate aim at a reb on a sorrel horse . . . and when I fired he fell from his horse." Muhlenberg could not determine whether the rebel he shot was just wounded or killed, but stated that several other of his comrades also claimed to have seen Confederates casualties.

Further evidence comes from Private A. Stanley Ulrich of Company E, who wrote that "during this skirmish we saw quite a number of rebels tumble from their horses." Samuel Pennypacker later visited the Witmer farm in 1881, and was told by its occupants that "a number" of bullet holes were found in their gate and fence. Additionally, after the skirmish two Confederates passed by, being supported on their horses; the Witmers assumed these men must have been wounded.[21] Therefore, it is safe to say that at least half a dozen to a dozen of French's cavalrymen fell from their horses at Witmer's farm.

4. The Prisoners

Now to be accounted for, as an extension of the previous section, are the 176 prisoners taken at both Marsh Creek and Witmer's, along with those who fell out due to exhaustion in the march between the former and the latter. First are Captain Forrest and his 20 men captured near Marsh Creek on the picket post. Arriving in Gettysburg early that afternoon, the rebels kept the frightened Pennsylvanians under care of the provost guard, the 31st Georgia, in the Christ Lutheran Church (also known as the College Church) on Chambersburg Street. Later they were moved to the lower floor of the Court House to spend the night. Henry Eyster Jacobs, the son of Professor Michael Jacobs, had watched his fellow students depart the town on the morning of June 26, and anxiously awaited, as did many Gettysburgers, news on the fate of the 26th. Upon asking a Southern officer, he was informed: "You will find some of the prisoners over there on the Church Steps." No objection was made to his visiting them, and he soon conversed freely with his friends and fellow collegians, now prisoners of war.

Corporal Charles Macdonald of Company F, who was one of the Pennsylvanians trapped inside the town upon Gordon and White's entrance, recalled that he and his comrades were "escorted good naturedly back to town and lodged in the Court House... We were greeted at the door of the Court House by several members of the 26th[.]" Macdonald "spent the night getting what information I could from my new found friends, the enemy." His "new found friends," however, could not resist even then from making puns at the Pennsylvanians. "Not being as well trained and practiced in running as the soldiers of Hooker's army," remarked one Georgian, "some few of them could not make the time required for their escape and were consequently captured."

General Gordon, meanwhile, delivered one of his ever-eloquent speeches to his Georgians, which brought "the wildest enthusiasm" on the receiving end.[22]

That evening, General Early rode to the courthouse and lectured the Pennsylvanians, musing quite offensively: "You boys ought not to be out here in the field where it is dangerous and you might get hurt." Other renditions of Early's mocking include that, with a grin, he mused: "Hi, you little boys must have slipped out of your mothers' band-boxes, you look so nice. Now be off home to your mothers. If I catch you again I'll spank you all." Early the following morning they were paroled.[23] According to an official tally by General Early, there were 47 Pennsylvania Militiamen captured at Marsh Creek and in Gettysburg.[24]

Two militia officers were locked in the courthouse and not released, detained as guides for Early's column as it moved eastward to York the following day.[25] Most likely, one of these officers was Hanoverian John S. Forrest, captain of Company I. Forrest was captured at Marsh Creek and therefore would have been one of the prisoners in town, and additionally as a Hanoverian he possessed knowledge of York County and could prove valuable as a guide. Forrest not would return to his company until July 23.[26] Only days after the engagement at Witmer's farm, rumors began to spread throughout the ranks of Company I, alleging Forrest was being sent south. "Capt Forrest is reported captured and on his way to Richmond by this time; and he is the only man who could have made us service able."[27]

The large number of men captured at Witmer's farm were kept several miles north of their captured comrades in Gettysburg. Immediately after the engagement, the prisoners from Witmer's farm were taken back into Confederate lines, where they were quizzed on sensitive matters. "They asked me how many men was about Harrisburg and how we came to Gettysburg," recalled Private William Few of Company E. Few also noted an arrogant attitude among his interrogators: "[T]hey seemed to think that it was time that we give up the fight and end the war," he wrote.[28] According to General Early, this group of prisoners captured around Witmer's farm numbered 123 men.[29] This roughly concurs with the estimate of two members of Company H—Privates William G. George and Joseph Dunnel, both from West Fairview—who estimated that "about 130 of our regiment fell into the hands of the Rebels" at Witmer's.[30]

The following morning, Early marched his division further east— Gordon and White remained on the turnpike, while his other three brigades, the balance of his artillery, nine of French's cavalry companies and his prisoners from the 26th continued east from Mummasburg, to Hunterstown. At the latter, Early paroled most of the prisoners of the 26th. "The following non-commissioned officers and privates of the 26th Regiment Pennsylvania Militia taken prisoners of war near Gettysburg, Penn.," read Early's order, "are hereby permitted to go to their homes upon their parole of honor not to serve in the United State Army, or in the other military organization under the state or U.S. Government until regularly exchanged."[31]

Ambrotype of Private Jeremiah Clinton Hill, Company A. A student at Pennsylvania College, Class of 1864, Hill was captured either in the town of Gettysburg or on picket at Marsh Creek on June 26. Hill was one of those held prisoner in the town of Gettysburg. (*J. Clinton Hill Memorial Collection, J. Howard Wert Gettysburg Collection*)

Chapter 5

Such an Awful Time I Never Had:
The March Back to Harrisburg

"[W]e halted after marching a mile [at the William Wert Farm] to let the balance of our men come up," wrote Private Henry Wirt Shriver of Company I. "[A]fter they joined us we kept on across the fields towards York Springs. I could not find out where we were and in fact nobody seemed to know[.]"[1] Jennings' first thought was to find an open railroad on which to ride back to Harrisburg; but he was too late—the Confederates had possession of the railroad and the town of Gettysburg. In a short time, Early's Confederates would torch the railroad bridge across Rock Creek on the eastern edge of Gettysburg together with reportedly burning seventeen rail cars. Among these cars was one which contained "government stores" for the 26th Militia, which was hastily looted by Early's soldiers. Consequently, wrote Captain Klinefelter, this meant that the regiment would have to "tramp it to Harrisburg."[2]

Since Early's Confederate patrols were prowling all the major thoroughfares, the 26th was forced to march by fields. Colonel Jennings decided for the time being to avoid all back roads as well, and whenever and wherever possible to stay under the cover of woods. Without a guide, Jennings used local farmers who would serve as guides for some time, replacing them as the regiment proceeded. "The excitement of the fight made us forget our fatigue for a while," wrote drummer Henry M. M. Richards, but hunger began to assert itself instead. The hungry men had no trouble getting water, however, as Richards remarked: "As for water to drink, all we needed was to stoop down and dip it out of the holes made in the ground by the feet of those going before, as it still continued to rain incessantly, and whenever we crossed a ploughed field each time we lifted a foot we left a hole large enough for a rifle pit."[3]

"[B]efore long," wrote Sam Pennypacker, "we were entirely concealed by the woods. Here we halted to have the roll called and among quite a number who were missing I was not sorry to learn the 'one-eyed sergeant' [Third Sergeant William S. Lessig] was included." The march continued, and at one point, when the regiment crested a wooded hill, several Confederate scouts were discovered "moving along the opposite fence." Colonel Jennings ordered the men to lie "prone upon the ground," and in a remarkable feat, the regiment managed to evade the eyes of the Southern scouts. Jennings and the other regimental officers cautioned for "absolute silence[.]" This was especially difficult, noted Pennypacker: "There was so little noise . . . that the least sound could be heard distinctly." The Confederate scouts passed, apparently oblivious to the regiment's presence. Captain Klinefelter was least sound could be heard distinctly." The Confederate scouts passed, apparently oblivious to the regiment's presence. Captain Klinefelter was convinced that the only reason they were not discovered was because the growing darkness concealed them.[4]

Even at this point, Colonel Jennings was still indecisive as to where he should fall back to—northeast to Harrisburg, to assist in defending the state capital, or east to York and Wrightsville, and assist Haller in preventing a Confederate crossing of the Susquehanna at that point. He sent an enlisted man to Hanover, only to learn it was occupied by the enemy. Lieutenant Colonel Jenkins was dispatched to York, and after hearing nothing from him for several days, the majority of the regiment assumed he had been captured.[5]

"There was something very thrilling and romantic to me then in the idea of our position, and the resemblance we had to hunted game endeavoring to elude their pursuers," fantasized Pennypacker. "A sense of danger gave intensity to the interest with which we watched the chances of being captured." Soon it became "very dark," and Pennypacker wrote that while the added darkness made many feel more secure, it also "increased the unpleasantness of travelling." Many of the militiamen had already thrown away their haversacks and accoutrements, either left behind at Witmer's farm or tossed aside during the retreat march because of the heavy burden it encumbered them with.[6] Unlike Pennypacker, the Maryland-native Shriver found little romanticism in this night march, penning in his diary: "Such an awful time I never had."[7]

About 9 p.m. in what Captain Klinefelter termed "a night of Egyptian darkness," the regiment neared the Conewago Creek about two and a half miles below (east of) the Harrisburg road. "We had descended a road between two woods," wrote Pennypacker, "and arrived at a stream of some size and depth, crossed by a shaky foot log which had formerly possessed a railing for the use of the hand, that the effects of time had partially destroyed, leaving gaps of several feet, so that in the dark it required a degree of care to walk over safely."

About half of Captain Klinefelter's Company A had crossed when "the tramp of horses was heard in our rear." "Immediately a panic seized upon the men and all made a rush for the log," recalled Pennypacker. "Not a single word was spoken, and as the stampede commenced from the rear it sounded to me precisely like the rustle of a sudden gust of wind. . . . In their eagerness to get over, several were pushed into the water, and some even jumped in from the bank and waded through up to their waists." Klinefelter and about half of Company A who had already crossed the creek and formed on the opposite side, almost fired on the men rushing into the water, nearly mistaking them for Confederate cavalry. For their coolness, bragged Private Edmund W. Meissenhelder of Company A, they were commended by the regimental officers.[8] Drummer Richards related;

Who the horsemen were we never learned, but {we} were told they belonged to our own scouts. They never reached us, but a few moments later a horseman did dash through the stream to the road immediately in front of us, and in an instant there was the click of some two hundred rifles as they were cocked and aimed, whilst various of the owners call in a low tone of voice, "Halt!" It proved to be a farmer who was frightened almost speechless, and had as narrow an escape from death as a human being may well want to experience.[9]

Another scare occurred shortly afterwards. The two rear companies of the regiment, under Major Greenawalt, had been separated from the rest of the unit after the debacle at the log bridge. Unable to cross the creek, they went about "wandering aimlessly through the woods until our approach, which they mistook for that of the enemy." By good fortune, the wandering of Greenawalt's two companies in surrounding woods neared the rest of the regiment, which was then in a roadway. Lieutenant William F. Hinkle of Company A (part of Greenawalt's group) commanded from "but a few feet ahead" of the regiment's main column: "Halt: who comes there?"[10]

This was quickly followed by "the blood-curdling click of numerous rifle hammers." A dash for the fence alongside the road was quickly enacted. Drummer Richards recalled that the command to halt:

{W}as so sudden that it was had very much the effect of a heavy thunder-bolt out of a clear sky. With just enough sense left in them to remember that our adversaries were probably cavalry, most of the regiment jumped for the fence. I felt my hair assuming a perpendicular position, leaped for the same place, managed to get my hands on two rails, and remembering that it was take less time to crawl through than jump over, I squeezed between them and there most ingloriously stuck. I had forgotten about the roll of blanket and shelter tent over my shoulder. Unable to get through or back, and expecting a bayonet or sabre thrust every moment, I kicked most vigorously until a good Samaritan, realizing my plight, pushed me through.[11]

Unlike the majority of the regiment, Samuel Pennypacker remained in the roadway. "Having learned something by my former escapade, I stood where I was, watching intently to see what was the matter."[12]

Fortunately Colonel Jennings had kept his head. In reply to Hinkle's "Halt: who comes there," Jennings remarked, "Friends[.]" Hinkle immediately recognized Jennings' voice, and "where just before that had been doubt, dismay and an ominous crashing of inoffensive rails, orders was restored and the march resumed." Because Greenawalt's force had approached the regimental column from the head, it consequently "brought the wrong end to the front." After the debacle was resolved, recalled Captain Klinefelter, "we opened order and passed them to their place, each laughing at the others' fears." However, Jennings and Greenawalt were not in the best of humor after this incident. "This episode nettled our brave colonel," recalled Private Edmund Meissenhelder, "and led him to use language certainly more for cible [sic] than polite." Major Greenawalt was heard to snipe, "Men, you act like a set of sheep."[13]

These two scares left the men of the 26th Militia with remarkably low confidence in themselves. "Had we actually been attacked at the time," thought Pennypacker, "I firmly believe twenty-five men would have cut us all to pieces." However, the future governor reasoned that considering the same "men who have since proven themselves as brave as any who ever fought, ran in the early part of the war all the way from Bull Run to Washington, I think we are at least excusable."[14] "[I]f the rebels had attacked us we would have been scattered like chaff in 2 minutes," wrote a rightly-pessimistic Shriver. On a similar note, Shriver logged in his diary: "[T]wice was there a false alarm and each time we ran like sheep[.]"[15]

Pennypacker recalled some of the march's miseries:

> *A drizzling rain kept falling through the night, and any one can easily imagine, as we blundered on, how fatiguing the marching became. In the woods we were continually stumbling over brush and stumps or being caught by bushes and briers; in the ploughed fields we were compelled to carry an extra weight of clay with each step. It was actually a pleasure to enter a grain field, for the long straw tramped down prevented us from sinking in, and made a good road. We left a trail through them like that of some huge roller. . . . At such times when a halt was ordered, each man would drop down in his tracks and snatch a few moments slumber while awaiting the command to proceed.*[16]

About midnight, the regiment "halted along a worm-fence in an open field for an hour." From their new location, the militiamen "could distinctly hear the sound of a Rebel bugle, borne to us through the oppressive stillness of that summer night." Scouts were dispatched, however they failed to return for a lengthy amount of time. "[A]fter half an hour's shivering in the . . . rain," penned Shriver, the scouts returned only to report the obvious, that the enemy was "near at hand," and admonished the importance of "absolute silence." Still raining, the unit continued to march until nearly 3 a.m., when they "turned in on the road side." Many men, related Captain Klinefelter, were "without even a blanket to soften the stones." "[W]e were so utterly used up," Shriver attested. The regiment had marched nine nearly-consecutive hours since their fighting debut at Witmer's farm—not to mention the hurried march from Marsh Creek—and only now lay down to rest.[17]

The 26th woke up scarcely an hour later. Their short slumber had done little to alleviate their grievances, and the majority of the men still felt "stiff and sore." Saturday, June 27, began as "we were at it again," hitting the roadway about 4 a.m. "[W]e had passed near Pinetown and were about 6 miles north of Oxford," detailed Shriver. "I had held on to [my] blanket and tent but about 8 oclock [a.m.] on Saturday (27th) I found I could carry them no longer—most of the men had thrown them away almost directly the day before—Dave [Winebrenner] and I left ours in a meadow for whoever might get them[.]" In his diary, Shriver recorded that he "could scarcely walk."[18]

For many of the militiamen, a level of desperate frustration overtook them. Drummer Henry M. M. Richards recalled what many men felt:

Would we never get clear of the bloodhounds who were straining every nerve to take us, and seemed bent on our destruction? Stiff and tired as we were, this persistent pursuit had the effect of enraging the men and bringing out a desire to meet the cursed 'Johnnies' and have it out with them once and for all. It seemed a very short hour, indeed, when we again struggled to our feet and moved on.[19]

"Those who worn out [and] were unable to go further dropped off one after another, and took shelter in the various farm houses," recalled Pennypacker. "Some were captured and others escaped by exchanging their clothing for a citizen's suit." Not only were they weary, stiff and sore, but hungry. "We had had nothing to eat the day and night before," wrote Frank Richards of Company A.[20] Drummer Richards recollected:

By this time that pangs of hunger were beginning to make considerable inroads on they 'boys,' so when daylight had fully appeared and we drew near to a sort of farm house, they made a 'dead break' for it and clamored for food. The inmates consisted of a mother and two daughters, who were comely young women. As soon as they espied us they first hung a large white sheet out of one of the windows in token of amity and then met us at the gate, with tears in their eyes, begging us to take all they had, but spare their lives. I recall yet, with a smile, the look of amazement on the faces of the men at the thought that anyone could even dream of our doing them personal injury. In fact, the grief of the women so worked on their feelings that I did not notice anyone helping himself to food, although badly in need of it.[21]

By 10 a.m., the hungry men of the 26th had marched several miles to the Colonel J. Wolford Farm, at the conjunction of the Bermudian and Latimore creeks, nearly eight miles south of Dillsburg. There the regiment bivouacked in a wood on the property. Drummer Richards could not help but remembering that a mere 24 hours ago the regiment was peacefully pitching its tents at Marsh Creek near Gettysburg, completely oblivious to the nearness of Early's Confederates. "Some of the command removed their shoes form their swollen feet and found it impossible to put them on again," Richards added. A fire was started, around which the Pennsylvanians dried their soaked clothing "as well as we could." Many simply crowded around the fire, using its' warmth to assist them in attaining some much-needed shuteye.

Their gracious host, Colonel Wolford and his neighbors, made sure the men would not go hungry. "[They] kindly entertained us with bread, butter, coffee and pies," admonished Captain Klinefelter. "The farmers are bringing plenty of good food for us," recorded Shriver. Perhaps the most telling statement of the effect this feast took on the wearied militiamen was what Shriver logged in his diary: "[W]e are doing very well[.]" Even despite the hurried retreat from Marsh Creek, the battle at Witmer's and the wearisome night march, a tasty repast served to silence their complaints for the time being.[22]

But one problem edibles could not fix was that of enemy forces. The rank-and-file of the 26th was convinced that Jubal Early was still intent on capturing the remainder of the regiment. However, the main threat the Pennsylvanians faced was actually coming from the north. No matter which direction their pursuers were coming from, several of the militiamen certainly aided the efforts of their foes. While at the camp in Colonel Wolford's woods "some booby fired off his gun to remove the load, and his foolish example was followed by perhaps fifty others before it could be stopped[.]" Consequently, a group of Confederate cavalry patrols who were within hearing distance were now aware of the 26th's location. Some of the regiment's stragglers—who had fallen out and been taken prisoner by the squad of Southern cavalry listening in—believed the firing signaled that the regiment had been overtaken by Confederate forces.[23]

"By some means," recalled Pennypacker, "the Colonel received intelligence that the 'rebs' were advancing on York, so upon leaving the wood [at Wolford's farm], we took the road for Harrisburg."[24] Shortly before 1 p.m. the march was continued. Private Shriver described the march from Wolford's:

{We were} so tired that every time we halted to rest we went to sleep as soon as we sat down—drinking water from every muddy pool we found in the road—I drank water during the night that was so muddy that I spat the mud out after I had swallowed the water and yet I felt not a bit of disgust—it tastes as sweet as if it had been clear spring water{.}[25]

After about an hour the unit came to a small, roadside tavern, where the locals fed them bread and apple butter. After the entire regiment was fed, the Pennsylvanians again continued northward. "From there we pushed on rapidly, and as evening approached," reminisced Pennypacker, "I began to feel that my powers of endurance would not hold out a great while longer, but was felicitating myself upon the prospect of our successful escape[.]" As the regiment neared the outskirts of Dillsburg, they received news which further dampened their spirits when several citizens informed the militiamen that Confederates were advancing from the north. "In my heart I cursed the rebels," evoked a weary Pennypacker, "for it seemed that just when we were in hopes of obtaining some rest, and were congratulating ourselves upon the favorable opportunity, we were called upon to make still further exertions to insure our safety."[26]

Colonel Jennings immediately formed the regiment inside Dillsburg. "In order to give them a worthy reception, the Colonel formed us in a solid square, blocking the street from curb to curb, Company A, with fixed bayonets, kneeling, plants the butts of their muskets firmly in the ground," wrote Captain Klinefelter, "while Company F was close behind them ready to fire over their heads, the others to follow in succession."[27] North of Dillsburg were various Southern scouting detachments from Brig. Gen. Albert Gallatin Jenkins' brigade of Virginia cavalry. The main body of Jenkins' brigade was proceeding east through Cumberland County towards Harrisburg. By June 27, they had captured the Cumberland County seat, Carlisle.[28]

"From the disposition of affairs," recalled Pennypacker, "it looked very much as if he [Colonel Jennings] expected an attack, and he made a short speech to us saying, that if we maintained that position firmly, all the cavalry in the rebel army could make no impression upon us." After about ten minutes, "without perceiving any hostile demonstrations," the regiment moved in "Company Front" to the northeast to a small hill situated about half a mile outside the town. The regiment was split in half, five companies facing one direction while the other five fronted the opposite way. From their perch, the Pennsylvanians could see several squads of Confederate cavalrymen operating in the distance. "Small scouting parties could be seen some distance off," recalled Pennypacker, "but not in sufficient force to render them dangerous."[29]

Corporal Charles Macdonald of Company F, who had been one of those captured and paroled in the town of Gettysburg, overtook the regiment at this location northeast of Dillsburg. He found Colonel Jennings sitting in a buggy wagon driven by a citizen, overly fatigued. Macdonald informed Jennings of the nearness of Confederate forces. Macdonald's statement was seconded by a civilian, and the exhausted Jennings took them for their word and determined that the regiment could not afford to remain in position that night.[30]

The civilians of Dillsburg had prepared a worthy feast for the Pennsylvania militiamen. However, because the regiment did not stay long enough inside the town to enjoy the meal, the citizens carried the charitable repast outside of town to the 26th's camp. "The citizens bro't [sic] out coffee[,] bread[,] butter[,] pies &c. and fed us well," logged Private Shriver in his diary. Captain Klinefelter mused that, despite the threat of Confederates roaming nearby, "Company A could never be scared out of a meal." "About night fall," recorded Shriver, "we turned into a road to the right [the Siddonsburg Road] and marched about 2 ½ miles where we encamped lying on our arms all night[.]" Colonel Jennings informed the regiment that "after a march of about four miles, we would halt long enough to get some rest and sleep, which he saw were now indispensable."[31]

About 10 p.m., the regiment crossed the Yellow Breeches Creek and encamped on the east side, comforting themselves with one more object between themselves and their antagonists. The militiamen bivouacked more than 100 yards south of the Siddonsburg Road, in a "semi-circular bend" of the Yellow Breeches. "It was surrounded by wooded hills, and approached by a foot log crossing the creek," Pennypacker later reminisced.

About a dozen men of Company F were detailed to guard the foot log which served as the main passageway across the creek. The remainder of Company F were instructed to "sleep under a large tree which stood there [near the creek], but were carefully cautioned to have our muskets in our hands with bayonets fixed, ready to jump up at a moment's notice." At one point during the night, the Pottstown guards were aroused by a false alarm; one of their own officers approaching. The pickets, although fumbling around with whose musket was whose, managed this alarm much better than the last time they had been near a log bridge, at Conewago Creek. This time, nobody got wet. Back in Dillsburg, Rebel cavalry arrived on the same hill northeast of Dillsburg which the 26th had recently occupied. There, the Southern soldiers enjoyed their dinner on the same hill which only a short time earlier had played host to the 26th and the feast provided them by the residents of Dillsburg.[32]

For once, the men were able to obtain several hours of sleep. Maryland-native Shriver wrote of his slumber on the evening of June 27:

> *You cannot imagine how excessive fatigue will accommodate one to any circumstances—I laid right on my back in my place in the ranks, me side on my gun; and my belt haversack and everything on, and the ground full of stones, all wet and dirty and yet I slept so soundly that the 5 hours we slept did not seem to be so many minutes{.}[33]*

At 2 a.m., in the early, predawn hours of June 28, the 26th fell in and resumed its march.[34] As the regiment set off, Colonel Jennings deployed part of Company A as skirmishers. Firing broke out as the unit neared Siddonsburg, nearly two miles northeast of their evening campsite. The 26th's skirmishers had shouted at a man on horseback to halt. When the man refused to halt, the skirmishers opened fire. "Tow [sic] shots were fired at him, but he made his escape," recorded Corporal William Henry Rupp of the skirmish detachment. While Rupp firmly believed that this was "one of the enemies scouts on horseback," the 26th was actually on the outer extension of the Union picket lines defending Harrisburg. A picket station had been placed in the barn of a tavern near Siddonsburg, and from there "a young fellow on guard" had ridden out, and according to one unconfirmed account, was slain by the fire.[35]

The regiment halted opposite the tavern for about fifteen minutes while the men filled their canteens. The early-morning darkness still filled the sky as the regiment passed through Siddonsburg, and arrived at Lisburn about sunrise. A halt was ordered for about an hour, as the militiamen devoured their breakfasts.

Meanwhile, Privates Joseph G. Rennard and Samuel Pennypacker of Company F sat down on a board with Major Greenawalt, and discussed the distance to Harrisburg. Optimistic news spread through the regiment when one lieutenant announced they were within twelve to fourteen miles of the coveted city. Greenawalt, however "cast a damper on our spirits," recalled Pennypacker. The Lebanon native informed the duo that "it was very uncertain" that the regiment would end up in Harrisburg, as the Confederates were already beyond neighboring Mechanicsburg. Greenawalt added that he and Jennings believed Harrisburg would be attacked and "perhaps captured before night," noting that "if we did reach it, it would only be by a long round-about march." Pennypacker elicited, "I began to think we were never going to get beyond the reach of the villains."[36]

It was true. Jenkins' brigade had reached Mechanicsburg early that Sabbath morning, and was skirmishing with the militia defending Harrisburg at a local road fork called Oyster's Point, about two miles west of the capital. Later that day, Jenkins would dispatch four companies of his 16th Virginia Cavalry Regiment to Dillsburg, under Maj. James Nounnan. Meanwhile, Jubal Early's division continued eastward through Adams and York Counties. Early captured York, and would skirmish with Yankee forces at Wrightsville. Ultimately, Haller's Federal forces burned the Wrightsville Bridge across the Susquehanna to prevent Early from crossing it.[37]

It is not surprising that Greenawalt was in such a pessimistic mood. Jennings and Greenawalt knew the regiment faced threats from its rear in Dillsburg, its south in Wrightsville and its north in Mechanicsburg. Therefore, Jennings led the regiment off the Lisburn Road, on which the regiment had been proceeding, and marched several miles to the east until he met the Northern Central Railway, very close to the Susquehanna River. The regiment followed the railway northward, towards Harrisburg. Company F had the duty of serving as the regiment's rear guard. The Pottstown boys were arguably the most fortunate rear guard the 26th had yet had— for once, there were no false alarms.[38]

"After several more weary hours and miles," recalled Pennypacker, "we were gladdened by the sight of Harrisburg at a distance over the hills and a faint cheer arose along the line." Some men cracked a laugh, and Colonel Jennings even smiled for the first time in what had seemed like years. Pennypacker observed that Jennings "appeared to be in the best of spirits[.]" Captain Klinefelter noted that the regiment startled the people of the nearby village of New Cumberland as they suddenly emerged from a nearby wood, "dirty, stiff, footsore, and hungry." The 26th appeared to be little more than a group of tattered hill-people descending on civilized life for the first time.[39]

The people of New Cumberland were compassionate, feeding the regiment well. After their tasty meal, the militiamen rested an hour before marching to near the Camelback Bridge, which connected the small villages of the Susquehanna River's west shore with Harrisburg. Here the regiment halted for about an hour, while Colonel Jennings crossed the river to report to General Couch. Corporal Charles Macdonald of Company F, who despite being paroled and released, had briefly returned to Gettysburg after warning Jennings of the nearness of Rebel cavalry at Dillsburg, caught up with the regiment at this time. "Found the Colonel lying, sound asleep on a flat rock by the road-side," Macdonald wrote, "and what was left of the boys strung along without much regard to military precision."[40]

Meanwhile, those who were not sound asleep took a moment to observe the scene around them. Parties of workmen were cutting down trees so as to provide no cover to attacking rebel forces, but at the same time destroying the picturesqueness of the once-beautiful landscape. Trees were laid across the roads to resist a mounted attack. All these preparations indicated that a serious attack on Harrisburg could come at any minute.[41]

Several regiments of militia "crowded" the 26th, asking questions ranging from who they were to where they had been. Some were heard to remark that "they look hard" and that they appeared "as if they had been out for a year." Samuel Pennypacker thoughtfully observed:

I expect we did present a pretty rough appearance. We had lost all the regimental baggage, drums, tents, blankets &c., and over two hundred men, and the remainder were dirty, stiff and foot sore, limping along like so many cripples. We were destitute of everything pertaining to comfort or convenience.[42]

Many took time to reflect upon their journey. "I never Thought I could bear what we have gone thro," penned Private Henry Wirt Shriver. "[O]ld soldiers[,] that is nine months men say they never saw anything or expected anything like it[.]" Two men who had been captured at this time met up with the regiment, and told fascinating tales of their capture and parole by the Confederates. Professor Michael Jacobs of Pennsylvania College did the math, and noted that the regiment had marched 54 out of 60 consecutive hours. Different companies held up better than others. The retreat only increased the admiration which Shriver and many others held for Captain Klinefelter's Company A. Shriver wrote, "The Gettysburg College Company held out wonderfully—Prof. Wolf . . . carried his blanket . . . thro' the whole march."[43]

Colonel Jennings returned about an hour later, and ordered the regiment up into Fort Washington, the main defenses of Harrisburg, around 3 p.m. The fort rested on a high bluff known as Bridgeport Heights, overlooking the capital city. Defending Fort Washington and its' surrounding subsidiary forts was imperative to the safety of Harrisburg.[44]

The 26th was quartered in "Camp Couch," a segment of the fort named for departmental-commander General Couch, nestled between Fort Washington and one of its' subsidiaries, Fort Couch. Here the Pennsylvanians stacked arms in a clover field along a "steep hillside," with only a small assortment of tents left in the entire regiment. The Pennsylvanians were encamped next to several New York State National Guard regiments, one of which was the 8th New York. The 8th had "an enormous quantity" of chickens they had stolen from farmers all along the Cumberland Valley. Despite their plentiful booty, the 8th declined to share any meaningful proportion with its' ragged Pennsylvanian comrades.[45]

Around 6 p.m. Jennings' men received rations. After supper, the Pennsylvanians bathed in the Susquehanna before settling in for the night. It would rain this evening—as if the regiment was not already used to hard nights. With tents and blankets a rarity among the 26th, a miserable night was in store for the militiamen. Private Henry Wirt Shriver laid down to procure some much needed shuteye with only "a piece of oil cloth" between him and the rain. He lay on the hillside and "shivered till morning."[46] In this, Shriver was most certainly not alone. The future-governor of the commonwealth of Pennsylvania, Samuel Pennypacker, recalled of his first night in Fort Washington:

During the night it rained, and . . . there seemed to be no alternative but to sleep out on the open bank, without any shelter whatever. I lay down spoon fashion, between Tucker {Richard Renshaw} and another man, and the former covered me over as well as he could with the lappels {sic} and tail of his overcoat.

Thus packed together, we kept each other warm, and I shall ever feel grateful to Tucker for kindness and goodness of heart he exhibited on that and the succeeding night. Thanks to his care and my own fatigue, I slept pretty well notwithstanding the circumstances.[47]

Many members of the 26th learned a lesson in physics that evening. "[L]ocated upon the side of a hill, at an incline of about 45 degrees, passing the night without shelter, and sleeping only on what we had saved in our weary flight," described Private Edmund Meissenhelder of Company A, "[t]he morning proved that we had illustrated the law of gravity by sliding down an inclined plane to near its base."[48]

The hasty retreat from Gettysburg northward was in some respects a fairly remarkable military feat. Marching 54 out of 60 consecutive hours, a regiment of roughly 500 largely inexperienced soldiers, who had been greatly distressed and demoralized after the actions at Marsh Creek and Witmer's farm, managed to maneuver their way back to relative safety in front of Harrisburg in so short an amount of time.

However, it came at a heavy price. On the evening of June 28, as the regiment entered Fort Washington, the 26th was no doubt the epithet of the word exhausted. Further, its ranks were diminished by numerous stragglers who were physically not able to keep up with the regiment. Corporal Mathias Henry Richards of Company A, the older brother of Drummer Henry M. M. Richards, had not made it the entire way to Harrisburg, instead being forced to halt at Colonel Wolford's farm some distance south of Dillsburg, Wolford being "an old acquaintance."

Young Richards had taken his place in line when he noticed his older brother "lying on the ground unable to move," as the regiment was departing Wolford's farm. "With the permission of my commanding officer I fell out of ranks and remained back with him." After spending the night at Wolford's, the two dodged Confederate horsemen near Dillsburg, at one point even borrowing some gray clothes from local farmers in place of their uniforms, eventually reuniting with the rest of the regiment on June 30 in Fort Washington.[49] In his own words, the elder Richards wrote several weeks later that he suffered "the most severe toil and exhaustion. Our march back to Harrisburg was most severe, officers and men hardly able to drag their weary limbs along."[50]

"Taking into consideration under a kind Providence," penned Captain George Rice of Company F, "we must thank our brave and energetic Colonel Jennings for our escape, and I cannot close this hasty and imperfect sketch without praying a well-deserved tribute to Major L. L. Greenawalt, and all who saw him as he marched along as our file leader with his calm, cool, and confident air, received encouragement to preserve and fresh hope was revived and strengthened. Indeed I may say that our whole regimental organization is a good one and satisfactory to all."[51]

In a letter home to his brother at Union Mills, Maryland, Henry Wirt Shriver reflected on the retreat:

We have certainly tasted the full quality of soldiers life-How vividly Home comforts appeared to our <u>minds</u> Even as we toiled thro the mud and mire from Gettysburg to Harrisburg-with all our Turnings and Windings we marched fully 60 miles between Friday noon and Sunday noon, a thing which I never would have undertaken to do for any regard whatever, and carry the load and did; but as I told Dave we don't know what we can do till we are tried-We were tried to the utmost{.}[52]

Chapter 6

We Are Treated Very Meanly Here:
Camp Life in Fort Washington

"We are treated very meanly here," wrote home a frustrated Shriver only a day after the regiment's arrival in Fort Washington. "The Fancy New York and Phila Reg'ts are fed on fresh beef[,] have good tents[,] plenty of fire wood &c while we get salt middling (which we have to boil off two or three times to get it palatable) and army crackers [hardtack] and coffee. If we only had good cooking arrangements 'twould do well enough but we must borrow kettles and almost everything from other companies and of course wait till it suits them to lend[.]"[1]

While they may have finally reached safety in Fort Washington, a bitter feud quickly grew between the 26th and some of the other regiments in the fort. Captain Klinefelter recollected that as they entered the fort, some of the "blue jays" (as they dubbed the New York National Guardsmen in their plush blue uniforms), taunted the men of the 26th, in one instance sneering that their retreat and performance was no better than their less-than-stellar appearance. The irritable Pennsylvanians, offended and disgruntled, threatened their New Yorker counterparts that if they did not return to their daily agenda of pilfering local farms, they would see the cartridges left over from their skirmish at Witmer's farm.[2]

The weather remained unpleasant in the early morning hours of June 29, but cleared up about sunrise. "If it rains [again] our condition will be truly deplorable," expressed Shriver in his diary. Company I made a fire, on which they warmed their "very stiff and sore . . . joints and feet[.]" That morning Colonel Jennings reported the regiment unfit for duty, stating that it needed a few days rest to regain its morale and strength, and also to give time for the stragglers who were now arriving in camp to rejoin the unit. "That we are unfit for duty is really so," commented Shriver, "for not one man can walk properly from stiffness or pain in the joints and galls on the feet."[3]

Rumors were flying around the camp. "The news is of the most conflicting character," penned Shriver. "The rebs are said to have Carlisle[,] Gettysburg[,] Hanover [and] York and to be advancing in full force on Harrisburg[.] Everybody is momentarily expecting an attack and every available space is fortified by entrenchments [and] well manned and supplied with artillery[.]" Word among the 26th was that if an attack was launched against their own state capital, due to their deteriorated condition, they would not participate—"I guess we'll be out," Shriver noted. Several times throughout the day officers informed the men that they were expecting an attack during the afternoon. "God Knows what will be the result," Shriver wrote, "but if they whip us here, we deserve it that's certain—as everything seems to be rumor no one knows but that this may be rumor too[.]"[4]

There was a small attack launched by General Jenkins shortly after noon on June 29. However, this minor scrapple was merely a diversion so that Jenkins could ride further south for an unobstructed view of Harrisburg's defenses. A detachment of Jenkins' Virginia cavalrymen skirmished with Yankee militia for nearly two hours at Oyster's Point, a road fork situated nearly three miles west of Fort Washington.[5]

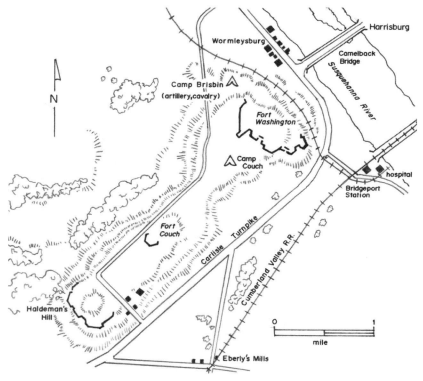

Bridgeport Heights and Fort Washington (*Map by John Heiser*)

The 26th was ordered to be prepared for a sudden Confederate advance. From their camp, the members of the 26th could observe within the fort the artillery pieces mounted and soldiers clutching their muskets and shaking nervously. Papers from Philadelphia had been brought into camp and circulated, which even worsened the morale and did away with what little confidence remained. "The Phila papers speak of 60,000 Rebs in Pa coming this way via the Cumberland Valley," recorded Shriver. The Marylander decided to take a brief stroll around the entrenchments, and was further discouraged with what he saw. "[F]ound the Artillerists drilling," he recorded. "[T]hey appear to be as green in the service as ourselves." An unconfirmed account also circulated around camp that General Couch "censured Colonel Jennings for not making a stand at Gettysburg."[6]

The regiment's quartermaster was among the missing, and since all requests for subsistence must be made through the quartermaster, the regiment had nothing to eat but hard tack, or what they were able to buy from the sutlers.[7] Money quickly became a necessity. "Whether will [sic] get any pay I do not know," Shriver reported. "It is certain however that we have to spend twice as much as we will get[.] [E]very little comfort we require we must buy and pay two prices for[.]"[8] Paying exorbitant prices for food was not what they had envisioned in return for volunteering their services.

"I must confess that I am disheartened (tho' not by any means frightened) at the aspect of affairs," Shriver confided. "I mean because our company is so inefficient that we can do nothing at all towards driving the invaders and I do not see how we ever will be, with our present company officers[.]" Captain Forrest had been captured leading a picket detachment at Marsh Creek, and the Hanoverians were again in turmoil. On a positive note, much of the regiment received blankets that evening, under which they "slept very well."[9]

But blankets cannot fight gravity. The regiment had learned the previous evening that the steepness of the slope caused them to slide down during their sleep. Several men who learned their lesson placed at their feet a piece of cordwood, with stakes to keep it in place. Henry Wirt Shriver remarked that this tactic allowed him a more pleasant slumber, "without the disagreeable sensation of slipping down the hill all the time, as it was the night before[.]"[10]

On June 30, the men of the 26th arose to a damp morning; it began to rain about 6 a.m. Many guns within the regiment were rusty, and had they gone into action, would have been of little use. Meanwhile, tensions continued to sprout within the fort. Shriver recorded in his diary: "We have rec'd no fresh beef since we are here—The New York and Phila companies have it every day[.]" The 26th was reduced to meat rations of the "roughest kind" and hardtack for food.[11]

Samuel Pennypacker found himself overtaken by "an irresistible craving for meat, and under the influence of it, on writing home to mother an account of our adventures, I asked her to send me a piece of dried beef." However, Pennypacker noted, "That was providing for the future[.]" The promise of meat in the future did little "towards alleviating present necessities," so the future-governor "went down over the hill to a small collection of houses on the bank of the river, and unsuccessfully endeavored to beg or buy some."[12]

That morning, the regiment's adjutant, Harvey W. McKnight, took down a morning report of the regiment. Samuel Pennypacker knew McKnight as a "young fellow from Co. A., who had a clear ringing voice, and pleasant agreeable manner."[13] McKnight's report shows the staggering number of men missing from the ranks four days after the regiment's debacle near Gettysburg. McKnight recorded[14];

Table II: Morning Report of the 26th PVM, June 30, 1863

Company	Present	Missing
A	52	17
B	45	37
C	48	24
D	53	14
E	55	40
F	67	31
G	45	24
H	44	14
I	40	30
K	37	25
Total	486	256

Adjutant Harvey Washington McKnight, Pennsylvania College Class of 1865, later served as Captain of Company D, 210th Pennsylvania Volunteer Infantry. From 1878 until his death in 1914, McKnight was director of Pennsylvania College. (*Special Collections, Gettysburg College*)

Among the regiment's company officers, McKnight's June 30 report shows only 4 of the 10 company commanders present.[15] These four officers are Captains Klinefelter (Company A), Pell (Company D), Rice (Company F) and Rishel (Company G). Many of the missing officers did not return for weeks. Captain Carnochan (Company B), who had been captured at Witmer's farm like so many others of his company, would not return to the regiment until July 27. Captain Forrest (Company I), captured at Marsh Creek, rejoined the 26th on July 23. By the following day, July 1, seven of the company commanders would be reported as present. Among this group were Captains Walker (Company C) and Morgan (Company H), who both had retired east from Gettysburg and fought at Wrightsville. Additionally, Captain Novinger (Company K) had returned. Captain Brooks (Company E) had rejoined the regiment by the morning of July 6.[16]

Around 1 p.m., the 26th received marching orders. The regiment exited the fort an hour later through a dirt pathway which served as an entrance/exit, and then continued west on the Carlisle Turnpike.[17]

While on the march westward, towards Oyster's Point, an incident occurred that disturbed Samuel Pennypacker for life. While the column had halted, "a negro servant of one of the officers came riding toward us on a Colonel's horse." As he approached, he was halted by the front of the regiment, and after a few moments received permission to pass. However, as he passed Company D, "a big stout bully" who is only identified as "Bill," caught the bridle of his horse, and "began to curse and abuse him in a most shameful manner. The negro replied very peaceably," recalled Pennypacker, "but Bill picked up several stones as large as he could well lift, and hurled them at him one after another with all his strength. One struck him in the middle of the back, and had it been his head must have knocked him senseless." The sight of this brutal act quickly infuriated others in the regiment. "Some of our fellows who were incensed at such a wanton outrage interfered," recalled Pennypacker, "and for a while it looked as if we were going to have a regular rumpus." "Bill" was taken to headquarters where he received only a reprimand from Colonel Jennings. Pennypacker could only comment that this incident represented the regiment "in a most shameful manner."[18]

The 26th marched about two miles west, halted and then marched about half a mile to the north, where the unit bivouacked in the middle of a grainfield. A deserted house lay about 200 to 300 yards nearby. Shriver added in his diary that they were camped "on a rising piece of ground." It is difficult to ascertain the regiment's exact position, but it was somewhere north of the Carlisle Pike and in the general vicinity of Oyster's Point. The 26th relieved a regiment which had held a similar position the day previous.[19]

It did not take long for the 26th to ransack the nearby house. While the New York and Pennsylvania militia regiments stationed here previously had certainly done their fair share, the 26th improvised to find something they might possible use. The Pennsylvanians brought out chairs, wooden boards, doors and even a stove. The latter, remarked Pennypacker "was perfectly useless to them." "The Farm house was searched throughout and not an onion or any vegetable in season was left in the garden," detailed Shriver.[20]

Also nearby was a cluster of ripe cherry trees, which the main body of the regiment had not noticed. A picket of another regiment was stationed nearby, and had made themselves especially useful by picking a large pile of cherries, and concealing it behind a tree until they returned. Shriver and several others who had wandered towards the trees quickly pitched into this pile and succeeded in devouring it before those who had picked them returned. Shriver realized the true extent of the militia's reckless rampage in this vicinity for the past two weeks when he found a beehive that had been punched open and the honey removed.[21]

While here, the regiment received their first pleasant surprise since they learned they could eat the cow that had derailed their train near New Oxford. Lieutenant Colonel Jenkins, along with many others who were supposed captured, came maundering back and rejoined the unit. The lieutenant colonel had not been heard from since he had been sent to York by Colonel Jennings immediately after the engagement at Witmer's.[22]

Shortly after Jenkins and the others rejoined the regiment, the unit moved to a clover field slightly north, but still "close by" their original location. Here they established Camp Jennings. Around sunset, a supply wagon arrived with shelter tents for the regiment. "[E]ach man gets ½ one— they are pieces of willed muslin about 4 ft[.] by 5-two or three men generally go Together, and button their pieces to each other, making a tolerable covering in wet weather," described Shriver. The men were required to find the pins and stakes for their tents themselves, scouring fences for these materials. Many also found firewood in a "fine wood" near the base of the rise on which they were encamped. Orders to cook rations for two days were issued, and the men were "kept in a continual state of excitement and expectation[.]" Meanwhile, about 100 negroes were at work cutting down trees all around the regiment, to render no hiding places for attacking Confederates (if their antagonists were to return and advance on Harrisburg, having since retired southward towards Gettysburg), and also doubling as defenses for the militiamen. As several veterans noted, this was the first time in four nights since they had enjoyed any significant cover over them, the last time being at Camp Wreck, near New Oxford.[23]

"Weather damp and drizzling[,] [we] are very comfortable in our tents," Shriver logged in his diary on July 1. Many prisoners from Gettysburg, notably from Company I, arrived in camp this day. "From their accounts I found that the rebel force was much stronger than I had believed," Shriver wrote, "being fully 6000 strong with cavalry and artillery—They were close upon us several times during our night march and we narrowly escaped being captured entirely—About 2000 of the infantry were within gunshot in the woods [on Bayly's Hill], during our skirmish, but fell back to the main body for orders after we fired on them—Had I known this during the march I would have felt much more weary than I did, for I firmly believed then, that we had been scared by a small cavalry squad whose numbers had been exaggerated by the farmers[.]"[24]

After breakfast, the regiment scoured their guns in an attempt to clean the rust that had formed from the continuous rain. "It was no slight task," recalled Pennypacker. Company I began target practice, each man firing one shot at a bull's eye 100 yards away. Shriver landed his shot "just on the edge of the mark which was second best[.]" However, the company, internally, was all but well. The company, originally numbering 72 men, had eighteen men captured and eleven missing. Among the latter were Captain Forrest and Second Lieutenant Alexander Barnes, who were still missing. Therefore, the only remaining company officer, First Lieutenant John Quincy Pfeiffer, was placed in charge. Pfeiffer's first attempt at leadership, during the retreat from Witmer's, quickly went awry. "Lieut Pfeiffer knows little or nothing so that we were our own masters and did as we Thought best," Shriver explained. "I am sorry to say [Pfeiffer] is a poor case for commanding 4 men let alone 40," Shriver confided. "We are miserably officered in our company and if I could be transferred, I would[.]"[25]

Further proof of the latter occurred when Pfeiffer ordered one of the company's corporals on duty, and received the courteous reply of "go to hell[.]" "The Lieut, then said he would have him punished for such language," recorded Shriver, "'punished and be damned,' said the corporal— The Lieut hasn't done anything with him[.] [T]he officers seem to have no power to enforce respect even if They tried, and I couldn't stand the treatment the officers get at the hands of some of the privates."[26]

That afternoon the regiment formed in ranks for regimental drill, but it began to rain and they were dismissed as soon as they had come. Towards evening, as the militiamen were preparing for a good night's sleep, they were ordered to strike tents immediately and march back to Fort Washington. When the 26th arrived in the fort they found wedge tents of a regiment that had just departed awaiting them. The 26th filled these tents in a comfortable fashion. One tent fit for eight was filled by three. Company A was detailed for picket duty about a mile out from the fort. The Gettysburgers were warned to expect Confederate cavalry to arrive during the night—fortunately for Captain Klinefelter and his men, none did.[27]

The next few days of early July became engulfed with newspapers and rumors pouring into the fort with news of a great battle near Gettysburg. "[I] felt very much concerned about the accounts in the papers this morning of fighting going on in Hanover at the Junction[,] Gettysburg and Westminster," Shriver commented. "We noticed our own movements so garbled in the newspaper accounts that we place no reliance on any of the accounts," he added.[28]

On the night of July 1, many men in the 26th had heard heavy firing from the southwest. News arrived in camp the following morning of the Shelling of Carlisle, and the Yankee victory at the latter city. Later in the day, the first reports of the Battle of Gettysburg filtered into the 26th's camp. "Heard today that a battle was fought at Gettysburg in which Gen Reynolds was killed," recorded Gettysburger William Henry Rupp of Company A in his diary. "[W]e are now anxiously awaiting the news from that quarter," Rupp added. Late on July 3, a rumor circulated about the great battle of the war between Meade and Lee, in which Lee "was badly beaten." However, many members of the 26th were hesitant to accept the rumors as fact. "[W]e have been receiving some news of the battle of Gettysburg but nothing definite yet," recorded Rupp, "but hope our forces may succeed in driving out Lee and his rebel horde."[29]

Wartime photograph of Private George Washington Frederick, Company A
(*U.S. Army Military History Institute*)

The companies of the 26th, meanwhile, rotated on picket duty outside of the fort. Shriver described his experience on picket duty;

Our company was ordered on picket duty in the afternoon and we marched out about 2 ¼ miles where we were posted in the woods near a farm house which like all others had been gutted of everything eatable- These outrages were committed while the people were absent tho' some of the soldiers committed the same things against the remonstrance of the owners- There was an old woman and a man staying at this home the rest of the family being across the river- I had several talks with the old woman who seemed to be aggravated even by the sight of a soldier at first, but I finally converted her opinion to a more favorable one of our Company at least-and she cooked me the best coffee before we left the post that I drank since in the service- She said that the soldiers who behaved so badly were the 30th Pa {Militia} Reg't who were enlisted in that very locality in fact a hired man who had lived with them and had enlisted was their guide to thro the premises-They broke open the desk expecting to find money which luckily the farmer had taken out the day before- destroyed or carried off all the eatables, Killed all the chickens, carried away even the books which the man said he would not have taken 50 dollars for—Their officers either could not or did nothing to restrain them- She said if the Rebels had come, and behaved that way every body would have made the greatest fuss about their barbarity but here our own men did it which was worse, and nothing was done- a regiment of New Yorkers were equally as rascally-the farmers told me that in a field which he pointed out they shot a fine steer dead leaving him lie to rot in the sun and at a neighbors house they shot several of his hogs from pure wantonness, and in defiance of his remonstrance-Had I read accounts of these things in the Southern Papers of Baltimore, I would have considered them malicious lies to injure the cause; but that it is really and truly the case; and worse than I have given you an idea, it is only necessary to be here to know- We had a pleasant time on picket duty our headquarters was in the woods we stationed, 3 or four men at some distance from the headquarters and the balance about 20-were off duty till their turn came which was about once a day and twice a night 2 Hours at a time- there was . . . excellent sour cherries just in their prime close by and we feasted on them to our hearts and stomachs content- we had hardly any rations with us only hard tack and a piece of cheese which I bought . . . we sent out a party on a foraging expedition who returned with two large loaves of bread and 2 pounds of butter which they bought for 75c and on which with our coffee we made a splendid meal- I went in duty at 9 oclock with my companion-we were to be relieved a 11. I thought we had been on the watch an awful long two hours-I finally called the sergeant of the Guard to know what time it was-I got no answer and at last called Dave who was at post no 3, who went with me to headquarters where we found our <u>whole party sound asleep</u>- we woke the sergeant that we had been on duty <u>4 hours</u> instead of two-we were relieved at once and did not go out again that night{.}[30]

At midnight on the evening of July 3, Company I was summoned back to Fort Washington, and upon arriving about 1 a.m. found "everything in confusion[.]" The regiment had received orders to board the cars of the Cumberland Valley Railroad, and be transported to Carlisle or beyond, where they would support the Federal forces currently pursuing Lee. When the Pennsylvanians arrived at the railroad depot, however, they found the cars already packed full with soldiers. There was nothing to do but stand by the tracks and wait. "It was raining in torrents and we stood there waiting for transportation for several hours," evoked Pennypacker. "But as there did not appear to be any provided, some of us went into a grain house by the railroad, and went to sleep." Sergeant Rupp of Company A recorded that the regiment had been standing in the rain "until 9 o'clock [a.m.] during which time we were completely drenched." It was around 9 a.m. when the cars finally arrived. "[T]he cars came—nothing but lumber cars with no windows," penned an irate Shriver. "We then got into the cars and waited with all patience for them to start," wrote Rupp. This wait—which Rupp estimated to be two hours—was certainly no pleasure, as Shriver wrote: "we were very hot being all in one car—we sat there or stood as best we could fully an hour more when we got orders to get out <u>again</u>!" Apparently they were no longer needed, and the disgruntled militiamen returned to camp shortly before noon.[31]

"And here we are on this 4th of July," penned Shriver. The regiment entered the fort just in time to catch a 30-plus gun salute, celebrating the Fourth of July. "[A] salute of 35 guns was fired shortly after we got here," recalled the Marylander. "I was on hand when they were fired and got some idea of artillery fighting—they make an awful racket when you are close by and the navy guns jump like little canine[.]"[32]

It was not long before the large majority of the Pennsylvania militia and New York State National Guard regiments which once crowded Fort Washington were sent to Carlisle and further down the Cumberland Valley to pursue Lee's retreating army. For the 26th, one of the few remaining regiments in the fortifications opposite Harrisburg, fort life grew into a monotonous daily routine. Colonel Jennings was named commandant of the fort, which in turn placed more responsibilities upon the 26th to garrison the hastily-constructed fortress. Company F was detailed to guard the gate, located at the eastern end of the fort. "That was much more agreeable than walking around the parapet," later reminisced Pennypacker, "and beside relieved us from the necessity of going on picket."[33] Pennypacker later described the guard station:

> *Two large marquee tents were arranged with board seats in them and other conveniences for guard quarters, and being just within the entrance of the fort, formed a very pleasant and capacious retreat for the reliefs off duty. My turn to go on guard came around once in every three or four days and I had no particular objection to it, save that it rained nearly every night and I was consequently very often soaked. The muskets too became wet and rusted and had to be cleaned very frequently, an operation which I always disliked or rather detested. . . . The guards are appointed for twenty-four hours and are divided into three reliefs so that each man is on duty two hours, and off the next four.[34]*

Many farmers who had fled during the invasion and were just now returning to their farms further down the valley as well as curious citizens from Harrisburg attempted to visit the fort. These bystanders served as "a regular nuisance" to those on guard. No non-military personnel were admitted unless they had with them a pass from the Provost Marshal stationed on the Camelback Bridge.[35] But as Pennypacker learned, the guards also had power with which they could hassle their superiors:

> Another time, at night, and it was a very dark night, the long roll sounded over in the woods. That, you know, is a signal of danger. Presently, there began a rattle of musketry in the same direction, and that attracted the attention of the officers. Colonel Jennings and Major Greenawalt came down to the gate to see what could be learned about it, and presently they went by me, a little out in the distance beyond. I was the guard. The lieutenant of my company, who had charge of the guard, came up to me and said, "Now mind; when they come back, you make them give you the countersign." I suppose he had read about such things in the books. You always find such incidents in the books, but I felt that I was called upon to do as he directed. The Colonel and the major presently came back. I presented my piece and said, "Halt, give the countersign," whereupon the Major said "Oh, don't be a fool," and he walked in.[36]

The regiment soon began a regular drill schedule. Squad drill took place in the mornings before breakfast, company drill in the morning from 9 to 11 a.m., regimental drill from 2 to 5 p.m. and dress parade led by Major Greenawalt at 6 p.m. every evening. "The latter [Dress parade] always possessed an attraction for me," wrote Pennypacker, "arousing all the military ardor and enthusiasm in my nature, and exciting emotions which it is difficult to describe, but somewhat akin to those which I suppose every one has experienced upon hearing a band of music play well 'The star spangled banner.' The sharp ringing tones of the Adjutant [McKnight] and the gruff bass voice of the Major [Greenawalt], who had command on such occasions, sound through my ears even yet." Roll was called at 5 a.m. by the beat of drums. "[I]f we miss roll call," noted Shriver, "we are put on extra duty of some kind." Pennypacker added that this "special duty," can make a man "swear most bitterly."[37]

There was a sutler in the fort from which small comforts could be bought at inflated prices. Another Sutler set up shop at the nearby Camelback Bridge and was known for selling quality butter. Much of the reason men would buy from the Sutlers was their sheer disgust with their issued rations, or homesickness for some little comfort. "How vividly home scenes come up before me during this distasteful life," wrote Shriver. "[E]very little thing has a double charm now-it seems like ages since we left [home][.]"[38]

J. Andrew Kirkpatrick of Clinton County was appointed chaplain of the regiment on July 2, and had prayer and preaching frequently in the evenings. Many "county people" also came into the fort selling fruit and berries, which were bought in abundance by the soldiers. Numerous Pennsylvanians made trips to the nearby town of Bridgeport where they found foods to their suiting for sale. One member of the regiment even printed a "poetical account" of the unit's June 26 skirmish near Gettysburg, entitled the "Battle of Bailey's [sic] Hill," and "made considerable money" by circulating it throughout the fort for ten cents a copy. Many men floored their tents with boards, but this did nothing to fix one large problem with Fort Washington—hygiene. "A large quantity of filth had accumulated about the fort," recalled Pennypacker, "rendering it unpleasant as well as unhealthy, and the time we spent in it was very disagreeable to me."[39]

Finding drinking water also arose as a daily dilemma for those who could not buy from the sutlers. The only water that was provided had been pumped up from the Susquehanna, into hogsheads that had previously contained coal oil, which gave the water a taste that made the men "so nauseous as almost to create vomiting." George Meigs of Company F discovered a sutler in camp that was selling delicious lemonade, and let several others in on the secret. Pennypacker, however, discovered, "under the bank a spring of good water with a narrow steep path, leading to it from the fort . . . ."[40]

Accurate reports were slow in reaching the 26th's camp of the "great battle" fought at Gettysburg. In the days immediately following the battle of Gettysburg, reports of a limited nature had found their way into the camp, the most detailed simply stating that things were going well. "We are still receiving cheering news from the army of the Potomac at Gettysburg," recorded Sergeant Rupp in his diary on July 5.[41] The Pennsylvanians would not learn for certain the result of the great battle until the evening of July 7, when Adjutant McKnight drew the regiment up in dress parade, and informed them that there would be a 36 gun salute for the simultaneous victories at Gettysburg and Vicksburg. Shriver described in a lengthy letter the events that unfolded:

{W}e were then marched to the top of the hill inside the fort and drawn up in divisions fronting towards Harrisburg-the artillery stationed just below us-the sun had been down just a little while and the sky was still full of color and I assure you it was as pretty a scene as you can imagine- The view from highest part of the fort is most extensive- probably 15 miles on all sides and the river forms a most beautiful feature in the picture Harrisburg too with the trees and houses well mixed is almost under us-our position is so high – a splendid Band belonging to one of the New York reg'ts played several national airs when the firing commenced each gun being fired in rapid succession the echo from the hills and town rattling back with a crash like thunder. While the firing was going on a beautiful wreath of smoke formed just over our heads, and floated slowly upwards, remaining perfectly defined and destined-till the last gun was fired when it gradually disappeared- Every soldier was watching it and you cannot imagine how queer it made me feel-It seems to symbolize that out of the smoke of war and confusion a union would be formed which would last; perfect in all its parts, gradually elevating itself in moral beauty and excellence, till lost in eternity. There was but this one, and the smoke from the guns was all round it at times, but twas still there as clearly defined a circle as could be marked with a company-what seemed *most singular, the other smoke went-past it with the air, while in the ring moved very slowly-Every one remarked the length of time it remained perfect;*

After the firing {Brigadier} Gen'l {William} Hall {of New York} made a short speech announcing the victory at Vicksburg and the almost certain capture of lee's army-we then gave three tremendous cheers, the band struck up Yankee doodle{.}[42]

This news was met with varied responses from the ranks of the 26th. Gettysburger William Henry Rupp, fourth sergeant of Company A, remarked that "[t]oday was a joyful and merry day in camp."[43] On another note, some of the other Gettysburgers and Pennsylvania College Students of Company A listened to the reports of a great victory at Gettysburg with mixed feelings. "How changed everything must be," Corporal Mathias H. Richards of Company A, a college student, wrote home on July 11. "[T]he peaceful cemetery, the [Lutheran] seminary, the college with the wreck of what was once my property and my room! Death all around staring at one in ghastly shapes."[44] Others pondered when their terms of service would expire. "Some began to think that the 'emergency' was nearly over," detailed Pennypacker.[45]

And soon the attention of nearly all the men in the 26th and other militia regiments which had enlisted "for the emergency" turned to this thought. Lee had been defeated, Vicksburg had fallen, Harrisburg was seemingly no longer threatened, and yet they were still being held in the service. An irritated Henry Wirt Shriver wrote home: "There are rumors this evening of our being moved up the valley but there is no certainty of it[.] I am very desirous to return home—There is nothing for us to do here, the rebels are out of Pa and the purpose for which we enlisted had been accomplished[.] . . . [I]f Lee is whipped altogether I presume we will be mustered out of service in a few weeks—I hope so at any rate—it is becoming rather monotonous here . . . . The news today looks as if Lee was going to make a stronger stand than ever on Maryland Heights—The 'Emergency' may not be over for some time if he succeeds in making a stand[.]" "We don't know how long it will be before we are mustered out," stressed a frustrated Frank Richards of Company A. "We were sworn in for the emergency. And now as Lee has been defeated and driven from the state, we wish to be mustered out as soon as possible."[46]

"During the following week the three months militia arrived from all parts of the State in great numbers, and trains were running day and night conveying them down the Cumberland Valley," recalled Pennypacker. "The people, who had never been thoroughly aroused until the State was invaded and the crisis upon them, then commenced to exert themselves in earnest, and a large force was organized and thrown into the field, though too late to be of very effective service. We, who had seen the rebels and been roughing it somewhat, felt ourselves to be of considerable consequence among the new comers, especially as many of them were of those who had previously refused to take the oath and returned home."[47]

Meanwhile, Company A found pleasantries while on picket duty in a barn about a mile outside the fort. "We are still on picket duty and prefer this place to that of Fort Washington on account of having good clear spring water," Sergeant Rupp recorded. "Whilst in the Fort we have to use the muddy water from the Susquehanna." Company A so enjoyed their tenure on picket that when their time on picket was about to expire, they sent a request to Colonel Jennings to extend their service for two more days. "And he (like a gentleman) granted it to us," wrote Rupp.[48]

Postwar photograph of Private John William Finkbinner of Company A, Pennsylvania College Class of 1869. (*Special Collections, Gettysburg College*)

Chapter 7

Another Trip Down the Valley

"It is unusual for those coming off of guard to be excused from drill, and all others duties on the following day," recalled Samuel Pennypacker. "When morning came, however," continued Pennypacker, "we were ordered to have everything prepared to strike tents and police the ground . . . . At the first sound of the Colonel's whistle, the pins were to be drawn; at the second, tents to be laid over; at the third, get to work." However, with storm clouds looming on this Saturday, July 11, Colonel Jennings delayed giving the signal, hoping for some better weather.

This unusual waiting continued for several hours, enough for Pennypacker to wash in the river and visit a sick friend in the fort hospital at the base of the hill. He returned and found the regiment still awaiting the whistle. It was later announced that the policing of the grounds would be delayed, but the men still tended to their tents. "[We] cleaned off all the old sod under the floor[,] dug a trench to turn off the water[,] laid the floor . . . and are now fixed very comfortably," logged Shriver. Later, the Pennsylvanians were informed that an inspection of arms by Major Greenawalt would occur the following morning.[1]

At 9 p.m. that evening (July 11), the men were awakened with ammunition being dealt out and marching orders; or rather in Company F, Captain George Rice flung a knapsack in each tent, and told them this must "answer the purpose of the whole party." In Company I, marching orders and ammunition were delivered to the men's tents. The muster roll was given to Lieutenant Pfeiffer, which greatly excited the Hanoverians, who momentarily believed they were about to be mustered out. However, when the excited militiamen eyed rations being distributed for three days, they knew that it meant yet another trip down the Cumberland Valley. At midnight the militiamen were ordered to cook three days rations and "pack up for marching[.]" Company A reluctantly left the barn which they had so cherished while on picket duty, and arrived in camp around midnight.[2]

About 4 a.m. the next morning, July 12, the regiment said a final farewell to Fort Washington, where they had spent two long weeks of their life. "Thank fortune, a last farewell," remarked a not-so-disparate Pennypacker. The regiment then marched down to the Cumberland Valley Railroad depot, and from there embarked on the cars about 7:30 a.m. The first stop was where a gutter ran along the tracks. There the Pennsylvanians jumped out of the cars and filled their canteens with the "cool and pleasant, but rather muddy" liquid.[3] Wrote Shriver:

Mechanicsburg was the first place we came to of any importance it is a real pretty place at least as much of it as could be seen from the cars-The Cumberland valley is a magnificent piece of country-The farms are of the very best kind, the land all level or slightly rolling and the crops in fine condition-hardly any of the grain has been harvested-We passed thro Carlisle which much handsomer town than I expected to see-It is really a beautiful place-We saw traces of the rebels along the road at several places, but the Farms were very little impaired-not nearly so much as there in the vicinity of Harrisburg, by our troops[.][4]

The regiment arrived in Shippensburg about noon, which was as far as the railroad had been repaired after being destroyed by Confederate forces. Stacking arms in the streets of Shippensburg, the Pennsylvanians sat at the doorsteps of the houses, each relatively close to his musket. Some soldiers found trouble by stealing food belonging to civilians, causing one woman to scold, "Yousens [sic] don't go and take what you want like the otherens [sic] [Confederates] did[.]"[5]

Shortly after 1 p.m. the regiment began a march on foot towards Chambersburg. "It was one of those hot and sultry days, which tend to make even a person in perfect inactivity feel feverish and unpleasant, when not a breath of air was stirring, and the very atmosphere we inhaled seemed almost to suffocate." Soon their clothing was soaked with sweat, "which rolled from us in streams." Men fell off from the column from pure exhaustion, and were evacuated to the nearest house to be cared for. The first halt was in an apple orchard about three miles from Shippensburg. "The men were very crabbed and made a fuss continually about the heat," lamented Shriver.[6]

About 5 p.m. that evening, the militiamen reached a small town called Green Village, situated along the Valley Turnpike roughly halfway between Shippensburg and Chambersburg. A large flag was strung above and across the roadway, causing wild cheering by the companies as they passed underneath it. Continuing on several miles and after some confusion, the regiment was ordered to encamp in a clover field owned by Colonel A. K. McClure, a prominent Chambersburg resident, on the outskirts of the latter town about 7 p.m. That evening the Pennsylvanians pitched their tents over 30 miles from Fort Washington, where they had been only a dozen hours earlier.[7]

As the men of the 26th looked around, they observed thousands of other militia with which they were to be cooperating—Pennypacker described their new comrades as a "large army of militia[.]"While near Chambersburg, Drummer Henry M. M. Richards found himself reunited with men from his native Reading. He recalled meeting "a number of Reading friends and relatives in the 42nd [Pennsylvania Militia] Regt." After roll call the following morning (July 13), "the boys went out on a scout to get . . . something good to eat." About 3 p.m., Colonel Jennings ordered the regiment to fall in, and "told us we would only have to march about three miles to a better location for a camp, where we would join our brigade. . . ." The 26th marched through Main Street in Chambersburg and continued south of town in the direction of Greencastle on the Valley Turnpike for "about a mile or two," before encamping in a wood that had previously been occupied by Confederate soldiers.[8]

"The woods in which we were, had been used as a camp by rebs and troops of every kind," recorded Shriver, "and the ground was filthy along with the others and after spreading a lot of fresh leaves over the ground laid our gum covers and slept on them very well tho the ground was soaked[.]" The Pennsylvanians shared their campsite with several other Pennsylvania Militia units and New York State National Guard units. That night heavy cannonading was heard from the south, but the cause was unannounced to the 26th, with the exception of an incorrect rumor spread through camp that "Meade had captured Lee's entire army at Williamsport, and we were going on to escort the prisoners back." This erroneous report was met with mixed feelings in the regiment. "We were very pleased at the news," wrote Pennypacker, "but the idea of making a double trip on foot across Maryland was not so agreeable." "[I]t seems too good to be true," Shriver logged in his diary.[9]

Alongside the Valley Turnpike was the Cumberland Valley Railroad, which had been destroyed by the Confederates for nearly seven miles. "The rails were laid in heaps along the road, all of them across gutters or hollow places so that both ends were supported upon the bank," recalled Pennypacker. "Then the sills were heaped underneath the centre, and set on fire, and when the iron became hot and soft it bent form its own weight." Pennypacker commented on the Southerners' work: "How those fellows managed to make such long daily marches, and at the same time scour the country so effectually for miles and accomplish so much hard labor, was more than I could understand." Shriver was so impressed by the coordinated destruction that he remarked: "[I]t must have been a job fully equal to laying the track[s] new[.]"

About 9 p.m., the regiment received orders to be prepared to march at 4 a.m. the following morning and to have one days rations cooked. However, the march was delayed four hours until 8 a.m. Before the regiment set off, Colonel Jennings gave a short speech, stating that they would for the first time march with their new brigade, "and from his acquaintance with our past performances he knew we could walk away from anything on the ground, especially as the greater number of the others were city chaps." As stated earlier in this study, Jennings had a strong distaste for the class of soldiers he referred to as "City Chaps," thinking them little worthy of the title of a soldier.[10]

Around 8 a.m. that morning (July 14), the regiment began its march, proceeding south, in the direction of Greencastle. "One regiment after another to the number of four or five came winding out of the woods and took position along the pike until all were stretched out in one long line... There was one wagon belonging to our regiment," recalled Pennypacker, "and those who were sick or unable to carry their baggage, were allowed to have it hauled." A guard was placed in the rear of each regiment to "pick up all who straggled without a pass from the Surgeon[.]" Because the Valley Turnpike was "so cut up" by wear and tear of many armies passing to and fro, the march was instead made on the fields on both sides of the road. On multiple occasions, the column was "compelled to make a detour by some side roads on the right, and in this way lengthened our journey considerably. Even then," lamented Pennypacker, "we marched a good part of the time in the fields on account of the ill condition of the roads."[11]

The 26th was not alone. They were in the rear of the column with their new brigade—the First Brigade, Second Division, Department of the Susquehanna. The brigade was commanded by Brig. Gen. Charles Yates of New York, and commanding the Second division was Maj. Gen. Napoleon Jackson Tecumseh Dana. The brigade consisted of the 20th, 35th and 45th Pennsylvania Militia as well as the 5th and 12[th] New York State National Guard Regiments, and was complimented by a battery of artillery.[12] The men of Company A were greatly impressed by the soldierly appearance of General Dana. "In marching along the road, I saw our Maj. Gen. (Dana) for the first time, and he presents a most soldier[l]y appearance," remarked Sergeant Rupp in his diary.[13]

Wartime image of Major General Napoleon J. T. Dana
(*MOLLUS-MASS Collection, U.S. Army Military History Institute*)

General Dana was born at Fort Sullivan in Eastport, Maine, on April 15, 1822, where his father—an artillery officer—was stationed. Entering the U.S. Military Academy at West Point at the age of 16, Dana graduated in 1842 and was assigned to the 7th Infantry. Engaged in the Mexican War, Dana was wounded so severely at Cerro Gordo that he was left on the field for dead until he found aid from a burial detail 36 hours later. In 1855, Dana resigned his commission in the army and partook in the banking business in St. Paul, Minnesota, but still maintained a commission as a brigadier general of Minnesota state militia. In October 1861, he was appointed colonel of the 1st Minnesota, which he commanded at Ball's Bluff. By spring 1862, Dana commanded a brigade in the Second Corps. While leading his brigade at the Battle of Antietam in September 1862, he was severely wounded and forced from the field for several months. In November 1862, Dana received a promotion to major general.[14] During the early stages of the Gettysburg Campaign, he had charge of the defenses of Philadelphia.[15] On July 11, Dana reported to General Couch at Chambersburg, and was assigned to command of the Second Division of the Department of the Susquehanna.[16]

Dana's newly-created Second Division consisted of three brigades, collectively totaling more than 12,000 men. The first brigade, under General Yates, was composed of Yates' 5th and 12th New York State National Guard, along with the 20th and 26th Pennsylvania Volunteer Militia and the 35th and 45th Pennsylvania Militia. Yates' brigade was supplemented by Lieutenant James W. Piper's Battery E, 5th U.S. Artillery. On July 13, the brigade totaled 3,865 men—the 26th numbered 467 men, and was the smallest regiment in the brigade. Colonel James Nagle commanded the Second brigade, which consisted of five Pennsylvania Militia units and Goodwin's New York State National Guard battery, totaling more than 4,000 men. Colonel Emlen Franklin's brigade of 4,762 men boasted six Pennsylvania militia regiments of 700 men or more.[17]

The brigade halted in a wood near Oak Grove Inn, about five miles north of Greencastle, around 1 p.m. The men rested at this spot for about two hours, during which time they slept, ate and conversed with each other. This also gave stragglers a chance to catch up. "The march that morning on account of the heat was very hard," recalled Pennypacker, "and before noon we were continually passing men lying in the fence corners and along the road completely overcome. Some of them died from the effects of the sun. I think fully one-fourth of the Philadelphia regiments straggled, and I overheard Colonel Jennings as he was looking at some of them, rather sneeringly remark 'city fellows,' a class for whom he apparently had a contempt."

About 3 p.m., two hours later, the column continued the march towards Greencastle. "The remainder of the march was comparatively easy," related Pennypacker. About dusk the regiment arrived near Greencastle, and camped on a hill about a mile north of and well in sight of the latter town. The top of the hill, where the regiment placed their tents, was flat, and after the night's rain would be unpleasantly muddy. General Dana established his headquarters in a farmhouse near the 26[18]'s camp. A miserable night awaited the militiamen, wrote Shriver:

> {T}he worst one we had since leaving Fort Washington . . . I concluded not to pitch our tents {because} it is so much trouble to get stakes, and as it did not look like rain we spread our tents on the ground without unpacking the blanket-using it for a pillow . . . and covered ourselves with the gums-about 2 o'clock I was waked by the raindrops pattering on my face-I pushed the cover over my head pulled my haversack under it and curled up under the cover . . . the rain fell in torrents, it pelted down on me where the cover touched almost like hail and thinks I if this continues I'll be floating in a little pond . . . It kept on about ½ an hour when I felt a cool sensation about my hip which was in a hollow place on the . . . ground and . . . I found that the water was filling up around me in a very disagreeable manner . . . .[19]

On July 15 the soaked Pennsylvanians awoke, expecting to march at 6 a.m. The orders were countermanded and instead the brigade remained in camp. Not much else occurred that day. "A large number of troops forming several brigades had arrived during the night and were continually coming in," detailed Pennypacker, "so that the hill was covered with them." Additionally, "[t]wo or three sutlers" arrived in camp "with loaded wagons, which were soon emptied. Among other things they had a supply of Philadelphia newspapers, a day or two old," Pennypacker recollected. "Cheese was a standing article with them and was greedily bought up at twenty-five cents per pound." On July 16, most of the regiments had marching orders towards Hagerstown, but after receiving news of Lee's retreat across the Potomac, the 26th was permitted to stay in camp. Colonel Jennings was appointed Acting Brigadier and placed in command of the camp. Governor Curtin paid a visit on this day, though he only managed to visit part of the 26th's camp.[20]

During his visit, Governor Curtin visited the camp of Company I. Marylander Henry Writ Shriver recorded of the governor's visit:

> Gov Curtin paid us a visit we all crowded round the carriage to hear what he had to say of the Emergency-He told us the news saying that Lee was across the river and Meade with him that Kirkpatrick had captured 1800 of the rear and 3 pieces of artillery-He said he was going back to Harrisburg to raise funds to pay us and that we could soon return to our homes —afterwards he made a speech in which he said that as soon as Lee's army was beaten and out of the way they would consider the Emergency over-He seemed to be somewhat intoxicated . . . .[21]

The morning of July 17 began as a number of cattle were brought into camp and shot for fresh beef. The Pennsylvanians discovered some of the natural pleasantries of their location, including a fresh water spring located at the base of the hill and abundant berries of every type, the latter which soon showed on the men's weight. "We had them almost daily at our meals for desert," lamented Pennypacker. The regiment was drilled regularly by Lieutenant Colonel Jenkins, "who had such an odd tone of voice that no one could understand his orders." Jenkins would give the order "shoulder arms, order arms, support arms," which was "entirely contrary to the manual, and would be obeyed by some reluctantly by others not at all." Once he cursed Adjutant McKnight for a mistake he made himself during a review of the brigade by Colonel Jennings. To take their minds off their bad-tempered lieutenant colonel were more rumors, one purporting that Charleston, South Carolina, had fallen. "[I] hope it may be true," remarked Private William S. Bordlemay of Company E.[22]

Private John C. Green enlisted in Company G at age nineteen. In this circa 1900 photograph, Green is standing under the gazebo, wearing a hat. (*Thomas T. Taber Museum of the Lycoming County Historical Society*)

While in camp near Greencastle, Private Richard Renshaw of Company F learned that his brother had died of wounds he suffered during the Battle of Gettysburg. "[W]ith considerable difficulty," Renshaw "succeeded in getting a furlough for a few days to attend his funeral and left for Phoenixville."[23]

This stress-free and enjoyable camp life continued until Tuesday, July 21, when about 9 a.m. the brigade struck tents, and with the 26th in the van, Colonel Jennings led his brigade north towards Chambersburg. It was a much easier march on this day, noted many Pennsylvanians, as a cool breeze blew in their faces. At 1 p.m. that afternoon the militiamen halted for an hour and a half in a wood between Greencastle and Chambersburg, and then shortly afterwards continued to their former campsite "a mile or two" south of Chambersburg.[24]

Another photo of Private John C. Green of Company G. In this photograph, Green is seated at left. (*Thomas T. Taber Museum of the Lycoming County Historical Society*)

On July 22, Major Greenawalt took the company officers "off some distance" to drill the in the military manual. Meanwhile, Sam Pennypacker was dispatched to deliver orders to the companies that the "best drilled Sergeant" of each company should take the enlisted men out do drill while Greenawalt was drilling the company officers. Some of the more clever "best drilled" sergeants felt no need to partake in a laborious drill when their company officers were busily engaged in drill of their own. In Company F, Sergeant George Scheetz's drill that morning, described by Samuel Pennypacker, began by marching "two or three fields off to be comfortably out of sight, formed under a large tree, 'shoulder arms, order arms, shoulder arms, stack arms, break ranks, march,' and we lay there on the grass until the two hours were over, and then returned to the tents. It suited the men exactly." This "company drill" lasted for several hours, although that afternoon the entire regiment participated in two and a half hours of regimental drill. "The sun was very hot and it made the boys sweat like fine fellows." Sam Pennypacker remarked that the Company F "paid up" for their morning slumber during the battalion drill under Lieutenant Colonel Jenkins. Dress parade was also held that evening.[25]

Throughout the day, "a great many women came into camp into camp with baskets of pies and molasses cakes for sale. Nearly all were sold, but they were miserable, unwholesome things. The crusts were almost as tough as sole leather, and the contents of the poorest kind as a general thing."[26]

July 24 found the 26th still in camp near Chambersburg. "Some of the boys are in a bad humor concerning our being mustered out," recorded Sergeant Rupp in his diary. Some men even threatened to stack arms if they had someone who would lead a mutiny. "They have not been in the service long enough to be acquainted with the manners and customs of camp life," Rupp, a veteran of the 87th Pennsylvania, critiqued, "and once the[y] have become acquainted with the rules and regulations of camp life they will not talk in this manner." The following day the complaints shifted to ration shortages. "Some say they will do no duty until they get something to eat," recorded Rupp. "For my part I do not see anything to complain about," Rupp continued. "It is true we do not get our full rations, but what is the use of complaining. Last evening we had quite a refreshing shower, and this morning it is cool and pleasant. . . . We had a very good dinner today of fresh beans and potatoes, and for a desert we had blackberries and milk."[27]

The morning of July 25 began with no drill, but instead "all [were] at work policing the ground, cleaning things up and burning the trash about the place." Many men considered this an indication of a movement, as before they had left all other camps, they policed the grounds first. Shortly before noon, they were informed not to get too comfortable for the evening, and "to be in readiness to move at short notice[.]" Haversacks were filled with hardtack in expectation of movement. The rain began to come down in torrents, and most supposed that as the sun set, the anticipated movement had been delayed. Many men were primarily focused on keeping their tents from blowing away in the not-so-mild rain storm.[28]

"The water runs through our tents in a perfect flood," Sergeant William Henry Rupp of Company A recorded. "Some of the boys had new potatoes in their tents and they went off when the tide was up...." Rupp was even more embarrassed by the reactions of a number of his comrades to the flooding. "Some of the boys said at the time it was raining: 'Oh I am drowning' when the water drove them out of their tents."[29]

Soon the storm ended, and the Pennsylvanians began to repair what they could. The officers informed the militiamen that they would be leaving that night for Harrisburg. "The men were in excellent spirits, with the prospect of going home," reminisced Pennypacker. The men of Company F, figuring the consequences would amount to little at this point, raided Captain Rice's tent of a large pile of potatoes, which they either ate or chucked at each other's heads "for amusement." Several companies made bonfires from nearby fence panels and brush to keep themselves warm as well as to dry their tents and blankets while they anxiously awaited the Colonel's whistle, which would signal the beginning of their return home.

Around 2 a.m. in the early, predawn hours of July 26, Colonel Jennings' whistle sounded through the camp and with a shout the regiment fell into line and commenced their march home. The skies still poured rain as the regiment marched towards Chambersburg on the Valley Turnpike. During their journey to the Franklin County seat, the militiamen were frequently obliged to take a detour from the turnpike to the fields surrounding the thoroughfare, due to the amount of mud occupying the roadway. "I had the pleasure of falling into a mud puddle which did not feel very pleasant," detailed Sergeant Rupp. Upon reaching Chambersburg, the Pennsylvanians were "packed in dirty freight cars, forty in each, so that in sitting down, our legs had to be intertwined." The cars of the Cumberland Valley Railroad did not move until closer to dawn, so, as Shriver logged in his diary, the men "spent an uncomfortable time sitting crowded in the freight car with no seats and trying to sleep as best we could[.]"[30]

At 4 a.m., the 26th departed Chambersburg via rail. The train halted about a mile north of the Franklin county seat to allow the 28th PVM and 32nd PM regiments to board the cars before continuing on to Shippensburg, where the train halted momentarily. However, the 26th was not intended to have been on this train. The 27th PVM was scheduled for the train, and Colonel Jennings was well aware of this. However, Jennings hastily put his regiment aboard the cars before the 27th arrived and then hurried the train forward before the mistake was noticed. The cars arrived opposite Harrisburg on the afternoon of July 26. The regiment disembarked and marched a short distance before establishing camp between the foot of Bridgeport heights (the site of Fort Washington), and the Carlisle turnpike. "We expected to be mustered out [the] next day," wrote Pennypacker, "but our past experience of the delay attending military matters should have taught us better."[31]

This photograph from the summer of 1863 shows a camp on the southern portion of Bridgeport Heights, a short distance outside of Fort Washington. Visible in the center background are cars on the Cumberland Valley Railroad line, by which the 26th Militia was transported down the Cumberland Valley in mid-July and back to the Harrisburg area on July 26. (*Cumberland County Historical Society*)

The afternoon of July 27 brought rumors that Southern forces had again invaded the state, and therefore an order arrived in camp as the muster rolls were being reviewed and finalized, that no more "emergency militia" were to be mustered out. "That the Emergency for which we enlisted, is over, is certain," expressed a frustrated Shriver, "but it seems that we are to be subject to every diversion which the rebels, in large or small force, may make in the direction of Pa[.]" To make matters even more vexing for the Pennsylvanians, many of the militiamen had already wrote or telegraphed home that they would be mustered out and at home "in a day or two." As far as the men of the 26th knew, it could be another month before they would be mustered out and return home.[32]

The men "slept very soundly . . . except [for] dreams of rebel frights," recorded Shriver. Many Pennsylvanians grew irate when they read issues the following evening of the Harrisburg *Evening Telegraph*, which pronounced the rumor that Confederate forces were reentering the state false—"The report, current in our streets last evening, of a raid of rebel cavalry into Pennsylvania, and the occupation of M'Connellsburg, Fulton county, turns out... to be a *hoax* [emphasis original]." This much to the chagrin of the rank-and-file of the 26th. They had come so close to being mustered out, but this "hoax" had derailed the efforts. However, this was nevertheless good news for the 26th— it meant there was no reason for which they should still be retained into service. "[E]verything looks cheerful now," recorded one militiaman. Throughout the day the men and their equipment were inspected, and after dinner the Pennsylvanians marched across the Susquehanna River over the Camelback Bridge to Camp Curtin. As the regiment marched to camp, it "stirred up such a cloud of dust that we were almost suffocated" and many later found themselves in need of a cleansing in the Susquehanna. In Camp Curtin they deposited their muskets in the same armory from which they had first drawn them.[33]

The regiment was scheduled to be mustered out on the afternoon of July 29, but it was postponed for another day. The men, therefore, washed themselves in the river, and later "climbed up the rocks and amused ourselves throwing stones into the river[.]" The reason for the delay was that the mustering officer, Captain Joseph Bush of the 13th U.S. Infantry, "was more fond of carousing about the hotels of Harrisburg than attending to his business." On July 30, Jennings "fastened on to him somewhere and brought him over [to Camp Curtin], determined that he should not escape until our regiment was mustered out." In typical fashion, Bush attempted to excuse himself: "Well, but Colonel, I must go over and get my dinner." "No you don't, Bush," Jennings was heard to reply, "I will order dinner for you here, chickens, turkey or anything you want."

Throughout the day, companies marched to the white farmhouse where Captain Bush was quartered, "answered to our names as the roll was called, and that ceremony concluded, bringing us one step nearer the end." "We were mustered out of service this morning," noted Sergeant Rupp of Company A, "and now the boys are in a very good humor and very anxious to be paid off." In Company I, after being mustered out by Bush, Captain Forrest and "4 or 5 of us took the discharges down to the Hotel and worked on them till almost dark when we finshed[.]" Warm weather made passing the night difficult, so several "Beadle's dime novels" were a pastime. Later that night, General Julius Stahel—formerly a cavalry commander in the Army of the Potomac, now serving under General Couch in the Department of the Susquehanna—was mistaken for the beloved General Frank Sigel as he rode through Camp Curtin, and was consequently given three cheers by the 26th.[34]

Friday, July 31, was spent in relative boredom and inactivity. Maryland-native Henry Wirt Shriver wandered over to Captain Klinefelter's headquarters, which he found empty. The Marylander noted a book left on the table, which he read "awhile," before returning to his company's camp. He soon met up with Captain Forrest, who he assisted in compiling a statement of articles lost in the debacle at Gettysburg on June 26. Perhaps pride was among this list. After completing this work, Shriver made his way into town, "drank some ale" at a hotel in the city before crossing the river to Bridgeport where he "ate some cheese and Rolls [and] then took a bath" in the Susquehanna. "[D]on't know what to do with myself," Shriver confessed, "we are to be paid off tomorrow so the Colonel says[.]"[35]

After breakfast on Saturday, August 1, the Pennsylvanians returned their tents, blankets, haversacks and canteens to the quartermaster. The men were left with nothing but their uniforms. In the case of Company F, their "accoutrements and knapsacks" belonged to the town of Pottstown. Until later that afternoon, the men spent another relaxing day, many going about town to dine and devour meals and other delectables they had savored for so long. Shriver noted that he "lived principally on cheese cakes, and lemonade to day[.]" Around mid-afternoon, Adjutant McKnight read a farewell from Colonel Jennings. "We gave three times three [cheers] to both of those officers," recalled Pennypacker, "and shouting good bye to Company A. we (F.) marched over to the farm house and were paid off." The men were paid sums all about $20—depending on when they were sworn in. Future governor Samuel Pennypacker received $19.26. The companies dispersed, some dining in Harrisburg before departing for their homes.[36]

Chapter 8

Returning Home

After receiving their pay, the men of Captain George Rice's Company F dispersed into the city of Harrisburg. There, the Pottstown soldiers dined at various places. Future governor Samuel Pennypacker sat down at a Harrisburg restaurant with comrade Cyrus Nyce. Also a private in Company F, it was Nyce who had convinced Samuel to join the Pottstown Company as the Phoenixville Company which Pennypacker had arrived in Harrisburg with deteriorated. "It was a very singular thing that many of the men said that Nyce and I resembled each other so much they could not tell us apart," wrote Pennypacker. "I was frequently saluted as 'Nyce' and he by my name, though he was nearly six feet high and much heavier."[1]

As they sat down to dinner in the city they had spent the last six weeks defending, the two must have reflected on their summer excursion. However, the time for dining and reflection was soon over, and around 7 p.m. the Pottstown Company—along with Major Greenawalt and Company E of Lebanon—boarded freight cars and proceeded down the Lebanon Valley Railroad, a line extending between Harrisburg and Reading. "Some of the fellows had taken the opportunity of imbibing enough to make them very drunk," recorded Samuel, "and getting on top of the cars, fell fast asleep there. They were in continual danger of tumbling off and the conductor told us that one fellow from Lebanon had rolled upon the track. He thought the man must have been killed, so the others were carried down and put inside. Two came staggering into our car, and, after vomiting all around in a manner to make themselves as disagreeable companions as could well be found, threw themselves down on the floor, and were snoring away in perfect unconsciousness of every thing."[2]

For those who were sober, they could peer out of the cars and be treated to a "beautiful" moonlight tint to the Pennsylvania countryside. "It was a beautiful, clear, and moonlight night," recalled Pennypacker, "the scenery along the road could be distinguished almost as readily as if it had been day[.]" Second Lieutenant Mark H. Richards and Samuel sat side by side at "the side opening of the car looking at the fields, woods and villages as they rolled rapidly by, without feeling the least inclination to sleep." Stopping at Lebanon, the Pottstown boys bade farewell to their beloved Major and their comrades in Company E. "The people of that place had very kindly provided a tub of ice-water with three or four dippers in it for Company F," recalled Pennypacker, "and we carried it on to our car thankful for the thoughtfulness displayed as well as the real benefit of the gift."[3]

Greenawalt would continue as a tanner in his native Lebanon for roughly three decades before leaving the Keystone State for California, where he had journeyed during the early 1850s. In December 1898, at age 72, Greenawalt was admitted to the Sawtelle Home for Disabled Volunteer Soldiers, near present-day Los Angeles. The Lebanon native had reportedly contracted a hernia while living in Pennsylvania in 1888. He died at the home due to heart disease on January 24, 1899, and was buried in the Home Cemetery.[4]

Corporal Conrad G. Gerhart of Company E, future Mayor of Lebanon
(From, *Biographical Annals of Lebanon County*, 1904)

For Corporal Conrad G. Gerhart of Company E, his term in the 26th was his second and final enlistment during the war. He had been born in Lebanon on September 16, 1841, the son of William and Elizabeth (Uhler) Gerhart. Early on, he entered a cigar-making business as well as assisting with his father's butchery. In September 1861, he enlisted as a musician in the 93rd Pennsylvania Infantry and was discharged in 1862. Upon returning from the 26th PVM in August 1863, he worked at his father's butchery, and in 1872 opened his own butchery. Elected to city council of Lebanon in 1896, Gerhart would be elected Mayor in 1899.[5]

It was between 2 and 3 a.m. when the train carrying Company F arrived in Pottstown. There the Pottstown boys were met with an early-morning hero's welcome. "The citizens had prepared an *extempore* collation in the yard of one of the hotels, after a speech from a minister, we attacked the viands and ate what we required [emphasis original]." Pennypacker and several others from Phoenixville turned over their accoutrements, which belonged to Pottstown, and boarded the engine of a coal train. "[S]oon after day light," the group came in sight of Phoenixville. Before returning to his home in the small, nearby village of Mont Clare, Samuel "bathed myself thoroughly" in the Schuylkill river. As he entered the gate to his home, the dog, Jack, failed to recognize the future-governor after six eventful weeks in the field— Pennypacker recorded that the canine "made such a noise that the whole household was aroused. Mother, Aunt Lib, Harry and Isaac came running to the door to welcome me—and thus was concluded my part of the 'Emergency.'"[6]

However, for many of Company F, the aftereffects of their six week excursion were not over. Captain Rice, First Lieutenant Henry Potts Jr., Privates John R. "Rolly" Caswell, Cyrus Nyce, Joseph G. Rennard and several others shortly afterwards became sick from the exposure during their service that summer. Privates Jerome Byer and Joseph L. Hays Jr. both later "died from the effects of the exposure."[7] Recovering from his ailments, Captain George Rice returned to his work as a successful civil engineer, and spent the rest of his life in Pottstown until his death there on September 26, 1918.[8]

For Samuel Pennypacker, his service in the 26th was his first and final military service. Born in Phoenixville on April 9, 1843, to Dr. Isaac A. and Anna Maria Whitaker Pennypacker, Samuel's father died when he was twelve years old, prompting his mother to take Samuel and her other three sons to live with her parents at Mont Clare, opposite of Phoenixville. Samuel attended a combination of public and private schools and prepared for the Sophomore Class at Yale. However, his grandfather, Joseph Whitaker, felt that he needed to prove himself first. Samuel taught school in a one room school house at Mont Clare during the winter of 1862 and spring of 1863. Following the school year, he enlisted in the 26th PVM. Upon returning from service with the 26th, the young scholar was drafted. However, Samuel's grandfather felt that he had proven himself enough during his service in the 26th and therefore paid the bounty for a replacement. Samuel graduated in 1866 with a Law degree from the University of Pennsylvania. In 1870, he married Virginia Earle Broomall and together they had six children of which four survived to adulthood. Samuel maintained a lifelong interest in history and authored his first book, *The Annals of Phoenixville and Vicinity*, in 1872. In his lifetime, Samuel authored over 90 pamphlets and books.

Pennypacker was associated with the Historical Society of Pennsylvania and was their president from the turn of the twentieth century until his death. In 1889, Governor and fellow Civil War Veteran James A. Beaver appointed him a Judge in Philadelphia and later that year Samuel was elected to the same position for a term of ten years. In 1902, the Republican party nominated him as their choice for Governor. Pennypacker defeated the Democratic nominee, Robert Pattison, who was twice governor before, by the largest majority up until that time. During Pennypacker's term of office, the State Archives and the State Museum were both created. He signed Pennsylvania's first clean stream act and first child labor laws. The State Forestry was doubled in size. Five new departments were created including the Department of Health, Department of Mines, Department of Fisheries, Department of Highways and the Department of State Police. The State Police was the first of its kind in the nation. The present capitol building in Harrisburg was built during his term and dedicated by him and President Theodore Roosevelt on October 4, 1906. After his term expired, Samuel took up residence at his home, Pennypacker Mills in Schwenksville, and went back to the practice of law and writing books until his death on September 2, 1916.[9]

For the remainder of his life, Pennypacker would never grow tired of describing his service with the 26th. In his postwar autobiography, Samuel pondered whether fate brought him to the battlefield at Witmer's:

> *It seems almost as though there were a fatality which determined that affairs should so be shaped. If my own {Phoenixville} company had not gone home, I should not have been in the regiment which went to Gettysburg and I would have experienced nothing of consequence. The Pottstown company had decided to connect themselves with another regiment in the camp, and only after much persuasion and considerable delay were prevailed upon by Colonel Jennings to change their association and unite with him. Had they not made this change I should not have gone to Gettysburg.[10]*

Company I of Hanover was seventh in line to be paid, and consequently the company would not be fully paid off until around 8 p.m. on August 1. Once the Hanoverians were all paid off, they had some transportation conflicts, but eventually, at 2 a.m., boarded an express train for Hanover Junction with their former captain, Lieutenant Colonel Jenkins. Marylander Henry Wirt Shriver of Company I noted that he "had a pleasant ride," which brought them to Hanover Junction around 4:30 a.m. However, at the junction the company found no trains waiting to transport them to the town of Hanover. Eventually the cars arrived, and they were welcomed into the town. Shriver decided to remain at Hanover for the evening, fearing he would be drafted if he returned home to Union Mills. Not surprisingly, the native Marylander felt "pretty sleepy" and "retired early" for the night.[11]

Shriver later married Mary Winebrenner of Hanover on October 2, 1866, and lived the remainder of his life in the old Shriver homestead at Union Mills, Maryland, where the couple had several children. Shriver died at midnight in his home in Union Mills on February 25, 1910, of an ongoing illness that had kept him confined to bed since October 1909.[12]

The original captain of the Hanover Company would not survive the war. Lieutenant Colonel Jenkins was born on November 10, 1832. He was killed in action on November 6, 1864, during the Siege of Petersburg, while serving in the 184th Pennsylvania as captain of Company G. He was 32 at the time of his death, which came only four days before his 33rd birthday. He left behind his widow Katherine and four children. The Major Jenkins Post #99 of the Grand Army of the Republic (founded May 7, 1878, in Hanover) was named in his memory.[13] Reflecting more than 40 years after the regiment's campaign, Drummer Henry M. M. Richards wrote: "Lieut. Col. Jenkins, from Hanover, did not have the same faculty of securing the good graces of those under him, but bravely sealed his loyalty to the Union with his life's blood, in front of Petersburg a year later."[14]

The College Guards boarded railroad cars at Bridgeport around 11 p.m. on the evening of August 1. The Gettysburgers remained in the cars until 3 a.m. the following morning, when they started for Hanover Junction. Arriving at the latter around 8 a.m., the Gettysburgers arrived around 10 a.m. in the town which had changed so much since they had last laid eyes on it.[15]

Fourth Sergeant William Henry Rupp of Company A—a lifelong resident of Gettysburg—would be considered 50 years after his service in the 26th as "one of Gettysburg's best known residents[.]" Rupp, also a veteran of the 87th Pennsylvania Volunteer Infantry, was a member of Corporal Skelly GAR Post 9. He died of an illness which had extended several weeks at 3:30 a.m. on February 25, 1913, at his home on Stevens street in Gettysburg.[16]

Twenty-two-year-old College Student and Private Frank Richards had already seen some of the devastating effects of the battle on the town and community of Gettysburg. He was granted a furlough in mid-July 1863 and visited his residence in Gettysburg. "All my clothing has been stolen by the rebels as also all my pictures which I had left in my trunk," he wrote. "My room is occupied by the rebel surgeon, and is in a comparatively good condition in comparison with the other rooms. My experience as a soldier taking into consideration the things lost at Gettysburg has cost me very dearly. I have no clothing left . . . but what I have on my back." A graduate of the Pennsylvania College Class of 1864, Richards later became a Lutheran clergyman in Chicago from 1867-1873, and later in Zanesville, Ohio, from 1876-1904. He edited and authored over five books. Richards married Caroline L. Super of Mansfield, Ohio, on February 10, 1869, with whom he fathered four children before his death on September 11, 1904, in Zanesville.[17]

The youngest member of Company A was returning to High School in Reading.[18] Drummer Henry Melchior Muhlenberg Richards was born on August 16, 1848. He entered Reading High School in 1860 at the head of all male applicants. At the age of 14, young Richards enlisted in the 26th as drummer boy of Company A, joining his older brother, Mathias. He graduated from Reading High School in 1864, and then reenlisted that same year in 195th Pennsylvania Infantry, and served under General Philip H. Sheridan in the Shenandoah Valley. Richards graduated from the U.S. Naval Academy at Newport, Rhode Island, in 1869. He was publicly complimented by Admiral David Porter and given his diploma by then-President Ulysses S. Grant. Richards was active in the Franco-German War 1870-1871.[19]

Another member of Company A to go onto prominence was Private George Washington Frederick. Born on April 4, 1837, in Shrewsbury, he was a graduate of the Pennsylvania College Class of 1863. During the Gettysburg Campaign, Frederick served on the staff of General Couch. He later raised a company of volunteers and for his efforts was commissioned second lieutenant of Company G, 209th Pennsylvania Infantry on September 1, 1864. Eight days later, Frederick had risen to captain of the company. His rapid promotion did not stop there—on September 17, Frederick became lieutenant colonel of the 209th. He was later brevetted a colonel of New York Volunteers on April 2, 1865, "for gallantry in action" at Forts Stedman and Sedgwick, near Petersburg.

Scarcely had Lee surrendered when Frederick was detailed for duty in the military trial of the conspirators involved in the Lincoln Assassination plot. Frederick was part of a group headed by Brevet Major John F. Hartranft to strictly supervise the imprisoned conspirators during their trial and the time leading up to their eventual execution. Afterwards, Frederick married Lavina Anna Culp of Gettysburg on January 18, 1865, and on April 27, 1871, remarried to Rebecca C. Hinkle of Philadelphia. After attending the Gettysburg Seminary from 1865 to 1866, he served as a Lutheran Clergyman at Zelienople from 1866-1867, and Chestnut Hill, Philadelphia, from 1867-1872, and later worked as manager of a Lutheran Book Store in Philadelphia from 1872-1898. He died on April 10, 1904.[20]

For Colonel Jennings, his service in the 26th was his last of the war. After the 26th was paid off and disbanded on August 1, Jennings returned to his iron foundry in Harrisburg. Later that same year, he was elected Sherriff of Dauphin County, a post which he held from 1864-1866, "but afterwards abandoned his official position and devoted himself once more to his foundry. Associating in partnership with J.M. Stover, he firmly established the Franklin Machine Works and Foundry of this city, as a successful enterprise."[21]

In 1875, Jennings was again elected Sherriff and served from 1876-1878. "It was during his last term that the great railroad riots occurred. Sunday, July 22, 1877, was a day of great suspense. The authorities, however, were quietly preparing for the emergency. Absent from home, Col. Jennings hastened to the State Capital, at once assumed control, organized the citizens, and restored peace to the city seriously threatened with mob violence. His action was favorably commented upon at the time, not only by the press, but by the Governor of the Commonwealth in his Annual Message, and was deserving of all praise for bravery and excellent judgment exercised at that critical moment."[22]

Postwar photograph of George Washington Frederick, Company A
(*U.S. Army Military History Institute*)

This group photograph pictures Brevet Major Hartranft and his staff. Frederick is standing, second from the left, while Hartranft is seated at center. (*Library of Congress*)

COLONEL WILLIAM W. JENNINGS.
Late Sheriff of Dauphin County.
President First National Bank.
President Commonwealth Trust and S. D. Co.
Harrisburg, Pa.
Died February 24th, 1894.

1893 Photograph of Colonel Jennings
(From, *History of the 127th Regiment Pennsylvania Volunteers*, 1902)

In 1880, Jennings was elected to be president of Harrisburg's First National Bank, "and subsequently was also chosen president of the [Commonwealth] Guarantee Trust and Safe Deposit company, both institutions having his constant supervision and direction. Under his management, these institutions have become two of the most successful banking houses in Central Pennsylvania," detailed a Harrisburg newspaper at the time of Jennings' death. Jennings also served as president of the Harrisburg Steam Heating Company, the first president of the Harrisburg Board of Trade, and director of the Cumberland Valley Railroad Company. "He was an excellent financier," detailed a 1907 county history, "and not a few of the business men of today in Harrisburg owe their success and prosperity to timely assistance and advice from him when they most needed it." "Generous and trustworthy, he drew men and women who gladly committed their financial interests unto him," praised Reverend C. W. Buoy, Jennings' pastor. "He put into the varied interests he served his best thought and heart[.]"[23]

As for Jennings' character, Buoy described him as "a leader in the world of finance and [he] bore off its prizes gracefully, modestly." The "modest" Jennings was "[g]entle in his nature, he was courteous, without distinction, accessible to high and low alike[.]"[24] His political affiliation was with the Republican party. In 1871, Jennings was the Republican candidate for Mayor of Harrisburg, but was defeated by "a small majority, after an exciting campaign by W. K. Verbeke."[25]

Colonel Jennings was married to Emma Jane Van Horn on December 17, 1861. At one point, his estate was reportedly estimated at $150,000 and it was claimed that he had his life insured for $80,000.[26]

Jennings died abruptly on February 28, 1894. The Harrisburg newspaper, *The Morning Call*, reported of Jennings' death:

The deceased left this city on Monday afternoon {February 26} with General D. H. Hastings, ex-Governor Beaver and J. L. Spangler, for Philadelphia on a business engagement. He was also to have gone to New York. When he left he was suffering with a cold, and this became worse, so that the same night his breathing was affected to such an extent as to require the attendance of a physician at his room at the Union League club. His illness became worse and he was removed to the Medico-Chirurgical hospital, and Dr. J. Ross Swartz of this city, the family physician, telegraphed for. The doctor, accompanied by Mr. Jennings' son William immediately responded and the Colonel was brought to his home in this city at an early hour yesterday morning {Wednesday, February 28}, the patient undergoing the journey without any apparent discomfort outside of that caused by the difficulty of breathing. The closest attention was paid to him at his home {at the corner of Third and Forster streets}, but a fainting spell overtook him, and all efforts failing to prevent it from reaching the heart, he died 20 minutes before noon, surrounded by his wife and all his children with the exception of Fanny, the youngest daughter, who was visiting at Orange, N.J. Col. Jennings had not been in the best of health for some time. About two years ago he was seized with a slight attack of paralysis which affected his speech to some extent, and from which it is said he never fully recovered.... The deceased leaves a wife and four children, Mary, William, Fanny and Harry.[27]

1894 Engraving of Colonel Jennings
(*The Morning Call*, Harrisburg, March 1, 1894)

Chapter 9

Reunion at Gettysburg

In the postwar years, Samuel Pennypacker, who had risen to prominence as a judge in Philadelphia, was named president of the 26th Pennsylvania Emergency Regiment Association. Samuel and other veterans of the 26th fought long and hard to have funds appropriated for a monument honoring the 26th at Gettysburg. However, the Board of Commissioners of Gettysburg Monuments were reluctant to do so, mainly because the 26th had not seen action in the Battle of Gettysburg, from July 1-3.

In the waning months of 1889, the Board of Commissioners of Gettysburg Monuments issued a resolution, informing Pennypacker and others that in their opinion, the 26th was ineligible for state funding for a monument. "[U]nder the provisions of the Act of Assembly Constituting this Commission, the Battle of Gettysburg is specifically referred to as a subject matter to be commemorated and the Commission are limited to the Regiments participating therein, which is confined in our judgment to the engagements of the 1st, 2nd and 3rd days of July, 1863, and does not include the events previous or subsequent to [the] same event[.]" Further distaste among veterans of the 26th came when they noticed the commission had mistaken their identity—in the resolution, they were referred to as the "25th Emergency Regiment."[1]

However, the secretary of the commission, Colonel John P. Nicholson, informed Pennypacker that "the Commission will be pleased to cooperate with the survivors in the accomplishment of their wishes[.]" Pennypacker wrote the commission in January 1890, requesting "that before taking final action upon the subject you will fix a time when it will be convenient for you to hear the reasons leading us to the conclusion that you are required to provide for the erection of a monument[.]" Pennypacker also informed the commission that "after a careful examination" of the Act detailing the appropriation of funds for monuments on the battlefield, he felt "quite confident" that the commission was legally obligated to hold a hearing before making a final determination. "It is quite natural that its [the 26th's] services should have been overlooked by the distinguished soldiers who constitute your body," Pennypacker harangued, "and it becomes therefore all the more important that the facts be presented to you by some one familiar with them."[2]

The first argument of the Commission was that the appropriations for monuments were given out "to commemorate the participation of Pennsylvania in the decisive battle of Gettysburg by definitely marking the position of her enlisted troops." Pennypacker countered, stating that "the deeds of the 26th Emergency Regiment were such as to eminently justify such commemoration. Though it has been classed with militia, it is improperly so classed. Its members responded to the call of the President of the United States, and were sworn into the United States like all other national volunteers." Pennypacker's second argument was that the 26th's actions changed the course of the battle. In reality, the unit made little to no difference on the outcome of the battle of Gettysburg. This argument may not have hurt the regiment's case in the late 19th-century with the limited perspective and reflection available on the campaign, but with historians in the present it has contributed to the negative stereotype against the unit.

Third, Pennypacker maintained that many have "a special and peculiar interest in the commemoration of the action of the 26th Emergency. Her other regiments went to Gettysburg as a part of the Army of the Potomac, leaning upon and supported by troops of other states."[3] The initial request for funds having been made in 1889, this debate continued well into 1891. Through all this, Pennypacker's exaggerated main pitch line was: "First force to engage the Confederates at Gettysburg and the first to shed Confederate blood in Penna. Delayed their advance one day."[4]

The board later issued a resolution which declared "[t]hat if the monument is to be erected as requested special legislative action and a special appropriation is required[.]"[5] At a board meeting held on January 16, 1891, Secretary Nicholson reasoned that the 26th was "acting under the orders of General D. N. Couch" when it was engaged at Gettysburg and that "[i]t is important for the history of the state that… the occupation of Gettysburg by a Pennsylvania Regiment prior to the arrival of the Army of the Potomac should be commemorated." Therefore, the board recommended to the State Legislature that an appropriation of $1,500 be made for the erection of a monument to the 26th.[6]

On April 30, 1892, the specifics of the monument were officially agreed upon. The Smith Granite Company of Westerly, Rhode Island, was contracted to construct the monument, which was to be completed before August 1, 1892. The agreement also specified the design, material and dimensions of the monument. "A bronze statue of an Emergency man surmounting a native Gettysburg boulder," outlined the agreement. "He is represented partly in uniform and partly in civil dress, having just leaped upon the boulder; where with musket firmly grasped he views the enemy in front." The boulder supporting the bronze figure would come from the Gettysburg Battlefield. "It shall be bedded to set on foundation and receive the statue." All text would "be on bronze panels and let into and fastened to the boulder by means of bronze bolts." Further, two "flanking posts" were placed on each side of the monument with more text. It was also agreed that the cost of the monument would not exceed $2,750.[7]

The 26th's monument was placed immediately west of the town square, at the intersection of Buford and Spring Avenues. In his speech at the dedication, Adjutant McKnight cited several reasons for "the appropriateness" of the monument's location. McKnight reasoned that "[i]t marks the point where we left the town on our march to Marsh Creek. It is separated from the other lines of battle on the field and cannot be confounded with them. It is near the town, the College and the Seminary, from which Co. 'A' of the regiment came. It stands, therefore, as a merited rebuke of the false criticism, iterated and re-iterated far and wide, that the citizens of Gettysburg were lacking in patriotic devotion at a time when their interests, as well as those of the country, were in jeopardy."[8]

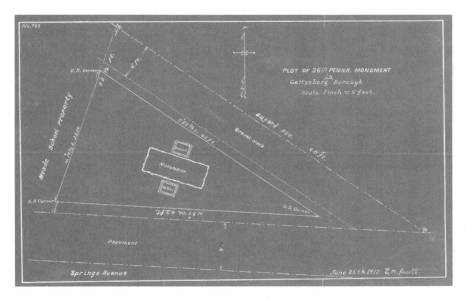

Blueprint showing the location of the 26th PVM's monument in 1912.
(*Pennypacker Mills Historic Site*)

In his postwar autobiography, Pennypacker described the monument as a "bronze figure of a young man clutching a musket, who had just run up upon the top of a native boulder[.]" Pennypacker had suggested that the monument "should show the trousers tucked into the boot-legs to indicate the sudden change from peaceful life to the battlefield."[9] Furthermore, the statue's artist attempted to portray a young Samuel Pennypacker. "While this statue at Gettysburg is in no sense a portrait," Pennypacker noted, "the artist endeavored to represent his idea of what was my own personal appearance when about nineteen years of age."[10]

Because of his role as president of the 26th Pennsylvania Emergency Regiment Association and the main proponent for the monument, Pennypacker was asked to be the keynote speaker at the dedication. Pennypacker agreed, and on June 8, 1892, sent the following printed circular to his fellow veterans;

26th **PVM Monument before the dedication**
(*Pennypacker Mills Historic Site*)

Comrade:

I have been requested by the Committee having the matter in charge to deliver the address at the dedication of the monument to commemorate the services of the Twenty-sixth emergency Regiment at Gettysburg. The monument selected is impressive and the location will be conspicuous. I should like the address, which will be printed and preserved for the future, to indicate clearly and fairly the unique position occupied by this regiment in that decisive battle. In order that it may be done will you kindly send me at once a brief memorandum, say on half sheet of foolscap paper, of what you saw in connection with out engagement with the enemy? Do you know of losses among ourselves or the enemy, and if so what did you see?

Very truly yours,
Saml. W. Pennypacker.[11]

In the months between then and the dedication in September, Samuel received dozens of letters from his fellow soldiers, recounting their service in the 26th, particularly the regiment's June 26 engagement at Gettysburg. Many remembered little 29 years later, some remembered precise details, while others sent Samuel copies of letters they had written while in the field in 1863.[12]

This was not the first reunion of members of the 26th Militia. In the years following the war, several reunions were held at Harrisburg. Unfortunately, little is known about these gatherings.[13]

On September 1, 1892, the survivors of the regiment attended the reunion in Gettysburg. Each man was given a bright blue ribbon which can be clearly seen adorning the chests of the veterans in the group photographs of the regiment's reunion. First to the podium was Corporal Edmund Jacob Wolf of Company A, who led the survivors in prayer. Music was played after Wolf and between each new speaker coming to the speaking platform. Sergeant Samuel H. Bentz of Company E delivered the opening address, and immediately afterward the monument was unveiled. Music roared, mixed with the applause of the now middle-age veterans.

Private J. Howard Jacobs of Company F officially presented the monument. Then came Adjutant McKnight, who gave a brief address praising the regiment and its' actions on June 26.[14] Located several paces south of the monument was a small, rudely-constructed platform, perhaps a dozen feet wide, used as either the speaker's platform or a stage from which music was played. Three wooden-poles fastened in a rudimental fashion with rope supported a cloth-like top about a dozen feet off the ground, which was proudly adorned with an American flag.[15]

Next to the podium was Pennypacker, the keynote speaker. In his ever-eloquent dialogue, the man who in a decade would be elected Governor of Pennsylvania puffed up his former comrades' confidence and somewhat comical belief, purporting they were the cause of the great victory at Gettysburg. The monument dedicated in the town well represented the men of the regiment. Depicting a young, 20-year-old Pennypacker, it truly characterizes the regiment's unpreparedness for the events that took place on June 26, 1863.

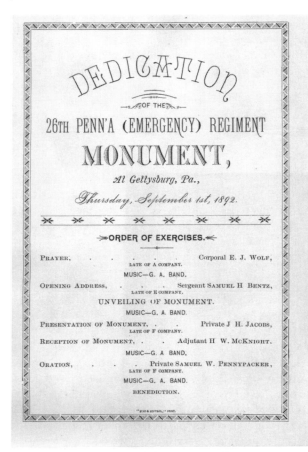

Items from the 26th's September 1, 1892, reunion belonging to Samuel Pennypacker. At left is a handout detailing the event schedule. At right is one of the distinctive bright-blue ribbons worn by all veterans who attended the reunion, clearly visible in the two reunion group photographs. At bottom is Samuel's permit to be admitted to the speaking platform. (*Pennypacker Mills Historic Site*)

A previously unpublished photograph of the 26th's reunion at Gettysburg, showing a platform in the far right of the photo. Colonel Jennings is in the chair in the left foreground, and Pennypacker stands behind him. This photo is angled slightly further right than the traditional reunion photo. (*Lebanon County Historical Society*)

This photograph is in several ways different from the previous. Colonel Jennings is standing, and no longer wearing a hat. Samuel Pennypacker, still standing immediately behind Jennings' chair, is also hatless, as is nearly the entire group compared to the last photograph. The view is angled slightly further left in this photograph, so that the platform at right is no longer visible. In both photographs, note the blue reunion ribbons prevalent among the entire group. (*Special Collections, Gettysburg College*)

An early William H. Tipton photograph of the 26th's monument. The two small tablets present today at the monument's sides are not present in this photograph. (*Lebanon County Historical Society*)

Circa 1893 Tipton photograph of the 26th PVM's Monument
(*Gettysburg National Military Park*)

This William H. Tipton photograph, taken facing southeast circa 1893-1895, shows the two tablets at the side of the monument. (*Gettysburg National Military Park*)

This 1913 view shows the 26th's monument from the rear, after improvements made on the site by the War Department. The small sign at the base of the monument reads "Keep off this Rock." (*Gettysburg National Military Park*)

Appendix A:

Samuel's Pennypacker's Anonymous Correspondence, 1863

During the regiment's service, Private Samuel Pennypacker wrote two anonymous letters to a Phoenixville newspaper. They are reprinted below[1];

Fort Couch, Harrisburg, July 3, 1863.

Dear Phoenix: Although I believe you goodly people of Phoenixville have no great partiality for the militia service and perhaps take little interest in it, still as there were about a dozen of us left behind when the time for which the rest came had expired, and it is fair to presume that each one of those has some personal friends who care for his welfare, I have taken the liberty of writing to you to narrate our brief military experience. And notwithstanding the fact that it has been but little more than two weeks since we bid farewell to Phoenix, we flatter ourselves that in proportion to the time, we have seen considerable of the elephant and been pretty well initiated into the mysteries of army life. As you are probably aware this company is principally composed of young men from Pottstown, generally of good families, and I am happy to state that I have not been able to find one 'Copperhead' among them. The officers are gentlemen who have left their business engagements in order to drive the invaders from the State, and who expect to remain until that work is accomplished. I have always found them obliging and willing to do a favor whenever it was possible. While in Camp Curtin, our company was Provost Guard and that duty, as a general thing not very laborious, was sometimes troublesome when hard cases were met with who had to be treated roughly.

On the morning of the 24th inst., we were awakened at 3 o'clock, A.M., by our orderly and commanded to prepare to march in three hours. The usual custom in the army is to draw the men up in line and keep them there until the cars are ready and all the other arrangements made; but we, perhaps in consideration of our greenness, were started off comparatively early on a special train. The principal towns which we passed on the route were York and Hanover, both of which struck me as being particularly neat and pleasant looking places. In the latter the predominance of a dark red color in the out-houses and barns about, which is so common through Montgomery and Berks counties, denoted the nativity of the inhabitants.

I noticed some pretty scenery as we came down the Susquehanna, but all along the road the crops appeared to me to be remarkably poor, it may have been on account of dry weather, but the wheat and oats were short and scattered, and the corn dwindling. About six miles from Gettysburg, the engine on the front train ran into a cow and was thrown from the track, but kept on its course for some thirty yards where the cars were completely wrecked and piled together in a heap. It happened very fortunately that none were seriously hurt, but the accident postponed our advance to Gettysburg, and we were compelled to encamp in the woods where the regiment remained over the next day. The first thing soldiers do after a halt is to scatter all about the neighborhood and hunt up every thing of an edible nature to be found. The nearer farm houses are soon drained of all the butter, milk and eggs they can furnish.

Thursday {June 25} evening a detail of one hundred and twenty men, of whom your correspondent was one, was made ostensibly for the purpose of going on picket, but really to advance to Gettysburg, and the rebels were said to be already in that vicinity. We then thought it a hard march, as the musket, cartridge-box, with ammunition, haversack, canteen and knapsack, in all making a heavy load to carry, and the accumulation of straps is very fatiguing. There had been no preparation made for our reception and we stood out in the street with the rain falling upon us until after midnight when we passed the remainder of the night in a filthy depot. To one who left home because the rebels were so near that he could stay there no longer, it was somewhat irritating to see the numbers of men lining the streets apparently as unconcerned as if no danger were near. I thought, however, I could perceive the reason of that when upon asking quite a small boy, "what a rebel was?" he replied, "a black abolitionist." He did not credit me when I told him that I acknowledged that title myself.

The next morning it rained very hard and the rest of the regiment having come up, we proceeded about four miles further and fixed our tents in a woods, lining them with shingles which were found near. We had just finished when the order came, strike tents and be ready immediately. It appeared that a rebel force of about eight thousand infantry, cavalry and artillery was so near to us that they had captured a few of our men who had gone a short distance for straw when they returned to camp. Of course we did not then know what was the matter, but we could easily suspect that something was not right, and consequently were soon ready. After traveling several miles through a muddy, sticky by-road, a number of the rebel cavalry overtook us and made some captures in the rear. We had a quite skirmish with them, firing off three or four rounds and it is said killing three men before they withdrew. Colonel Jennings then led us to the mountains, and we kept up the march with intermissions of a few minutes all night over hills, through fields, across the creeks and in every imaginable direction. The rebels were so near on both sides that they could be seen and heard; and once the whole regiment laid down among the trees in almost breathless silence so that the jingle of a tin-cup was audible from one end to the other. Our retreat was continued in the same manner all the next day and night, and on Sunday {June 28} about 2½ o'clock, P.M., we arrived at Harrisburg foot sore and completely worn out with fatigue.

Along our line of march the people were everywhere very kind, coming out of their houses and supplying us with a sufficiency of excellent provisions, and giving information in regard to the whereabouts of the rebels. We found this place in imminent danger of attack, but after our arrival the "rebs" soon fell back, when we were again pushed forward two or three miles, but on the 1st inst. returned to the Fort. How long we will remain here it is impossible to tell. As I have already protracted this letter too much, I will now close.

Yours Truly, XOM.

{Handwritten initials "S. W. P." underneath in scrapbook.}

***

Camp Near Greencastle, Pa., July 20th, 1863

Dear Phoenix:--When I last had the pleasure of addressing you, we were stationed in Fort Couch, or as it was designated in General Orders, Fort Washington, opposite Harrisburg. The Camp there was situated on a high bluff, overlooking the river and affording a fine view of the mountains surrounding the city, which stretch away to the right and left as far as the eye can reach; while the Susquehanna, a wide and rather shallow stream, flows quietly along at their feet. A bridge of great length {Camelback Bridge}, and apparently in a very insecure condition crosses at the foot of the fortifications, which are approached by a wagon road winding up the hill from the rear. The position would have been very pleasant, had it not been for the amount of filth which had accumulated from the numerous regiments continually arriving and departing, and the foul condition of the river water, which exercised a very deteriorating influence upon the health of the troops. Generally the men evaded the guards and procured the drinking water from springs without the fort; but that used for cooking purposes was pumped up from the river, and was the vilest I ever had the misfortune to taste.

While there we were visited by several of the people of Phoenixville, who were on their way to the battle-field of Gettysburg. I believe nothing brightens the spirits of a soldier more, and affords him greater pleasure, that to meet with familiar faces and inquire in regard to matters at home.

Sometime during the night of the 12th we received orders to march, and early on Sunday morning we started on a troop train down the Cumberland Valley, and reached Shippensburg about noon. Unfortunately, the fog was very heavy for the greater part of the distance, and consequently the opportunity for observing the country was limited to a small space on each side of the track.

At Carlisle, noticing that every now and then a man passed by with a large slice of bread in his hand, and thinking that I might be able to make an addition to my commissary stores, I jumped off the cars, and tracing the line back, made my way about a square until I reached a kitchen, where an old lady was distributing bread and meat as fast as she could cut it, and so she continued until all her supplies were exhausted. It is one of many instances which shows the gratitude and kindness which the people of this section of the country exhibit toward the soldiers.

We were unable to go beyond Shippensburg by rail, as the road had been repaired but a short distance further; so we commenced our march at that point, and arrived at Chambersburg late in the evening. The afternoon was hot and sultry, and numbers of the men gave out on the road, lying down in the fence corners or any convenient place, while some fell senseless from sunstroke. All along the route the people came out to their gates with buckets and tubs of water, and gave drink and sometimes food to us as we passed by. At a small place called Greenville, where the column halted to rest, I was much impressed with two little boys not more than four or five years, who came out to fill our canteens, and one of whom told us very sorrowfully that the rebels took his black dog. He seemed to feel the loss severely, and in all probability will never forget the rebels as long as he lives.

We encamped over night on the north side of Chambersburg, in the midst of an army of militia. The next morning, though it rained heavily, a companion and myself, bidding defiance to the weather, and running the risk of being left by the regiment, went into town and surveyed the scene of rebel depredations there We found all the railroad property—consisting of the depot, several large warehouses, and other buildings—in ruins; and it seemed to me strange, that instead of setting fire to them and consuming them quickly, they had preferred the laborious method of ramming bars of iron against the brick walls, until they gave way and the roof fell in. the principal part of the machinery had been previously removed, but that which was left was broken up and destroyed; and even large pieces of wrought iron, which it was impossible to break, bore upon their surfaces marks and indentations made by heavy sledges. We were told that one of the rebels was crushed under a falling building , and was still buried beneath some of the ruins.

Several miles of the track between Chambersburg and Greencastle had been torn up, and the rails bent out of shape, by placing them across hollows with the ends supported, and then piling the sills on top, and setting them on fire. When the rails became heated they were bent in the middle from the weight above.

In Chambersburg we took dinner with a lady who refused to receive any compensation whatever, saying that she would be ashamed to charge a Union soldier for a meal while she had anything to give. That afternoon we continued our journey a mile and a half, and the next day proceeded to our present camp, nearly a mile from Greencastle.

The pike is the direct road between the two towns, but it was so cut up by the wagons of both armies, and in such a bad condition from the recent heavy rains as to be almost impassable, so that we travelled by one of the side roads, and thereby considerably increased the distance. The usual orders to the men after a hard day's march had been accomplished, and the spot selected for a camp reached, is to "break ranks and make yourselves comfortable," which under some circumstances, (a pouring rain for instance), has very much the air of a joke.

Our quarters here are far more pleasant than any we have yet been in, being on the edge of a large wood, where we can enjoy the shad of the trees, and in a country fruitful and abounding in springs of excellent water—a consideration of the utmost importance. In this neighborhood the springs are really wonderful for the strength and temperature. Inexhaustible quantities of ice-cold water gush out of the hills in perfect streams. The crops are generally good, and the corn especially looks very well. Much of the wheat, though dead ripe, remains uncut, and a large proportion of that which has been bound remains stacked in the fields, as the rebels have scarcely left a horse in all this region, and the farmers have no way of hauling in their grain. For miles the farms have been almost totally stripped of horses, cattle and fowls, and the barns are entirely empty. I was surprised to see how philosophically the people endure the loss of so much property, and how willingly those who have been deprived of nearly everything, share what they have remaining. They say that while a few of the rebels made their exactions in a polite manner, the majority were very impudent, wantonly destroying what they could not use. They would fill their canteens from the molasses barrels, and leave the rest to run out upon the cellar floors. Vinegar, and all such articles, for family use were wasted. The farming utensils, such as shovels, spades, forks, scythes, ploughs, and many things which could be of no advantage to them at all, were either carried away or rendered useless.

They were particularly harsh toward those who expected to be exempt on account of copperhead proclivities, and appeared to hold them in the utmost contempt, telling them that if they favored the Southern cause, they ought to take arms and fight for it, and adding further that they had lived and acted in Davis' dominions as they did in the North, he would have hung every one of them long ago. It is my opinion that the invasion has a very good effect politically, upon our border counties, and that copperheadism, crushed to the earth, will never raise its venomous head here, while the memory of wasted crops and ruined property remains.

Gov. Curtin paid us a visit a few days ago, and was enthusiastically received by the soldiers. He made an address to each regiment, praising them for the promptness with which they responded to his call, and saying that he sympathized with them in all the privations which they had endured. He added that no man did his duty who enjoyed his sleep in quiet while the inhabitants of his own State were driven from their homes and deprived of their possession{s}. He considered the emergency almost over, and told the men that they would soon be returned to their homes, so that you may expect to see some of us in Phoenixville before a great while.

Yours Truly, XOM.

Appendix B:

Colonel Jennings' Official Report

Colonel Jennings likely wrote his Official Report regarding the regiment's actions near Gettysburg on June 26 in early July 1863, while the regiment was in Fort Washington. He never submitted his Official Report, instead retaining it for himself. In his later years (likely in 1892 prior to the Regiment's Monument Dedication), Jennings gave Pennypacker his report. Pennypacker placed the report in his original, handwritten manuscript of his memoir, "Six Weeks in Uniform." The report was addressed to General Couch, and therefore the second-person language refers to Couch. Jennings' previously unpublished report follows[2];

In obedience to your orders, we left Harrisburg on board cars. In the morning of 24th of June, for Hanover, York County, at which place I received orders to proceed to Gettysburg, Adams County. When about six miles this side of that place the engine struck a cow, and was t{h}rown from the track, breaking a number of cars, but fortunately without seriously injuring any one. On account of this accident I encamp{ed} in the woods near that place and sent a message to Major Haller, informing him of what had occurred, and was commanded by him to await further orders. On the morning of the 25th of June I received orders to have my command ready to fall back to Hanover at a moments notice. During the day Major Haller sent some orderance {sic} stores by: Muskets, equipments, ammunition and one small cannon, with orders to make whatever disposition of them I thought proper. I immediately placed them upon the cars and sent them to Hanover in charge of four men, belonging to a house guard, with orders to report to the Provost Martial {sic} of that place. There were numbers of rumors, during the day, of the enemy being in force, ten miles above Gettysburg. At ten o'clock on the night of the 25th, I received notice that the cars would be ready to move my command to Gettysburg at 5 A.M. the following morning, and that I should have my command ready to move at that time. Next morning we embarked upon the cars and arrived at Gettysburg at about 7 a.m. I immediately reported to Major Haller, and inquired of him the position of the enemy, and whether his scouts were reliable, offering, if they were not, to furnish men from my reg't, who would go forward and discover the position of the enemy, and was assured by Major Haller that they were reliable, and that there was no enemy within ten miles. Major Haller then ordered me to move my command to a place three miles above Gettysburg, which order I immediately proceeded to exicute {sic} and after having advanced about one mile and a half, was met by one of Major Haller's scouts, who informed me that the enemy was advancing in force with Artillery, Cavalry, and Infantry, but Capt. Bell, who was in command of the scouts assured me that this could not be correct, and that this scout as no reliable. I continued my march and encamped at the place designated by Major Haller and immediately sent out a reliable Lieut. {Captain John S. Forrest} with twenty picked men to discover if the enemy was advancing or not, which party was captured about one mile from that point. The Camp had not been formed when Capt. Bell rode up to me in great haste and informed me that the enemy was three fourths of a mile from my encampment, and were advancing rapidly. I then asked him if he considered scouts who allowed the enemy in as large force as his representative (which was five thousand) within three fo{u}rths of a mile of my command without giving me information reliable. The only excuse which he could give was that the heavy rain, which had set in on the night of the 25th of June, and which still continued, prevented them from discovring {sic} the enemy at a great distance. I then asked him if he could furnish me a man from his command to act as {a} guide, as I was unacquainted with the country and was assured that we could not, as he was the last of his command and was required to report to Major Haller. Believing the enemy to be to{o} strong for my command and having orders from you in such case to fall back, I ordered my men to fall in, and started in the direction of Hunterstown, feeling assured that this was the <u>only</u> course by which I could save my command, avoiding the main roads. After marching about three miles, I halted in woods from which I had a view of the country, for a considerable distance and by the assistance of my glasses, I discovered a body of the enemy (Infantry) numbering about 800 or 1000, moving in a direction which would bring them in contact with my command, should {I} continue {to} march in the course which I had intended to take. Just at this time {I} were informed that the enemy's cavalry were advancing on my rear. I took a course more to the left in order to avoid the infantry on my right, and after having marched about half mile I again halted to reconiter {sic}. The men being very tired sat down in the road during this halt. Whilst in this position the enemy's cavalry and infantry, numbering about 300, attached {sic} my rear guard and captured most of the men composing it. I immediately formed my Regt. in the field to the right {south} of the road, and opened fire on them, which checked them and caused them to move of the left of the road and fall back on the infantry following them, taking with them a number of prisoners of the rear guard and men who were not able to endure the march. Believing that Infantry, which I had previously seen moving to my right, would cut off my retreat, should I remain there any great length of time. I marched my Regt. through the fields between the two forces. Thus I continued my march night and day, avoiding the enemy, which was frequently on my flanks, and which pursued me to within ten miles of Bridgeport, by halting my Regt. in secluded places, and arrived at Bridgeport at 12 o'clock Sunday, June 29th {28th}. From paroled prisoners, who have since arrived, I leave that the enemy was very confident they {would} capture my command, and that they appeared to be fully acquainted with my force and movements up to the time they attacked me. The conduct of the men under my command was such as could be desired.

Appendix C:

Samuel Pennypacker's 1863 Campaign Equipage

"On the wall at Pennypacker's Mills there hang together the knapsack I carried, the shoes I wore," wrote Samuel Pennypacker, "a broken carbine made in Richmond in 1862 and picked up at the scene of our conflict, and a ramrod I found in a rebel camp a few days later at Chambersburg on our way to join Meade."[3] Additionally, Samuel also preserved his kepi, containing the lettering, "F 26."

Knapsack and shoes used by Governor Pennypacker in the Gettysburg campaign, June and July, 1863.

"Knapsack and shoes used by Governor Pennypacker in the Gettysburg Campaign, June and July 1863" (Philadelphia *Public Ledger*, November 29, 1917)

Samuel Pennypacker's kepi from his service in the 26th PVM.
(Collections of Pennypacker Mills Historic Site, Photo by the Author)

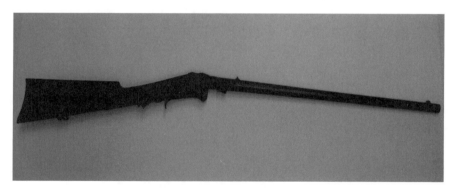

Samuel recorded that he later recovered this broken carbine from "the scene of our conflict." The carbine was made in Richmond in 1862 by "S.C. Robinson Arms Manufactory." *(Collections of Pennypacker Mills Historic Site)*

Appendix D:

Addresses Delivered at the Monument Dedication, 1892

Officially, Adjutant Harvey W. McKnight of the 26th was to "receive" the monument on behalf of the Gettysburg Battlefield Memorial Association.[4] In his address at the dedication, McKnight includes several inaccuracies. For one, he claims that the 26th Militia "was the first to meet and engage the enemy in Pennsylvania[.]"[5] That honor belongs to a detachment of the 1st New York Cavalry, who engaged Southern Cavalry a short distance north of Greencastle on June 22. McKnight's address was not included in the two-volume compilation, *Pennsylvania at Gettysburg*, which contains the addresses delivered at the dedication of Pennsylvania monuments on the battlefield, because Pennypacker's speech was the keynote address at the dedication, and therefore was the only address included. McKnight's address later appeared in the *Pennsylvania College Monthly*, doubtless by the influences of McKnight being the college's director at the time, as well as the rich, intertwined history the college had with the 26th PVM. McKnight's address follows;

> *In performing the part assigned to me in these exercises, I cannot refrain from expressing my gratification at having been connected with the organization represented here to-day, whose memorial I am now to receive on behalf of the Battlefield Memorial Association. Through the terms of military service many of us identified us with other regiments, of whose records we have just reason to be proud, yet there are peculiarities marking connection with the "26th Penna. (Emergency) regiment" which should render it specially gratifying to all survivors. But for it we should have had neither part nor lot in the most decisive campaign and the greatest battle of the war.*
>
> *To those unfamiliar with the facts, it may seem that our relation to the "Battle of Gettysburg" is much like that of the recently discovered moons of Mars to the planet itself, subordinate and diminutive; that we are indebted for recognition on this field to the valor and the achievements of the men who, on the granite ridges around us, met the foe and hurled him back, broken and shattered; that but for three days of fierce battle here and of ultimate victory for the defenders of the Union, our presence at Gettysburg on the 26th of June, 1863, and our subsequent engagement and retreat might never have attracted special notice or received deserved record. It may be that even we have not fully appreciated the real and helpful relation we sustained to the stirring events which have made the ground on which we stand historic and sacred—events which involved the very life of the nation and have made possible its unity, growth, grandeur and happiness.*

But, as the orator on this occasion will doubtless indicate and prove, our part in the Gettysburg campaign, resulting, as it did, in a brief check to the enemy and in time thereby gained the advancing Union forces, was a matter of the utmost moment in determining the issues of the battle that followed and of the war itself, especially in rendering successful the movements for the defense of Pennsylvania's capital.

It is needless to inquire anew into the causes of the war and to dwell upon the antagonistic ideas embodied in the great armies which confronted each other on this field. "In one view," as George William Curtis has aptly expressed the fact, "it was a war of Constitutional vindication, in another of Constitutional interpretation. But in any view it was an inevitable war, if ever such a phrase may be used. * * The issue at stake was ostensibly by the nature and vitality of a great political union. But beneath and beyond lay the problem of a social and industrial system inextricably involved by the compromises of the Constitution with the national conscience and the national life. It was a war without precedent for the grandeur of it significance, for the vastness of its resources, and for the stern tenacity of its combatants. It was a contest, not of regular armies nor of mercenary levies to gratify dynastic ambition or to extend ruthless conquest, but of republican citizens self-organized into military hosts to maintain conflicting principles held with equal sincerity and defended with equal courage." In its progress it came at last to yonder hill-tops and into these valleys with armies almost equal in numbers, bully equal in valor, and equal in determination. On the one hand, Lee, encouraged by the victories of Fredericksburg and Chancellorsville, pushed his army, which had been reinforced by two of Longstreet's divisions from the James' river and a large number of conscripts from Richmond, northward into the valley of Virginia, across the Potomac, into Maryland, and finally into the Cumberland valley, intent upon an invasion which should be decisive of the issues of the war. On the other hand, Hooker, at first, and Meade, later, directed the "Army of the Potomac" in pursuit to arrest this bold northward movement, but, embarrassed by the unconditioned order to protect Washington, were compelled to march cautiously and slowly, thus giving the enemy and opportunity to threaten Harrisburg, and even to plan and move for its capture. On the 21ˢᵗ of June Lee ordered Ewell, then in Maryland near Hagerstown, to march as far as Harrisburg, and to take possession of it if possible, and by the evening of the following day the camp-fires of Rodes' division were burning in Pennsylvania around Greencastle, while Early was moving his division towards Greenwood and yonder mountain pass to cooperate with Rodes by way of Gettysburg, York and Wrightsville in the capture of our capital city.

A great emergency had thus been created. Consternation prevailed among the people of the North, particularly in the threatened districts and cities of Pennsylvania. The President of the United States issued a call for volunteers to repel the invaders—a call which was urgently indorsed and repeated by the Governor of this Commonwealth. No tempting bounties were offered. The appeal was made to the patriotism of the people. The term of service was to be during the emergency—a very indefinite and uncertain period as affairs then stood. It might have been for a month, or for a year, or for the remainder of the war. No one could tell. The duties involved in obedience to this call were plainly of the sternest and most hazardous sort. The invasion to be repelled was being accomplished by a brave, disciplined and mighty army, in the flower of its strength and flushed with recent victories, under the command of one of the greatest chieftains of modern times. It was manifestly no holiday excursion, no easy task to meet and repel such a foe. Yet when the call involving such hardships and risks came, the men of the "26th Regiment" promptly responded. They came at once from school and office and store and shop and field. Home, business, study, ease—all were left for the field of patriotic duty and service.

The "26th" was the second regiment organized at Harrisburg under this call for emergency men. It was the first, save a troop of cavalry, on the field of Gettysburg, to which it came on the morning of June 26th, preceded by a detachment the evening before. It was the first to meet and engage the enemy in Pennsylvania, checking as general Early admits, the advance of his division towards York and Wrightsville. It did as well as any unsupported single regiment, however disciplined and experienced, could have been expected to do against an entire division of Lee's army, and for its forced and successful retreat to Harrisburg it deserves commendation, not censure.

It is not a part of my duty to give in detail the movements of the regiment, but, if the Colonel were not present, I would give my estimate of his coolness and courage and skill as a commanding officer. As his adjutant, I had special opportunities to know the good fortune that was ours in being under his leadership. His prompt obedience to the order to advance to Marsh Creek, when he knew that mistake was made and after courteously remonstrating with his superior officer; his quick comprehension of the situation when the enemy was reported to be in force within three-fourths of a mile of our position at Marsh Creek; his ready decision to cross the Mummasburg road by the most direct route, giving it as his judgment that another column of the enemy was moving on that parallel road and unless we anticipated his movement, we would be caught between his columns and forced to surrender; his prompt and wise disposition of the regiment for successful defense when attacked by the Confederate cavalry on the Hunterstown road; his selection of a safe route to Harrisburg on the meager information he could get; his care for his men, and his calm, courageous, soldierly bearing which inspired them with confidence—all marked him as the true soldier, the skillful commander, the man for the occasion. To him, I believe, we are indebted for our escape from a most hazardous situation.

A word now in reference to the location of the monument. The appropriateness of the spot must easily be apparent to all. It marks the point where we left the town on our march to Marsh Creek. It is separated from the other lines of battle on the field and cannot be confounded with them. It is near the town, the College and the Seminary, from which Co. "A" of the regiment came. It stands, therefore, as a merited rebuke of the false criticism, iterated and re-iterated far and wide, that the citizens of Gettysburg were lacking in patriotic devotion at a time when their interests, as well as those of the country, were in jeopardy. And I may add that for all time the people of the town, to be true to themselves and appreciative of their *own part in meeting the responsibilities of that crisis-period, should feel intelligent and patriotic pride in this memorial.*

But there is another feature of appropriateness in this location which should not be overlooked. Yonder stands the home of John Burns, who, when the battle of the first day was being fought, took up his gun, and, though aged, hastened to the front to join 'the boys in blue' in their brave and patriotic war effort to hold back the foe and save the day, and whose heroic service has been recognized and praised throughout the nation and made a part of the nation's history. Here, in nearness to the old hero's home, without intention on part of the Committee, will stand properly the memorial of "the 26th Pennsylvania (Emergency) Regiment." There is a self-evident fitness in this conjunction. What did he more than you? He left his home, so did you. If he took up arms in defense of his country, so did you. If he went to the front and engaged the enemy, so did you. If he, a citizen, realizing that a great emergency existed, that the cause of his country was endangered, voluntarily exchanged his ordinary employment and experiences for military duty and danger, so did you. If he, imbued with a patriotic spirit, did what he could for his country in a trail-hour, so did you. The only difference between him and you was one of age and the fact that your service was rendered under military oath and regulations and directed by properly constituted authority, while his was offered according to his own pleasure. In spirit and occasion the service in both instances was the same.

But I most not detain you longer. Twenty-nine years have wrought many changes. Many who were with us then as we marched out his road are with us no more. We remember them affectionately to-day, and dedicate this monument to their memory. We have all grown older. Experience has enlarged, perhaps changed, our views on many points. As citizen soldiers, we tried to do our duty, and as soldier citizens, few regiments have exerted a more extended influence for good. On bench, at the bar, in the pulpit, in the professor's chair, on the rostrum, in the field of politics and in the halls of legislation, in all the learned professions and useful walks of life, the "26th" has many representatives and is still rendering a wide and blessed service. And may I not say that, whatever changes of experience or opinion the years may have brought, on one point we remain united and unchanged, that treason is odious and that patriotism is a duty—a duty which binds us to right, virtuous, worthy living and working, and which holds us in constant readiness to meet any emergency created by threatening evils and to stand loyally for the preservation of the unity, peace, prosperity and Christian character of our country.

It affords me unfeigned pleasure, my comrades, as the representative of the Gettysburg Battlefield Memorial Association, to accept this monument and to promise, in the name of the Association, that is shall be constantly guarded and cared for.[6]

Samuel Pennypacker's address is lengthy, and for that reason will not be reprinted here. It can be found in: *Pennsylvania at Gettysburg*, (Harrisburg, PA: Wm. Stanley Ray, State Printer, 1914), Volume 2.

Appendix E:

Muster Roll of the Regiment

Field & Staff
Jennings, William W. Colonel.
Jenkins, Joseph H. Lieutenant Colonel.
Greenawalt, Lorenzo L. Major.
McKnight, Harvey W. Adjutant.
Sayles, Charles. Quartermaster.
Kirkpatrick, J. Andrew. Chaplain.
Horner, Edward H. Surgeon.
Hill, Charles M. Assistant Surgeon.
Royer, John W. Sergeant Major.
Harvey, Henry T. Quartermaster Sgt.
Keiser, Daniel. Commissary Sergeant.
Lenberger, Joseph L. Hospital
    Steward.

Company A
Klinefelter, Frederick. Captain.
Hinkle, William F. First Lieutenant.
Slater, Luther M. Second Lieutenant.

Sergeants:
Frey, Henry C.
Shindle, Harry C.
Schmacker, Samuel D.
Rupp, William Henry
Fegley, Orlando L.

Corporals:
Fount, David H.
Pritchard, Thomas C.
Rank, David F.
Koller, Jesse C.
Dizinger, John C.
Wolf, Edward J.
Irryang, John
Richards, Mathias H.

Privates:
Albert, Daniel
Beeber, John A.
Boyer, Mathew G.
Billhimer, Thomas C.
Branson, Phineas A.
Beltzhoover, George M.
Belch, Raphael A.
Baugher, Frederick W.
Biymyer, Joseph P.
Bishop, William O.
Berkstresser, John E.
Culley, Joseph R.
Collins, Samuel B.
Crossman, John J.
Cook, Herman L.
Canter, Davis G.
Combs, Charles H.
Culp, Rufus R.
Chritzman, George
Dover, Philip
Dohner, Henry J.
Eaton, Frank
Finkbinner, John W.
Frederick, George Washington.
Gotwald, William A.
Garver, Charles F.
Garver, Martin L.
Garver, Theodore F.
Gotwald, William A.
Hartein, Charles A.
Heilman, Jacob S.
Heagy, Charles A.
Heilig, Charles A.
Henry, Samuel.
Hill, Jeremiah C.
Hummell, Charles C.

Jacoby, Amandus.
Jacobs, Luther D.
Krauth, John Morris.
Meissenhelder, Edmund W.
Muhlenberg, Frank.
Miksel, Simon P.
Morrison, Henry C.
Myers, George B.
Moorehead, Charles C.
McLaughlin, Alexander.
McKnight, Harvey W.
Parson, William E.
Rowe, Eugene L.
Richards, Frank.
Richards, HenryMelchior Muhlenberg.
Rodman, John M.
Rodolp, Theodore F.
Reily, Andrew J.
Rank, Silas W.
Schaffer, William C.
Swope, Luther A.
Seip, Theodore Lorenzo.
Schindle, Jacob D.
Shuey, Dennis Bashore.
Shuey, Theodore F.
Schick, Rudolph M.
Steck, William A.
Weills, John C. S.
Wells, James G.
Wolf, Franklin B.
Young, John M.
Ziegenfuss, Henry L.

Company B
Carnochan, Warner H. Captain.
Smith, Francis. First Lieutenant.
Humphrey, George H. Second Lt.

Sergeants:
Orwan, William B.
Long, Albert.
Runyon, Charles W.
Mosher, Hugh.
Dewey, Edwin H.

Corporals:
Ross, Alonzo.
Newman, A. Scott.
Fanning, Wallace.
Rockwell, Myron A.
Gates, Marcus A.
Adams, Jeremiah.
Murry, Charles W.

Privates:
Adams, Otis.
Alvord, Royal.
Beebe, Benjamin F.
Barret, Lewis.
Bishop, Charles.
Bassett, Thomas.
Buck, Herman T.
Bement, Rufus B.
Buell, Perry.
Brooks, Ralph.
Buffam, Edward T.
Baxter, Uriah.
Bungon, Frank.
Brooks, Waldo.
Chase, William R.
Carnwright, Daniel.
Campbell, Chancey C.
Doan, Langdon H.
Dove, Thomas J.
Greene, Amos.
Griswold, Darius.
Gifford, Hiram H.
Gates, George L.
Guild, Joseph R.
Greenleaf, Edmund Q.
Kendall, Charles.
Kiff, Charles S.
Long, G. Dudley.
Leonard, Israel.
McCabe, Charles E.
McKean, James.
McKean, Norman.
McKean, Davis.
Newberry, George N.
Putnam, Harvey.
Pomroy, Elijah.

Phillips, William H.
Pierce, Albert A.
Redington, Robert F.
Ruggle, Archibald.
Rockwell, Delos.
Ross, Thomas.
Rockwell, Joseph.
Ruttan, David C.
Slade, Bryon B.
Slade, Eben.
Seymore, Jerome S.
Sawyer, John D.
Smead, Reuben.
Sullivan, Cornelius O.
Sullivan, Cornelius.
Teter, Charles.
Tromain, Francis E.
Vosberg, Edward.
Vandorn, Edward.
Vroman, Sidney Van Horn.
Vroman, Stephen.
Whiteman, William W.
Williams, Edwin D.
Williams, Hubbard H.
Wolf, John N.
Waiborn, Aaron.
Williams, Charles C.
Walden, John.
Watkins, Benjamin.

Company C
Walker, C. Wilson. Captain.
Sands, William H. First Lieutenant.
McCormick, Edward S. Second Lt.

Sergeants:
Donaldson, Oliver.
Furst, Robert H.
Wise, George O.
Bussell, Calvin P.
Sloan, James D.

Corporals:
King, William C.
Deise, James M.
Hipple, Torrence C.

Hudson, Theodore R.
Bower, Daniel T.
Nyhart, John G.
Mackey, John.

Privates:
Allen, William.
Arnold, John A.
Bisel, William F.
Bridgens, William H.
Bitner, John.
Bricker, Charles W.
Bent, Charles.
Best, Ellery C.
Corbit, Thomas.
Campbell, George W.
Caldwell, Green M.
Crispin, Willard.
Dailey, Thomas H.
Daley, Millard H.
Dobler, Aaron A.
Fertig, William R.
Fickes, Andre J.
Foster, Hiram.
Ferrar, Jacob.
Gheer, William A.
Gross, Edward P.
Gramow, John E.
Garth, John S.
Gibney, William.
Gray, John.
Hipple, Henry G.
Hilcher, Edward.
Hass, Edward D.
Hill, William.
Higo, Peter H.
Jenkin, Salothie L.
Loder, Henry A.
Lohiff, James.
Myers, Jeremiah.
Mill, Robert.
Moore, John H.
Moore, Alfred J.
McGhee, Robert.
McFerren, Cassius M.
Nelson, Robert.

Nidy, John.
Pank, Samuel.
Parkes, John S.
Richardson, George.
Smyth, James L.
Sheaver, James C.
Seward, Andrew G.
Storns, James C.
Todd, William.
Wickwire, George.
Welsh, William S.
Wolf, Michael R.

Company D
Pell, James L. Captain.
Jones, William J. First Lieutenant.
Miller, Edward. Second Lieutenant.

Sergeants:
Pettiger, John.
Foster, Benjamin R.
Bitterman, Thomas.
Fenton, Isaac.
Miller, Samuel.
Keeser, Daniel.

Corporals:
Umberger, Benjamin.
Hoffman, Michael.
Matter, Henry S.
Stonewood, Emanuel.
Lines, Howard.
Spangler, Henry.
Troutman, Martin.

Privates:
Albert, John.
Albert, Jacob.
Armstrong George.
Batley, Hiram.
Butdorf, Philip.
Bitterman, Cyrus.
Bueck, Hiram.
Binestine, John H.
Feree, Jacob F.
Ferguson, John.

Ferguson, James.
Fuller, William.
Hocklander, Cornelius A.
Hoffman, Jonathan.
Hope, John W.
Heiney, Samuel B.
Israel, David.
Keiser, George.
Kareher, John F.
Keiser, Jonas.
Keudle, William.
Knight, Richard.
Maurer, Henry.
Mark, John.
Matter, Samuel.
Mummy, Martin.
Myers, Joel.
McCoy, Jeremiah.
Naylor, Daniel.
Nash, William.
Parpet, James.
Parpet, George.
Pell, Peter.
Pell, Henry.
Regle, Obed.
Russler, Andrew.
Russler, Benjamin.
Ristinger, John.
Row, Jonas.
Russel, David H.
Shire, Lewis.
Snyder, William.
Snyder, Israel.
Stevens, John.
Swigards, John S.
Soilers, Charles H.
Thomas, James.
Troutman, Elias t.
Updegrove, Aaron.
Updegraph, Solomon.
Workman, Levi.
Wylie, Arthur.
Witmer, John W.
Walcot, Oliver.
Zerley, Edward.

Company E
Brooks, John C. Captain.
Moyer, Lemuel. First Lieutenant.
George, David S. Second Lieutenant.

Sergeants:
Embich, W. H. Harrison.
Hughes, Samuel L.
George, Cyrus S.
Boger, Cyrus.

Corporals:
Weldman, Mason.
Byle, Franklin.
Redsecker, Jacob C.
Stout, Isaac.
Warren, Lucien R.
Gerhart, Conrad G.
Grittinger, Henry C.
Shunk, Casper.

Privates:
Allwine, Jonathan.
Biecher, Emanuel.
Brooks, James T.
Bruce, Jonathan Z.
Brunner, John.
Beck, Charles W.
Bentz, Samuel H.
Barto, Penrose.
Barto, Reuben.
Bordlemay, William Shuey.
Byle, John.
Coffman, Jacob.
Darrach, Edgar.
Derr, Cyrus.
Dampman, Anthony W.
Embich, Jacob J.
Embich, George.
Eggers, Luther F.
Few, William.
Forney, Stehman.
Fernsler, John.
Gleim, George.
Garrett, Henry.
Garret, Benjamin F.

Geary, Joseph W.
Geiger, Henry H.
Holsberger, Daniel B.
Harter, Jacob J.
Hecker, Adam A.
Hostetter, David C.
Howard, George W.
Hay, Ismal.
Kahle, Isaac.
Kartz, Franklin.
Karmany, James M.
Krumbine, Reuben.
Kline, Jacob W.
Light, Abiah C.
Londen, Henry.
Light, Henry C.
Light, Edwin.
Louden, Peter B.
Leininger, George.
Mark, Milton.
Moyer, Ezra.
Maguire, Milton.
Moore, James H.
McConnel, Israel.
McAdam, William.
McConnel, Simon.
McGinley, Edward.
Nesbit, Robert.
Neber, William.
Pfleger, George.
Reinoehl, Cyrus W.
Rank, Titus H.
Rohrer, Andrew H.
Rentz, Cyrus.
Strickler, Franklin G.
Schuler, Henry W.
Steinman, Daniel.
Schrop, Henry J.
Shuey, Allen.
Smith, William C. J.
Ulrich, A. Stanley.
Uhler, John E.
Weldman, W. Morris.
Weaver, Armand.
Weit, Martin.
Wentz, William J.

Wilhelm, John.
Yordy, Henry K.
Zimmerman, Percival

Company F
Rice, George. Captain.
Potts, Henry Jr. First Lieutenant.
Richards, Mark H. Second Lt.

Sergeants:
Dyer, William A.
Scheetz, George.
Lessig, William S.
Meigs, William G.
Lessig, Englebert.

Corporals:
Smith, Mahlon V.
Loyd, Jon S.
Evans, Miller D.
Corbert, John.
Richards, Henry.
Guesr, John.
Davis, D. W.
Macdonald, Charles W.

Privates:
Auchey, John.
Byer, Jerome.
Buckley, William P.
Bair, Christian G.
Bechtel, Edwin R.
Bickel, Nathaniel.
Binder, William J.
Caswell, John R.
Custer, Horace A.
Collar, Mahlon.
Collar, Hiram.
Daub, Samuel S.
Derolf, Abram.
Ennis, Robert.
Ellis, Daniel E.
Fritch, Jonas D.
Fryer, John H.
Feger, Thomas W.

Fray, Jonathan.
Frock, Benjamin.
Frick, Charles.
Ford, John B.
Fry, John.
Fryer, Michael.
Graham, Daniel F.
Hitner, Henry C.
Heizall, Samuel.
Huber, Jefferson F.
Hays, Joseph L. Jr.
Herring, Levi.
Herring, Paul.
Herring, Isaac.
Hollowbush, John W.
Hummel, Jonathan.
Huber, Henry.
Hobart, Henry J.
Hobart, Nathaniel P. Jr.
Huber, Josiah.
Jacobs, J. Howard.
Kraner, Cyrus.
Kemerling, Henry.
Lessig, George B.
Liggett, George.
Landis, David R.
Lachman, William.
Lessig, Michael.
Moyer, George.
Meigs, George.
Missimer, Van Buren.
Missimer, Merit.
Morrow, George.
Murshall, Patterson.
McKane, Theodore.
Nice, Cyrus.
Prutzman, Henry A.
Pennypacker, Samuel W.
Rahn, Henry G.
Rhodes, John.
Renshaw, Richard.
Rennard, Joseph G.
Rowe, Benjamin S.
Ruddy, Thomas.
Sponsler, Calvin B.
Smith, Edwin F.

Shaner, George W.
Small, Robert F.
Spancake, Israel.
Schrope, Ephraim.
Steele, George.
Shick, Augustine W.
Thomas, William J.
Thomas, Werner.
Welles, Joseph K.
Wyun, William W.
Wagoner, Frank.

Company G
Rishel, Elias C. Captain.
Bryan, Ellis. First Lieutenant.
Warn, Monroe C. Second Lieutenant.

Sergeants:
Rogers, Melvin H.
Biddle, Edward M.
Hill, Harvey J.
Snell, Charles.

Corporals:
Corson, Milton.
Sampsel, Charles H.
Handshaw, Daniel.
Huling, Lewis G.
Steck, Frank.
Green, John C.
McCarty, George M.
Smith, Dallas J.

Musician:
Goover, William.

Privates:
Bubb, David.
Babb, James.
Barrett, William D.
Bodine, Milton.
Barto, Henry.
Barto, Jacob J.
Corr, Henry.
Cooper, Abraham.

Dent, Thomas A.
Donley, George B.
Doner, William.
Edkin, Henry B.
Edkin, Thomas J.
Fawcett, Lemuel.
Fague, George W.
Falls, Andrew J.
Flick, John.
Gower, George.
Howlett, Charles.
Heart, Joseph.
Kahler, Pierson D.
Kraus, Franklin J.
Kepner, Isaac.
Laylon, James.
Lorah, Jacob.
Little, George W.
Laurenson, John.
Montague, Bodine.
Mader, Benjamin.
McCarty, Silas.
Norton, William.
Reeder, John V.
Rogers, John W.
Rogers, Edward A.
Rook, Esbon F.
Snell, Franklin B.
Stevens, John R.
Stroup, James L.
Stroup, John W.
Smith, Charles.
Sauder, John C.
Van Buskirk, Oscar.
Veilengruber, George.
Vough, David.
Yeakel, John W.

Company H
Morgan, John T. Captain.
Reese, David. First Lieutenant.
Manson, George H. Second Lt.

Sergeants:
Knighton, William C.

Sanders, Emanuel R.
Brown, William.
Dunbar, Joseph Jr.

Corporals:
Kraber, John O.
George, John C.
Buchanan, Peter.
McCabe, William.
Millen, Howard.
Stevens, Dennis.
Taylor, Joseph.
Dunbar, Hiram.

Privates:
Able, William.
Bowman, George W.
Brooks, Daniel.
Barr, Walker.
Doyle, Joseph.
Doulin, Michael.
Dunnel, Joseph.
Eckart, John.
Ehrman, Francis.
Eckart, Solomon.
Fry, Horace.
Givler, George.
George, John H.
George, William.
Hartman, John.
Hass, Henry.
Jackson, Henry.
Keys, David.
Kilhetler, Daniel.
Keys, Stephen.
Keys, Jacob.
Lewellan, John.
Lingerfield, John.
Newman, William.
River, Ell.
Rapp, Levi.
Ripley, Abram.
Shannon, Albert.
Standerman, Henry.
Sunderling, Gabriel.
Shoemaker, Edward.

Sugars, Henry.
Strabauch, Philip.
Stack, Jeremiah.
Taylor, John.
White, Charles.
Waxler, James.
Yous, Henry.
Zinn, George.

Company I
Forrest, John S. Captain.
Pfeiffer, John Quincy. First Lt.
Barnes, Alexander T. Second Lt.

Sergeants:
Henry, Joel.
McCausland, William H.
Deitrick, Howard N.
Carver, Napoleon B.
Young, Charles.

Corporals;
Rinehart, Josiah.
Sneeringer, Thomas.
Shultz, Henry.
Winebrenner, David E.
Bueher, Henry C.
Klinefelter, Amos F.
Kump, Charles T.
Thomas, Charles W.

Privates:
Althoff, William.
Allison, Noah.
Bair, William.
Bastres, William H.
Baum, William F.
Beard, William A.
Blair, James.
Blair, John F.
Bollinger, Edward.
Bond, John.
Forney, David F.
Forney, William G.
Freet, Jacob.

Gautz, William
Gardner, Jacob.
Graybill, Martin.
Heathcote, Lewin.
Hitzol, Martin.
Herman, Addison M.
Hersh, John J.
Hersh, Josiah D.
Himes, Barthabus.
Hinkle, John H.
Holter, Lewis V.
Holter, William H.
Johnson, Washington J.
Jones, Lewis B.
Jones, Isaac.
Leader, William.
Louchs, Isaac.
Metzgar, Henry C.
Michael, Jacob H.
Myers, Michael D.
Myers, William A.
McLean, Aaron.
Nail, Mahlon H.
Ports, Hezekiah.
Pfeiffer, Henry H.
Sanders, John J.
Sherman, George W.
Sherwood, George E.
Shriver, Henry Wirt.
Snyder, William H.
Snyder, Eli.
Snyder, Daniel J.
Stahl, Ovid.
Trone, George E.
Trone, Olvier.
Trone, Samuel E.
Wagener, Fabius N.
Weigle, Samuel.
Willing, John.
Wirt, Calvin.
Wolf, William C.
Young, Cornelious.
Zimmerman, Martin.

Company K

Novinger, Marcius. Captain.
Campbell, Peter A. First Lieutenant.
Kepler, Joseph W. Second Lieutenant.

Sergeants:
Huff, John H.
Lenker, Daniel Y.
Bordner, William.
Miller, Preston.
Fegley, Henry W.

Corporals:
Enterline, Jeremiah.
Klinger, Jonathan.
Fox, Italian J. W.
Boyer, Henry F.
Cutterman, Josiah.
Hoffman, Jacob F.
Ditty, Thomas M.
Rathboon, John J.

Privates:
Bartholemew, Charles.
Brock, Byron.
Bariet, Nathan.
Bean, Solomon L.
Catherman, Isiah.
Culby, Isaac.
Deibler, Emanuel.
Dolby, Abraham.
Forney, Jacob.
Groff, Hiram F.
Groff, W. D.
Heinninger, Henry.
Henry, Samuel L.
Hinkle, George W.
Huff, George.
Jury, Lewis.
Jackson, John W.
Klinger, Jacob.
Klinger, Daniel.
Linker, Jacob H.

Leibo, Isaac.
Lerch, William F.
Lerch, Simon F.
Lerch, John F.
Longsdorf, Henry H.
Morris, Brock.
Martz, Cornelius.
Meek, John W.
Miller, John J.
Martin, William.
Miller, Perry.
Mercer, Francis.
Poith, Joseph.

Roop, John.
Ricker, Samuel.
Swab, Jeremiah.
Sarge, Franklin.
Spotz, John S.
Stewart, John.
Weist, Samuel L.
Wingert, John W.
Wingert, John.
Woodsides, Alfred.
Wisner, Smith J.
Yerger, Joseph F.

Bibliographic Note

In researching this study, a variety of different manuscript and book sources were examined—a significant amount of these references were, prior to this study, untapped sources, as far as they relate to the 26th Pennsylvania Volunteer Militia. First and foremost, a number of late-nineteenth and early-twentieth century books were analyzed. These include county and genealogical histories (which often provide biographical accounts or in some cases even reminisces of veterans), as well as books and memoirs written by veterans themselves. Further published resources utilized include the invaluable late-nineteenth century War Department publication, the *Official Records*, which contains the official reports and correspondence of both Union and Confederate commanders.

Many manuscript sources were used in compiling this volume. The largest and arguably most valuable manuscript collection utilized includes the staggering and voluminous assemblage of pertinent papers at the estate of Governor Samuel Pennypacker, a member of the 26th Militia. This archival goldmine holds Governor Pennypacker's original, handwritten version of his memoir recounting the time he spent in the field with the 26th, entitled "Six Weeks in Uniform," which was published in 1883. Further, it contains a number previously untapped sources, among which include several dozen letters written to Pennypacker by other veterans of the 26th during the summer of 1892. These letters were in response to a request by Pennypacker, who was gathering information on the regiment's June 26 encounter at Gettysburg in order to deliver the keynote address at the dedication of its' monument in September 1892. Additionally, Pennypacker Mills holds the previously unpublished official report of Colonel William W. Jennings of the 26th, which greatly adds to the history of the regiment.

Two more manuscript collections were so useful in this work that they too deserve especial note. In the Shriver Family Papers at the Maryland Historical Society are the detailed letters and diary of Henry Wirt Shriver. Written while he was in the field with the 26th Militia in June and July 1863, Shriver's detailed accounts provide a rare look into the daily lives, thoughts and opinions of the men in the 26th. Further, the holdings at the U.S. Army Military History Institute at Carlisle Barracks proved an instrumental part of this study. The Institute holds several valuable accounts from men in the 26th. However, the Institute's archives also holds dozens of accounts from men in other 1863 "Emergency Militia" Units, which also offer insight relative to the "Emergency Militia" in general. Furthermore, the Institute's massive photo archives, including the celebrated "MOLLUS-MASS" albums, have proved extremely useful.

More specifically, the two key sources from the ranks of the 26th Militia utilized to complete this study were undoubtedly the Shriver Papers and Pennypacker's "Six Weeks in Uniform" memoir. Pennypacker began his memoir several months after his service with the 26th had ended. "My only reason for writing the following narration of the events which transpired," he wrote on November 22, 1863, "relating particularly to myself, during a short term of military service, is that the scenes and occurrences may be described while they are still fresh in memory, and the impression of them vivid and distinct. It must have been noticed in the experience of every one, that however deep and strong the marks which particular circumstances have made upon our feelings, marks which particular circumstances have made upon our feelings, time will gradually erase one point after another, wear off the edges, and render the whole dim and uncertain. I have therefore determined to write truthfully, minutely, and as clearly as possible, whatever occurred within my own observation during that time, thinking that in future year it may be a satisfaction for me to read what has here been transcribed."[1]

Handwritten title-page to Pennypacker's original "Six Weeks in Uniform" manuscript. (*Collections of Pennypacker Mills Historic Site*)

By the time Pennypacker completed the manuscript, it numbered 80, handwritten pages. In 1881, Pennypacker informed early Gettysburg historian John Bachelder of his manuscript "which I have had bound and put away for my children." Pennypacker believed that "[i]t is probably the only contemporary record of the war of that regiment. Of course it is very personal in its character." Further, the future-governor invited Bachelder to review his memoir. "If you think it would be worth your while to examine it, the ms is at your service any time that you may happen to be in Philadelphia."[2] In 1883, when Pennypacker finally published the memoir, he did so only "after much hesitation and with many misgivings," due to how "so very personal in its character" the memoir was. "Several considerations have had weight in inducing me to commit what may seem to be an impropriety," he wrote. "Col. John P. Nicholson, and other friends, who are students of the military history of the rebellion, and whose judgment is worth much more than my own in such matters, have earnestly urged me to print it."[3]

First handwritten page in Pennypacker's "Six Weeks in Uniform."
(Collections of Pennypacker Mills Historic Site)

However, Pennypacker had other motivations as well. "A Pennsylvanian naturally resents the statement, so often made in prose and verse, that John Burns was the only man in Gettysburg to display loyalty and courage, and information concerning a regiment, one of whose companies came from that town, and which was the first force to engage the rebel army there when it entered the State, ought not, perhaps, to be withheld." But perhaps what makes Samuel's "Six Weeks in Uniform" memoir so remarkable is the fact that it was entirely unchanged from the time Pennypacker penned the original manuscript in the waning weeks of 1863—just several months after his discharge from the 26th Militia—to the time of its' publication 20 years later, in 1883. "An effort was made to recast the paper," Pennypacker admitted, "but it was soon found that the result was to destroy all of the color and freshness which constituted its only literary merit, and the attempt was abandoned. It is hoped that he freedom of comment upon men and affairs will be excused and the quick and enthusiastic impressions of a boy of twenty."[4]

Furthermore, a difficulty encountered in documenting any historic affair is that of the eroding memory of its' participants. A number of the accounts from the 26th Militia are written in 1892, in response to a request by Pennypacker. By then, it had been 29 years since the regiment's stint in the field. Many memories had by then largely faded. Additionally, often the ability of those engaged in battle to comprehend what is happening is meager. This is especially so for largely inexperienced troops, which composed the greater part of the 26th Militia. Private William Few of Company E remarked in a July 1892 letter "that it has been so long ago that I have almost forgotten what did transpire[.] I was very young at the time[.]" 29-years later, all Few could remember of the march to Witmer's farm and the engagement there was "marching out of the woods on the Cashtown [Chambersburg] road, and meeting the advance of Earlie's [sic] Corp and I remember having an engagement with them and they charging on us and I was one of the unfortunate in being taken Prisoner."[5]

Despite such difficulties, there is still a phenomenal amount of primary source material relating to the 26th Militia's short but eventful summer in the field. For a more complete listing of the bibliographic sources used in this study, the reader is directed to the Bibliography.

Bibliography

BOOKS:

The Alumni Record of Gettysburg College, 1832-1932. (Gettysburg, PA: Gettysburg College, 1932).

Alexander, John and Slade, Jim, *Firestorm at Gettysburg: Civilian Voices*, (Atglen, PA: Schiffer Military/Aviation History, 1998).

Beers, J. H. & Co., *Biographical Annals of Lebanon County, Pennsylvania*, (Chicago: J. H. Beers, 1904).

Breidenbaugh, E. S., *The Pennsylvania College Book, 1832-1882*, (Philadelphia: Lutheran Publications Society, 1882)

Dawson, John Harper, *Wildcat Cavalry: A Synoptic History of the Seventeenth Virginia Cavalry Regiment of the Jenkins-McCausland Brigade in the War Between the States*, (Dayton, OH: Morningside, 1982).

Early, Jubal Anderson, *Narrative of the War Between the States*, (reprint, Da Capo Press, 1989).

Gregg, J. Chandler, *Life in the Army, in the Departments of Virginia, and the Gulf, Including Observations in New Orleans, With an Account of the Author's life and Experience in the Ministry*, (Philadelphia: Perkinpine & Higgins, 1868).

Haller, Granville O. *The Dismissal of Major Granville O. Haller*, (Patterson, NJ: Daily Guardian, 1863).

Harris, Nelson, *17th Virginia Cavalry*, (Lynchburg, VA: H. E. Howard, 1994).

Hefelbower, Samuel Gring, *The History of Gettysburg College, 1832-1932*, (Gettysburg: Gettysburg College, 1932).

Heverly, C. F., *History of Albany Township, 1800-1885, With Biographical Sketches of the Pioneers, Her Soldiers and Statistics and Matters of General Interest Connected with the Township*, (Towanda, PA: Bradford Republican Print, 1885).

Jacobs, Michael, *Notes on the Rebel Invasion of Maryland and Pennsylvania, and the Battle of Gettysburg*, (Phila: J.B. Lippincott & Co., 1864).

Kelker, Luther Reily, *History of Dauphin County Pennsylvania, With Genealogical Memoirs*, (New York/Chicago: Lewis Publishing Co., 1907)

Kesterson, Brian Stuart, *Campaigning with the 17th Virginia Cavalry Night Hawks at Monocacy*, (Washington, WV: Night Hawk Press, 2005).

Lee, Francis Bazley (ed.), *Genealogical and Personal Memorial of Mercer County New Jersey*, (New York and Chicago: The Lewis Publishing Company, 1907).

McClure, A. K., *Abraham Lincoln and Men of War-Times: Some Personal Recollections of War and Politics During the Lincoln Administration*, (Philadelphia: The Times Publishing Company, 1892).

Mingus, Scott L. Sr., *Flames Beyond Gettysburg: The Confederate Expedition to the Susquehanna River, June 1863*, (New York and California: Savas Beatie, 2011).

Morris, John G., *Fifty Years in the Lutheran Ministry*, (Baltimore: James Young, 1878).

J.W. Muffly (ed.), *The Story of Our Regiment: A History of the 148th Pennsylvania Vols.*, (Des Moines, IA: The Kenyon Printing & MGF Company, 1904).

Myers, Frank N., *The Comanches: A History of White's Battalion, Virginia Cavalry*, (Baltimore: Kelly, Piet & Co., 1871).

Frank Myers, *The Comanches: A History of White's Battalion, Virginia Cavalry, Laurel Brigade, Hampton Div., A.N.V., C.S.A.*, (Kelly, Piet & Co., Baltimore, 1871, reprint by Butternut Press, Baltimore, 1987).

Pennypacker, Samuel W., *Historical and Biographical Sketches*, (Philadelphia: Robert A. Tripple, 1883).

Pennypacker, Samuel W., *The Autobiography of A Pennsylvanian*, (Philadelphia: John C. Winston Company, 1918).

Regimental Association, *History of the 127th Regiment Pennsylvania Volunteers, Familiarly Known as the "Dauphin County Regiment,"* (Lebanon, PA: Report Publishing Company, ca. 1902).

Richards, Henry Melchior Muhlenberg, *Pennsylvania's Emergency Men at Gettysburg*, (Reading, PA: n.p., 1895).

Shuey, Dennis B., *History of the Shuey Family in America From 1732 to 1919*, (Galion, OH: By the Author, 1919).

Warner, Ezra, *Generals in Blue: Lives of the Union Commanders*, (Baton Rouge: Louisiana State University, 1964).

Wells, Clark H., *The Reply of Lt. Com. C.H. Wells, U.S.N., To A Pamphlet Recently Published by G.O. Haller, late a Major U.S.A.*, (York, PA: H. Young, 1865).

Wingert, Cooper H., *The Confederate Approach on Harrisburg: The Gettysburg Campaign's Northernmost Reaches*, (Charleston and London: The History Press, 2012).

GOVERNMENT PUBLICATIONS:

Heitman, Francis B. (compiler), *Historical Register and Dictionary of the United States Army, From Its Organization, September 29, 1789, to March 2, 1903*, (Washington: Govt. Printing Office, 1903).

U.S. War Dept., *The War of the Rebellion: A Compilation of the Official Records of the Union and Confederate Armies*, (Washington: Govt. Printing Office, 1889).

various, *Pennsylvania at Gettysburg*, (Harrisburg, PA: Wm. Stanley Ray, State Printer, 1914).

ARTICLES & PERIODICALS:

Anonymous, "Addendum to History of 'Co. A,'" *Pennsylvania College Monthly*, 3:4, (May 1879).

Bradford County Historical Society, "Annual," (Towanda, PA: Bradford Star Print, 1910), 4.

Malone, Bartlett Yancey, "The Diary of Batlett Yancey Malone," in *The James Sprunt Historical Publications*, (Chapel Hill: University of North Carolina, 1919), 16:2.

Mingus, Scott L. Sr., "Jenkins' Cavalry Raid Through Northwestern York County, Pennsylvania," *The Gettysburg Magazine*, 44 (January 2011).

Nye, Wilbur Sturtevant, "The First Battle of Gettysburg," *Civil War Times Illustrated*, 4:5, (August 1965).

Parson, W. E., "History of 'Co. A,' 26th Regiment, P.V.M.," *Pennsylvania College Monthly*, 3:3, April 1879.

Parson, W. E., "History of 'Co. A,' 26th Regiment, P.V.M.," *Pennsylvania College Monthly*, 3:4, May 1879.

Pennypacker, Samuel W., "Fort Washington in 1863", *Transactions of The Historical Society of Dauphin County, Pennsylvania*, 1:1, (1903).

Richards, Henry M. M., "Lebanon County's Emergency Volunteers at Gettysburg", in *Proceedings of the Lebanon County Historical Society*, 3:7, (1905).

NEWSPAPERS:
Evening Telegraph, Harrisburg, PA, 1863-1864
Gettysburg *Compiler*, Gettysburg, PA, 1866-1961
The Compiler, Gettysburg, PA, 1857-1866
Gettysburg *Times*, Gettysburg, PA, 1904-present
The Montgomery Ledger, Pottstown, PA, 1857-1921
The Morning Call, Harrisburg, PA, 1885-1898
Pennsylvania Telegraph, Harrisburg, PA, 1864-1864
Philadelphia *Press*, Philadelphia, PA, 1857-1880
Philadelphia *Public Ledger*, Philadelphia, PA, 1836-1925

MANUSCRIPTS:
ANTIETAM NATIONAL BATTLEFIELD LIBRARY, SHARPSBURG, MD:
130th Pennsylvania Volunteer Infantry File

DICKINSON COLLEGE, WAIDNER-SPAHR LIBRARY, CARLISLE, PA:
Charles F. Himes to Dear Rood, October 2, 1863

GETTYSBURG NATIONAL MILITARY PARK LIBRARY, GETTYSBURG, PA:
26th Pennsylvania Militia File
26th Pennsylvania Militia Monument File
17th Virginia Cavalry File
William Hamilton Bayly Account
Mrs. Joseph Bayly Account

Sarah Broadhead Diary

Henry Eyster Jacobs Memoir

Frederick Klinefelter, "An Historical Sketch of 'Company A,' 26th Penna. Volunteer Militia"

John C. Wills Reminisce

GETTYSBURG COLLEGE, SPECIAL COLLECTIONS AND COLLEGE ARCHIVES, MUSSELMAN LIBRARY, GETTYSBURG PA:

William Henry Rupp Diary

HISTORICAL SOCIETY OF DAUPHIN COUNTY, ALEXANDER FAMILY LIBRARY, HARRISBURG, PA

Phillip German Scrapbook

Pamphlet, *Zion's Path Through History*

LEBANON COUNTY HISTORICAL SOCIETY, HAUCK RESEARCH ARCHIVES, LEBANON, PA:

Henry M. M. Richards Autobiography, 1883

MARYLAND HISTORICAL SOCIETY, H. FURLONG BALDWIN LIBRARY, BALTIMORE, MD:

Shriver Family Papers (MS 2085);

Henry Wirt Shriver Diary

Henry Wirt Shriver Letters

NATIONAL ARCHIVES AND RECORDS ADMINISTRATION, WASHINGTON, DC:

Records of the Department of Veteran Affairs, RG-15;

Historical Register of National Homes for Disabled Volunteer Soldiers, 1866-1938

NATIONAL SOCIETY OF THE SONS OF THE AMERICAN REVOLUTION, LOUISVILLE, KY:

Sons of the American Revolution Membership Applications:

Lorenzo L. Greenawalt Application

NEW HAMPSHIRE HISTORICAL SOCIETY, CONCORD, NH:

John Bachelder Papers:

Samuel Pennypacker to John Bachelder, August 26, 1881

PENNSYLVANIA STATE ARCHIVES, PENNSYLVANIA HISTORIC AND MUSEUM COMMISSION, HARRISBURG, PA:

Record Group 19, Records of the Dept. of Military and Veterans Affairs, Civil War Muster Rolls & Related Records;

26th Pennsylvania Militia Muster-In and Muster-Out Rolls

127th Pennsylvania Volunteer Infantry Muster-Out Roll

Adjutant General's Papers on the Regiment

Adjutant General Thomas J. Stewart to General St. Clair A. Mulholland, June 16, 1909

Consolidated Morning Report Book, 26th Regt. State Militia, June 30, 1863-July 28, 1863

Pennsylvania Civil War Veteran's Card File, 1861-1866

Samuel Pennypacker Papers (MG 171)

PENNYPACKER MILLS HISTORIC SITE, SCHWENKSVILLE, PA:

Letters to Samuel Pennypacker;

Joseph L. Lenberger, July 4, 1892

A. Stanley Ulrich, July 6, 1892

William Few, July 6, 1892

J. H. Jacobs, July 7, 1892

Samuel S. Henry, July 8, 1892

Charles Macdonald, July 11, 1892

Edward S. McCormick, July 11, 1892

William G. George and Joseph Dunnel, August 10, 1892

Augustine W. Shick, August 17, 1892

Hiram J. Dunbar, August 20, 1892

Frank Muhlenberg, August 27, 1892

Rudolph M. Schick to Dear Cousin, July 5, 1863

Pamphlet, "Before the Pennsylvania Commission on Gettysburg Monuments: In reright of the 26th Pennsylvania Emergency Regiment to a Monument at Gettysburg"

Samuel W. Pennypacker to Dear Mother, June 29, 1863

Photograph, "26th Pennsylvania Emergency Regiment Monument"

Printed Circular, June 8, 1892

Monument Dedication Materials

Colonel William W. Jennings Manuscript Official Report

Newspaper Scrapbook

STATE LIBRARY OF PENNSYLVANIA, RARE COLLECTIONS LIBRARY, HARRISBURG, PA:

"In Memoriam: William Wesley Jennings," MOLLUS-Pennsylvania, Circular No. 8, 1894

C.W. Buoy, "Address by C.W. Buoy, Grace Methodist Church, Harrisburg, PA, Saturday, March 3, 1894"

U.S. ARMY MILITARY HISTORY INSTITUTE, CARLISLE BARRACKS, CARLISLE, PA:

John W. Ames Papers;

John W. Ames to dear Mother, June 15, 1863

Robert L. Brake Collection;

26th Pennsylvania Militia Regimental Papers

Civil War Document Collection;

William S. Bordlemay to Respected Friend, July 18, 1863
Civil War Miscellaneous Collection;
    John S. Weiser Letters, October 11 and December 17, 1862
Randy Hackenburg Collection;
    Robert S. Simington Biographical Sketch
    Samuel Yorks Thompson Biographical Sketch
Harrisburg Civil War Round Table Collection;
    Mathias H. Richards Letters
    Haas-Jones-Curry Family Papers
    Peter A. Filbert Diary
Elliot Hoffman Collection;
    Charles F. Sayles Papers
Nicholas Rice Papers:
    Nicholas Rice, "Memoir"
PA Save the Flags Collection:
    Samuel P. Conrad to Mr. Lewis J. Strickler, Dear Friend, January 20, 1863

UNIVERSITY OF MICHIGAN, WILLIAM L. CLEMENTS LIBRARY, ANN ARBOR, MI:
    James Schoff Collection;
        William Seymour Journal

VERMONT HISTORICAL SOCIETY, LEAHY LIBRARY, BARRE, VT:
    William F. Smith Papers
        William Smith Typescript Memoir.

YORK COUNTY HERITAGE TRUST, YORK, PA:
    Frederick Klinefelter File
    Hiram H. Gifford Declaration for Disability Pension

PRIVATE COLLECTIONS
AUTHOR'S COLLECTION
    "GWS" to Dear Brother and Sister, June 29, 1863

J. HOWARD WERT GETTYSBURG COLLECTION
    J. Howard Wert Scrapbook

Abbreviations

GC   Special Collections and College Archives, Musselman Library, Gettysburg College, Gettysburg, PA

GNMP   Gettysburg National Military Park Library, Gettysburg, PA

HCWRT   Harrisburg Civil War Round Table Collection, U.S. Army Military History Institute, Carlisle Barracks, Carlisle, PA

HWS   Henry Wirt Shriver

JHWGC   J. Howard Wert Gettysburg Collection, Private Collection

LCHS   Lebanon County Historical Society, Hauck Research Archives, Lebanon, PA

MDHS   Maryland Historical Society, H. Furlong Baldwin Library, Baltimore, MD

ML   *The Montgomery Ledger*, Pottstown, PA

O.R.   U.S. War Dept., *The War of the Rebellion: A Compilation of the Official Records of the Union and Confederate Armies*, (Washington: Govt. Printing Office, 1889), Series I.

PASA   Pennsylvania State Archives, Pennsylvania Historic and Museum Commission, Harrisburg, PA

PCM   *Pennsylvania College Monthly*

PPM   Pennypacker Mills Historic Site, County of Montgomery, Schwenksville, PA

RG 19   Record Group 19, Records of the Dept. of Military and Veterans Affairs, Civil War Muster Rolls & Related Records, PASA

SFP   Shriver Family Papers

SWP   Samuel W. Pennypacker

USAMHI   Archives, U.S. Army Military History Institute, Carlisle Barracks, Carlisle, PA

YCHT   Archives, York County Heritage Trust, York, PA

Endnotes

Introduction: "Great Stir and Excitement Among All Classes"

[1] *O.R.*, 27:3, 79-80.

[2] *Ibid.*, 54-55.

[3] William F. Smith Typescript Memoir, W. F. Smith Papers, Vermont Historical Society.

[4] Philadelphia *Press*, "The Invasion," June 26, 1863.

[5] *O.R.*, 27:3, 914.

[6] *Ibid.*, 145; Cooper H. Wingert, *The Confederate Approach on Harrisburg: The Gettysburg Campaign's Northernmost Reaches*, (Charleston and London: The History Press, 2012), 16-23.

[7] Samuel W. Pennypacker, "Six Weeks in Uniform, Being the Record of A Term of Military Service of the United States in the Gettysburg Campaign of 1863," in Samuel W. Pennypacker, *Historical and Biographical Sketches*, (Philadelphia: Robert A. Tripple, 1883), 307-397.

[8] *Ibid.*, 309-310; In his autobiography, which was published posthumously, Pennypacker described Lloyd as "an upright, narrow and methodical clerk in the bank[.]" See, Samuel W. Pennypacker, *The Autobiography of A Pennsylvanian*, (Philadelphia: John C. Winston Company, 1918), 73.

[9] Pennypacker, *Autobiography*, 76-77.

[10] *Ibid.*, 77-78.

[11] Pennypacker, "Six Weeks in Uniform," 309-310.

[12] Samuel Gring Hefelbower, *The History of Gettysburg College, 1832-1932*, (Gettysburg: Gettysburg College, 1932), 179-203; E. S. Breidenbaugh, *The Pennsylvania College Book, 1832-1882*, (Philadelphia: Lutheran Publications Society, 1882), 420-421; W. E. Parson, "History of 'Co. A,' 26th Regiment, P.V.M.," 90-91, in *PCM*, 3:3 (April 1879); Anonymous, "Addendum to History of 'Co. A,'" 125-126, in *PCM*, 3:4, May 1879; In 1921, the college changed its' name from Pennsylvania College to Gettysburg College, the latter name it still bares today.

[13] Parson, "History of 'Co. A,' 26th Regiment, P.V.M.," *PCM*, 3:3, 90-91.

[14] Frank Richards to Henry Warren Roth, July 24, 1863, 26th PVM File, GNMP.

[15] Sarah M. Broadhead Diary, June 15, 1863, GNMP.

[16] Hefelbower, *The History of Gettysburg College*, 179-203; Breidenbaugh, *The Pennsylvania College Book*, 420-421; William Henry Rupp Diary, June 16, 1863, GC; Frederick Klinefelter, "An Historical Sketch of 'Company A,' 26th Penna. Volunteer Militia," 26th PVM File, GNMP; Hereinafter cited as, Klinefelter, "An Historical Sketch," GNMP.

[17] Rupp Diary, June 17, 1863, GC; Klinefelter, "An Historical Sketch," GNMP; Breidenbaugh, *The Pennsylvania College Book*, 420-421.

[18] Rupp Diary, June 17, 1863, GC; Richards to Roth, July 24, 1863, GNMP; Breidenbaugh, *The Pennsylvania College Book*, 421; Parson, "History of 'Co. A,' 26th Regiment, P.V.M.," *PCM*, 3:3, 90-91; J. Howard Wert Scrapbook, JHWGC.

[19] HWS Diary, June 15-17, 1863, SFP, MDHS.

[20] James F. Haas, "A Pennsylvania Family Goes to War," a talk presented to the Harrisburg Civil War Round Table, February 22, 1985, typescript in Haas-Jones-Curry Family Papers, HCWRT, USAMHI.

[21] *Ibid.*

[22] *National Tribune*, Daniel F. Graham, "Pennsylvania Emergency Men," April 25, 1907.

[23] Peter A. Filbert Diary and Biographical Sketch, HCWRT, USAMHI.

[24] Robert S. Simington Biographical Sketch, Randy Hackenburg Collection, USAMHI.

[25] M. H. K. Snell to Lyle K. Snell, January 5, 1919, Robert L. Brake Collection, USAMHI.

[26] Samuel Y. Thompson Biographical Sketch, Hackenburg Collection, USAMHI.

[27] Nicholas Rice, "Memoir," 77-78, Nicholas Rice Papers, USAMHI.

[28] John W. Ames to dear Mother, June 15, 1863, John W. Ames Papers, USAMHI.

[29] HWS to Mary Winebrenner, July 9, 1863, SFP, MDHS.

[30] "GWS" to Dear Brother and Sister, June 29, 1863, Author's Collection; The author of this letter continues to declare that "I expect to start for Pittsburg in the morning" to enlist with the Department of the Monongahela.

[31] Muster-in Roll of the 26th PVM, RG 19, PASA.

Chapter 1: A Regiment is Born: The Regiment Forms at Camp Curtin

[1] HWS to Frederick Augustus Shriver, June 17, 1863, HWS to Uncle, June 20, 1863, SFP, MDHS.

[2] *Ibid.*

[3] *Ibid.*

[4] *Ibid.*

[5] *Ibid.*

[6] Rupp Diary, June 17, 1863, GC; Mathias H. Richards Letters, HCWRT, USAMHI.

[7] *Ibid.*; Klinefelter, "An Historical Sketch," GNMP; Parson, "History of 'Co. A,' 26th Regiment, P.V.M.," 3:3, 92; For more information on the conflict regarding the terms of service of Pennsylvania militia, see, Wingert, *The Confederate Approach on Harrisburg*, 31-35.

[8] Klinefelter Commission, Klinefelter File, YCHT; Adjutant General Thomas J. Stewart to General St. Clair A. Mulholland, June 16, 1909, RG 19, PASA;

John G. Morris, *Fifty Years in the Lutheran Ministry*, (Baltimore: James Young, 1878), 398.

[9] J.W. Muffly (ed.), *The Story of Our Regiment: A History of the 148th Pennsylvania Vols.*, (Des Moines, IA: The Kenyon Printing & MGF Company, 1904), 92-93.

[10] Richards letters, HCWRT, USAMHI.

[11] *Ibid.*; Breidenbaugh, *The Pennsylvania College Book*, 422; Meissenhelder was born on February 22, 1843, in Dover, York County. After graduating from Pennsylvania College in 1864, Meissenhelder served as a Second Lieutenant in the 210th Pennsylvania Volunteer Infantry. After the war, he practiced Medicine in East Berlin from 1868-1871 and in York from 1871 until his death on December 1, 1917. During this period, he also served as a U.S. Pension examining surgeon. See, *The Alumni Record of Gettysburg College, 1832-1932.* (Gettysburg, PA: Gettysburg College, 1932), 61.

[12] Richards letters, HCWRT, USAMHI; Breidenbaugh, *The Pennsylvania College Book*, 422.

[13] Breidenbaugh, *The Pennsylvania College Book*, 422; Rupp Diary, June 18, 1863, GC.

[14] Pennypacker, "Six Weeks in Uniform," 311-312.

[15] *Ibid.*, 312-313.

[16] *Ibid.*

[17] *Ibid.*, 313-314.

[18] *Ibid.*, 312.

[19] Charles F. Sayles to Dear Caroline, June 18, 1863, Elliot W. Hoffman Collection, USAMHI.

[20] *Ibid.*

[21] *Ibid.*

[22] HWS to Uncle, June 20, 1863, SFP, MDHS.

[23] Parson, "History of 'Co. A,' 26th Regiment, P.V.M.," 3:3, 92.

[24] HWS to Uncle, June 20, 1863, SFP, MDHS.

[25] Breidenbaugh, *The Pennsylvania College Book*, 422.

[26] HWS to Uncle, June 20, 1863, SFP, MDHS.

[27] *Ibid.*

[28] Breidenbaugh, *The Pennsylvania College Book*, 422; Klinefelter, "An Historical Sketch," GNMP.

[29] Rupp Diary, June 21, 1863, GC; HWS to Uncle, June 20, 1863, SFP, MDHS; Pamphlet, *Zion's Path Through History*, Historical Society of Dauphin County.

[30] Henry Eyster Jacobs Memoir, GNMP.

[31] Henry M. M. Richards Autobiography, LCHS.

[32] Henry M. M. Richards, *Pennsylvania's Emergency Men at Gettysburg*, (Reading, PA: n.p., 1895), 7.

[33] Pennypacker, "Six Weeks in Uniform," 314-315; HWS Diary, June 22, 1863, SFP, MDHS; Sketch of Camp Curtin, Philip German Scrapbook, Historical Society of Dauphin County.

[34] Luther Reily Kelker, *History of Dauphin County Pennsylvania, With Genealogical Memoirs*, (New York/Chicago: Lewis Publishing Co., 1907), 3:9-11; Regimental Association, *History of the 127th Regiment Pennsylvania Volunteers, Familiarly Known as the "Dauphin County Regiment,"* (Lebanon, PA: Report Publishing Company, 1902), 10-13.

[35] Regimental Association, *History of the 127th Regiment*, 23-29

[36] *Ibid.*, 34-35, 42, 48-53, 61-62.

[37] *Ibid.*, 69, 76, 82, 93, 98.

[38] *Ibid.*, 13-14, 102-110.

[39] "In Memoriam: William Wesley Jennings," MOLLUS-Pennsylvania, Circular No. 8, 1894, Rare Collections Library, State Library of Pennsylvania.

[40] Regimental Association, *History of the 127th Regiment*, 13-14, 102-110.

[41] *Ibid.*, 116-145.

[42] Samuel P. Conrad to Mr. Lewis J. Strickler, Dear Friend, January 20, 1863, Pennsylvania Save the Flags Collection, USAMHI; Conrad wrote that during his previous endeavor as a member of the color guard, "[a] glanced bullet hit me at my left knee... but there it stopped then I put it in my pocket and there it is yet[.]

[43] "In Memoriam: William Wesley Jennings," Rare Collections Library, State Library of Pennsylvania.

[44] Regimental Association, *History of the 127th Regiment*, 180-181.

[45] J. Chandler Gregg, *Life in the Army, in the Departments of Virginia, and the Gulf, Including Observations in New Orleans, With an Account of the Author's life and Experience in the Ministry*, (Philadelphia: Perkinpine & Higgins, 1868), 98-101.

[46] *The Morning Call*, "Col. Jennings Dies Suddenly," March 1, 1894.

[47] Pennypacker, "Six Weeks in Uniform," 319-320.

[48] Klinefelter, "An Historical Sketch," GNMP.

[49] Richards, *Pennsylvania's Emergency Men at Gettysburg*, 7.

[50] Richards to Roth, July 24, 1863, GNMP.

[51] Pennypacker, "Six Weeks in Uniform," 327.

[52] C.W. Buoy, "Address by C.W. Buoy, Grace Methodist Church, Harrisburg, PA, Saturday, March 3, 1894," Rare Collections Library, State Library of Pennsylvania.

[53] Pennypacker, "Six Weeks in Uniform," 319-321.

[54] Muster-in Roll of the 26th PVM, RG 19, PASA

[55] *O.R.*, 27:2, 215.

[56] HWS Diary, June 23, 1863, SFP, MDHS; Rupp Diary, June 23, GC; Pennypacker, "Six Weeks in Uniform," 323-324.

[57] Charles MacDonald to SWP, July 11, 1892, PPM.

[58] Muster-in Roll of the 26th PVM and Muster-out Roll of the 127th Pennsylvania Volunteer Infantry, RG 19, PASA

Chapter 2 With A Pie in Each Hand: The Journey to Camp Wreck

[1] HWS Diary, June 24, 1863, SFP, MDHS.

[2] Pennypacker, "Six Weeks in Uniform," 326-327.

[3] *Ibid.*, 327-328.

[4] 130th Pennsylvania Volunteer Infantry File, Antietam National Battlefield.

[5] John S. Weiser to dear Sisters and Brothers, October 11, 1862, Civil War Miscellaneous Collection, USAMHI.

[6] 130th Pennsylvania Volunteer Infantry File, Antietam National Battlefield; Weiser to dear Parents, December 17, 1862, Civil War Miscellaneous Collection, USAMHI.

[7] Pennypacker, "Six Weeks in Uniform," 328.

[8] Lorenzo L. Greenawalt Application, Sons of the American Revolution Membership Applications, National Society of the Sons of the American Revolution.

[9] Muster-in Roll of the 26th PVM, RG 19, PASA.

[10] Pennypacker, "Six Weeks in Uniform," 328.

[11] Henry M. M. Richards, "Lebanon County's Emergency Volunteers at Gettysburg," in *Proceedings of the Lebanon County Historical Society*, 3:7 (1905), 175; The 1852 California State Census concurs with Richards' statement, listing Greenawalt as 27 years old and a resident of Sacramento County. See, California State Census, 1852, California State Library, Sacramento, CA.

[12] Regimental Association, *History of the 127th Regiment*, 67.

[13] *Ibid.*, 190.

[14] *Ibid.*, 245-248.

[15] *Ibid.*, 139-140.

[16] *Ibid.*, 274-275.

[17] *Ibid.*, 225.

[18] Pennsylvania Civil War Veteran's Card File, 1861-1866, PASA.

[19] Francis Bazley Lee (ed.), *Genealogical and Personal Memorial of Mercer County New Jersey*, (New York and Chicago: The Lewis Publishing Company, 1907), 276; Francis B. Heitman (compiler), *Historical Register and Dictionary of the United States Army, From Its Organization, September 29, 1789, to March 2, 1903,* (Washington: Govt. Printing Office, 1903), 1:283; Bradford County Historical Society, "Annual," (Towanda, PA: Bradford Star Print, 1910), 4:31-32, 35; C.F. Heverly, *History of Albany Township, 1800-1885, With Biographical Sketches of the Pioneers, Her Soldiers and Statistics and Matters of General Interest Connected with the Township*, (Towanda, PA: Bradford Republican Print, 1885), 360.

[20] Pennsylvania Civil War Veteran's Card File, 1861-1866, PASA

[21] *Ibid.*

[22] *Ibid.*; Regimental Association, *History of the 127th Regiment*, 69; *Pennsylvania Telegraph*, "From the Two Hundred and First Regiment," September 9, 1864; In 1864, Morgan became Major of the 201st Pennsylvania Volunteer Infantry. On September 7, 1864, while in Camp Couch, near Chambersburg, with the 201st, Morgan "was the recipient of a magnificent sword, belt and sash, from his numerous friends and admirers, of West Fairview, Cumberland county." Morgan replied; "I am not accustomed to public speaking; yet I cannot

refrain from expressing my sincere thanks to my friends of West Fairview, for this token of their esteem and good will. I pledge them my word and sacred honor, that I will wield it with a firm hand strong arm, should occasion require it." See, *Pennsylvania Telegraph*, "From the Two Hundred and First Regiment," September 9, 1864.

[23] Pennsylvania Civil War Veteran's Card File, 1861-1866, PASA.

[24] Pennypacker, "Six Weeks in Uniform," 329.

[25] Klinefelter, "An Historical Sketch," GNMP.

[26] HWS Diary, June 24, 1863, SFP, MDHS.

[27] Pennypacker, "Six Weeks in Uniform," 329.

[28] *Ibid.*

[29] *Ibid.*, 329-330; HWS Diary, June 24, 1863, SFP, MDHS.

[30] Granville O. Haller, *The Dismissal of Major Granville O. Haller*, (Patterson, NJ: Daily Guardian, 1863), 65; Hereinafter cited as Haller, *Dismissal*.

[31] *Ibid.*

[32] Scott L. Mingus, Sr., Flames Beyond Gettysburg: The Confederate Expedition to the Susquehanna River, June 1863, (New York and California: Savas Beatie, 2011), 27-30.

[33] Clark H. Wells, *The Reply of Lt. Com. C.H. Wells, U.S.N., To A Pamphlet Recently Published by G.O. Haller, late a Major U.S.A.*, (York, PA: H. Young, 1865), 12-15; Wells' reply to Haller's *Memoir*—a booklet written by Haller to defend himself from Wells' claims, which was published in the fall of 1863—was prepared in December 1863, but his "friends earnestly entreated him not to publish his Reply to Haller's infamous Pamphlet, as the latter had sealed his condemnation by his own statements. But he has since learned, while on the blockade off Mobile, that several officers of the Army and Navy at New Orleans had seen his pamphlet, and they were glad to read my manuscript 'Reply,' which gave them a different impression altogether, pronouncing Haller's pamplet [sic] as an infamous one and unworthy of belief." See, Wells, *The Reply*, 4-5.

[34] Broadhead Diary, June 24, 1863, GNMP.

[35] *The Compiler*, Gettysburg, "The 26th Regiment P.V.M.," June 29, 1863.

[36] Newspaper Scrapbook, PPM; Richards to Roth, July 24, 1863, GNMP; Klinefelter, "An Historical Sketch," GNMP; Breidenbaugh, *The Pennsylvania College Book*, 422-423; ML, "Keystone Guards," July 14, 1863; HWS Diary, June 24, 1863, SFP, MDHS; Herman L. Cook Account, Gettysburg *Times*, September 21, 1943.

[37] Pennypacker, "Six Weeks in Uniform," 330.

[38] *Ibid.*, 330-331.

[39] ML, "Keystone Guards," July 14, 1863.

[40] Klinefelter, "An Historical Sketch," GNMP; Parson, "History of 'Co. A,' 26th Regiment, P.V.M.," *PCM*, 3:4, (May 1879), 121; Breidenbaugh, *The Pennsylvania College Book*, 423; Pennypacker, "Six Weeks in Uniform," 331; Rupp Diary, June 24, 1863, GC.

[41] HWS to Mary Winebrenner and Frederick Augustus Shriver, June 29, 1863, SFP, MDHS.

[42] Newspaper Scrapbook, PPM.

[43] Haller, *Dismissal*, 65.

[44] *Ibid.*, 66.

[45] Parson, "History of 'Co. A,' 26th Regiment, P.V.M.," *PCM*, 3: 4, 121.

[46] HWS Diary, June 25, 1863, SFP, MDHS; *ML*, "Keystone Guards," July 14, 1863; Pennypacker, "Six Weeks in Uniform," 331-332.

[47] HWS Diary, June 25, 1863; Breidenbaugh, *The Pennsylvania College Book*, 423.

[48] Pennypacker, "Six Weeks in Uniform," 332.

[49] Klinefelter, "An Historical Sketch," GNMP; Richards, *Pennsylvania's Emergency Men at Gettysburg*, 8.

[50] Pennypacker, "Six Weeks in Uniform," 332-333.

[51] *Ibid.*; Klinefelter, "An Historical Sketch," GNMP; Richards, *Pennsylvania's Emergency Men at Gettysburg*, 8; Breidenbaugh, *The Pennsylvania College Book*, 423; Harrisburg *Evening Telegraph*, "The Situation," June 25, 1863; Rupp Diary, June 25, 1863, GC.

[52] Colonel Jennings' Manuscript (MS) Official Report, located in the original handwritten copy of Pennypacker, "Six Weeks in Uniform," at PPM. Colonel Jennings never submitted his report to the War Department, instead retaining it for himself. Hereinafter cited as, Jennings MS Report, PPM.

[53] Broadhead Diary, June 25, 1863, GNMP.

[54] John C. Wills Reminisce, GNMP.

[55] *Ibid.*

[56] Haller, *Dismissal*, 66-67.

[57] *Ibid.*

[58] Pennypacker, "Six Weeks in Uniform," 335.

[59] Parson, "History of 'Co. A,' 26th Regiment, P.V.M.", *PCM*, 3: 4, 122.

[60] Pennypacker, "Six Weeks in Uniform," 335-336; J. Howard Wert Scrapbook, JHWGC.

[61] Haller, *Dismissal*, 68; Michael Jacobs, *Notes on the Rebel Invasion of Maryland and Pennsylvania, and the Battle of Gettysburg*, (Phila: J. B. Lippincott & Co., 1864), 13-14.

[62] Pennypacker, "Six Weeks in Uniform," 336; Rupp Diary, June 25, 1863, GC.

[63] Newspaper Scrapbook, PPM.

[64] HWS Diary, June 25, 1863, SFP, MDHS.

Chapter 3: Such A Confusion I Never Saw: The Battle of Witmer's Farm and Bayly's Hill

[1] *ML*, "Keystone Guards," July 14, 1863.

[2] Jennings MS Report, PPM.

[3] Rupp Diary, June 26, 1863, GC; HWS Diary, June 26, 1863, SFP, MDHS; *ML*, "Keystone Guards," July 14, 1863.

[4] Jacobs Memoir, GNMP.

[5] J. Howard Wert Scrapbook, JHWGC.

[6] Wills Reminisce, GNMP.

[7] Rupp Diary, June 26, 1863, GC; Pennypacker, "Six Weeks in Uniform," 337-339; *ML*, "Keystone Guards," July 14, 1863; Klinefelter, "An Historical Sketch," GNMP; HWS to Mary Winebrenner and Frederick Augustus Shriver, June 29, 1863, HWS Diary, June 26, 1863, SFP, MDHS; Haller, *Dismissal*, 68;. Parson, "History of 'Co. A,' 26th Regiment, P.V.M.," *PCM*, 3:4, 122; Jacobs, *Notes*, 14; Richards, *Pennsylvania's Emergency Men at Gettysburg*, 9; Samuel S. Henry Account, Gettysburg *Times*, September 21, 1943; Hefelbower, *The History of Gettysburg College*, 190-191.

[8] Richards, *Pennsylvania's Emergency Men at Gettysburg*, 9; Haller, *Dismissal*, 68-70; Jennings MS Report, PPM.

[9] Haller, *Dismissal*, 68-70; Breidenbaugh, *The Pennsylvania College Book*, 423; Gettysburg *Compiler*, "Citizens of Gettysburg in the Battle," March 8, 1887.

[10] Jennings MS Report, PPM; Samuel S. Henry to SWP, July 8, 1892, PPM; Concerning this lone rifle shot, Henry wrote; "About 4 years ago I met Capt. Forrest at Hanover, and asked him what it [the shot] meant. He replied, as nearly as I can now remember, that the firing was done by a soldier who had been in—or had belonged to the Potomac Army. I think he also said, that he fired without orders. Now whether he had been formerly a member of the Potomac Army—e.g. one of the 9 months men—, and having been discharged and afterwards joined our Reg't;—or whether he still belonged to the Army of the Potomac, I can not state."

[11] Frank N. Myers, *The Comanches: A History of White's Battalion, Virginia Cavalry*, (Baltimore: Kelly, Piet & Co., 1871), 192-193.

[12] Samuel S. Henry Account, Gettysburg *Times*, September 21, 1943; Richards to Roth, July 24, 1863, GNMP; Rupp Diary, June 26, 1863, GC; HWS Diary, June 26, 1863, HWS to Mary Winebrenner and Fredrick August Shriver, June 29, 1863, SFP, MDHS; *ML*, "Keystone Guards," July 14, 1863; Klinefelter, "An Historical Sketch," GNMP; W. E. Parson, "History of 'Co. A,' 26th Regiment, P.V.M.," *PCM*, 3:4, 122-123; Pennypacker, "Six Weeks in Uniform," 340; Jacobs, *Notes*, 14; Richards, *Pennsylvania's Emergency Men at Gettysburg*, 9; Rudolph M. Schick to Dear Cousin, July 5, 1863, PPM.

[13] Breidenbaugh, *The Pennsylvania College Book*, 424.

[14] Newspaper Scrapbook, PPM.

[15] "Ruddy Taught Penny to Paddle in Water," Newspaper Scrapbook, PPM.

[16] Jennings MS Report, PPM.

[17] Pennypacker, "Six Weeks in Uniform," 341.

[18] *Ibid.*; Breidenbaugh, *The Pennsylvania College Book*, 424; HWS to Mary Winebrenner and Frederick Augustus Shriver, June 29, 1863, SFP, MDHS; *ML*, "Keystone Guards," July 14, 1863.

[19] Richards, *Pennsylvania's Emergency Men at Gettysburg*, 9.

[20] Klinefelter, "An Historical Sketch," GNMP.

[21] Richards, *Pennsylvania's Emergency Men at Gettysburg*, 11; Rupp Diary, June 26, 1863, GC.

[22] Jennings MS Report, PPM.

[23] *O.R.*, 27:2, 465; Bartlett Yancey Malone, "The Diary of Bartlett Yancey Malone," in *The James Sprunt Historical Publications*, (Chapel Hill: University of North Carolina, 1919), 16:2, 36.

[24] *O.R.*, 27:2, 465; Jubal A. Early, *Narrative of the War Between the States*, (reprint, Da Capo Press, 1989), 256-257; Malone, "The Diary of Bartlett Yancey Malone," 16:2, 36.

[25] Nelson Harris, *17th Virginia Cavalry*, (Lynchburg, VA: H.E. Howard, 1994), 2-3, 15, 39-40, 70; After resigning in June 1864, French returned to Mercer County, where he spent the remainder of his life as a "successful gentleman farmer." He died in Mercer County in 1872.

[26] Information provided by Brian Stuart Kesterson, Lubeck, WV.

[27] OR 27:2, 465; Brian Stuart Kesterson, *Campaigning with the 17th Virginia Cavalry Night Hawks at Monocacy*, (Washington, WV: Night Hawk Press, 2005), 34-36.

[28] *OR* 27:2, 465; William J. Seymour Journal, June 26, 1863, James Schoff Collection, University of Michigan.

[29] Pennypacker, "Six Weeks in Uniform," 341.

[30] William Hamilton Bayly Account, GNMP; Also see Mrs. Joseph Bayly's Account, GNMP; Mrs. Bayly was home during the engagement at Witmer's Farm, and recalled hearing "firing apparently about half a mile from the house . . . ."

[31] Richards, *Pennsylvania's Emergency Men at Gettysburg*, 11; Rupp Diary, June 26, 1863, GC; Jennings MS Report, PPM; Wilbur S. Nye, "The First Battle of Gettysburg," *Civil War Times Illustrated*, 4:5, (August 1965), 16.

[32] Richards, *Pennsylvania's Emergency Men at Gettysburg*, 11; Jennings MS Report, PPM; Richards to Roth, July 24, 1863, GNMP; Klinefelter, "An Historical Sketch," GNMP; Parson, "History of 'Co. A,' 26th Regiment, P.V.M.," *PCM*, 3:4, 123-124; Rudolph M. Schick to Dear Cousin, July 5, 1863, PPM; Breidenbaugh, *The Pennsylvania College Book*, 424.

[33] Jennings MS Report, PPM; Richards to Roth, July 24, 1863, GNMP; Samuel W. Pennypacker, "Dedication of Monument 26th Emergency Infantry, September 1, 1892," *Pennsylvania at Gettysburg*, (Harrisburg, PA: Wm. Stanley Ray, State Printer, 1914), 2:767; Hiram Gifford Declaration for Disability Pension, Vertical Files, YCHT.

[34] HWS to Mary Winebrenner and Frederick Augustus Shriver, June 29, 1863, SFP, MDHS; Richards, *Pennsylvania's Emergency Men at Gettysburg*, 11.

[35] HWS to Mary Winebrenner and Frederick Augustus Shriver, June 29, 1863, SFP, MDHS; Richards, *Pennsylvania's Emergency Men at Gettysburg*, 11; SWP to Dear Mother, June 29, 1863, PPM; Klinefelter, "An Historical Sketch," GNMP; Dennis B. Shuey, *History of the Shuey Family in America From 1732 to 1919*, (Galion, OH: By the Author, 1919), 107.

[36] Richards, *Pennsylvania's Emergency Men at Gettysburg*, 11; Richards to Roth, July 24, 1863, GNMP; Rupp Diary, June 26, 1863, GC; *ML*, "Keystone Guards," July 14, 1863; Klinefelter, "An Historical Sketch," GNMP; HWS to Mary Winebrenner and Frederick Augustus Shriver, June 29, 1863, SFP, MDHS; Parson, "History of 'Co. A,' 26th Regiment, P.V.M.", *PCM*, 3:4, 123-124; Pennypacker, "Six Weeks in Uniform," 342-343; *History of the Shuey Family*, 107; Rudolph M. Schick to Dear Cousin, July 5, 1863, PPM; Breidenbaugh, *The Pennsylvania College Book*, 424.

[37] Hiram J. Dunbar to SWP, August 20, 1892, PPM; The company's captain, John T. Morgan of West Fairview, had been detached with "8 to 12 men in the town [Gettysburg] to follow [the regiment] with two wagon loads of provisions." The group was forced to retire eastward, eventually participating in the affair at Wrightsville. See, J. H. Jacobs to SWP, July 7, 1892, PPM.

[38] HWS to Mary Winebrenner and Frederick Augustus Shriver, June 29, 1863, SFP, MDHS; Richards to Roth, July 24, 1863, GNMP.

[39] Pennypacker, "Six Weeks in Uniform," 344.

[40] Shuey, *History of the Shuey Family*, 107; After the "strenuous" retreat march back to Harrisburg following the engagement at Witmer's, Dennis Shuey was unable to stand on his swollen and weary feat. Reporting to the surgeon, he was remanded to the hospital "on account of articular rheumatism, which he had contracted and from which he has suffered ever since." Despite describing himself as "not well," he left the hospital on July 10 and rejoined the regiment. After participating in the regiment's efforts to pursue Lee's Army down the Cumberland Valley, he was discharged on July 30. After the war, Shuey maintained a "close friendship" with future-governor Samuel Pennypacker. The two were tent mates during the 50th Anniversary of Gettysburg in July 1913, in Tent 311 on the 10th Street. Shuey sent Samuel several photos of the reunion, and Samuel thanked him, writing; "I thank you very much indeed for sending me the photographs, and I am much pleased to have them." See, Shuey, *History of the Shuey Family*, 108-109; D. B. Shuey to SWP, November 24, 1902, and Photographs, July 1913, signed D. B. Shuey, Samuel Pennypacker, Private Papers, MG 171, PASA; SWP to D. B. Shuey, February 6, 1914, PPM.

[41] Rudolph M. Schick to Dear Cousin, July 5, 1863, PPM.

[42] Kesterson, *Campaigning with the 17th Virginia Cavalry Night Hawks at Monocacy*, 34-36.

[43] *Ibid.*; Richards, *Pennsylvania's Emergency Men at Gettysburg*, 11; Pennypacker, "Six Weeks in Uniform," 342-344; Joseph L. Lenberger to SWP, July 4, 1892, George B. Lessig to SWP, July 18, 1892, Frank Muhlenberg to SWP, August 27, 1892, PPM; Hospital Steward Joseph L. Lenberger, who was inside the Witmer farmhouse at the outset of the affair, later reported that he was captured while attempting to cross the Goldenville road and rejoin the regiment. See, Lenberger to SWP, July 4, 1892, PPM

[44] Richards, *Pennsylvania's Emergency Men at Gettysburg*, 11.

[45] *Ibid.*

[46] James Hodam Account, 17th Virginia Cavalry File, GNMP.

[47] Richards, *Pennsylvania's Emergency Men at Gettysburg*, 12.

[48] Pennypacker, "Six Weeks in Uniform," 342-344.

[49] Parson, "History of 'Co. A,' 26th Regiment, P.V.M.," *PCM*, 3:4, 124; Klinefelter, "An Historical Sketch," GNMP; Hiram J. Dunbar to SWP, August 20, 1892, PPM; Rudolph M. Schick to Dear Cousin, PPM; Jennings MS Report, PPM.

[50] Parson, "History of 'Co. A,' 26th Regiment, P.V.M.," *PCM*, 3:4, 124; HWS to Mary Winebrenner and Frederick Augustus Shriver, June 29, 1863, SFP, MDHS; Klinefelter, "An Historical Sketch," GNMP; Hiram J. Dunbar to SWP, August 20, 1892, Rudolph M. Schick to Dear Cousin, PPM; Jennings MS Report, PPM.

[51] *ML*, "Keystone Guards," July 14, 1863; Pennypacker, "Six Weeks in Uniform," 344-356.

[52] Kesterson, *Campaigning with the Seventeenth Virginia Cavalry*, 34-36.

[53] Hodam Account, 17th Virginia Cavalry File, GNMP.

[54] Charles F. Himes to Dear Rood, October 2, 1863, Waidner-Spahr Library, Dickinson College.

[55] Augustine W. Shick to SWP, August 17, 1892, PPM.

[56] Charles Macdonald to SWP, July 11, 1892, PPM.

[57] *O.R.*, 27:2, 996; Pennypacker, "Six Weeks in Uniform," 361; Mingus, *Flames Beyond Gettysburg*, 237.

[58] Pennypacker, "Six Weeks in Uniform," 361.

[59] Consolidated Morning Report Book, 26th PVM, June 30, 1863-July 28, 1863, RG 19, PASA.

[60] *Ibid.*; J. H. Jacobs to SWP, July 7, 1892, PPM; Jacobs also wrote that shortly after the men of the Philadelphia City Troop passed, the group captured a rebel spy. "[O]ur boys took him back, [and] he was afterwards sent to York and from there to Harrisburg." Jacobs also recalled several incidents during their retreat east from Gettysburg; "On our retreat, we captured a lot of horses—being taken into the rebel camp at Gettysburg (I think on Wolf's farm [east of Culp's Hill]) by a citizen farmer, who showed us a pass and an order from rebel General Early, thinking we were rebels. When I told him he was in the wrong camp, and demanded a surrender, a Captain, Ball, I think, rode up to me, and said that if I did not let him go through he'd shoot me, at the same time drawing his revolver, not having even a gun with me, I was compelled to let him go, and Early got those horses. The farmer told me that Early said if he'd get him a lot of horses, his own should not be taken." Jacobs believed that the "Captain was a traitor, and the farmer a sneak, and of course a democrat." See, Jacobs to SWP, July 7, 1892, PPM.

Chapter 4: Analyzing Witmer's Farm

[1] Richards, *Pennsylvania's Emergency Men at Gettysburg*, 11.

[2] SWP to Dear Mother, June 29, 1863, PPM.

[3] Seymour Journal, June 26, 1863, Schoff Collection, University of Michigan.

[4] John Alexander and Jim Slade, *Firestorm at Gettysburg: Civilian Voices*, (Atglen, PA: Schiffer Military/Aviation History, 1998), 28.

[5] Early, *Narrative of the War Between the States*, 257-258.

[6] J. Howard Wert Scrapbook, JHWGC.

[7] Pennypacker, *Autobiography*, 94.

[8] Jacobs, *Notes*, 14.

[9] Jennings MS Report, PPM.

[10] Harvey W. McKnight, "Twenty-Sixth Regiment P.V.M.," *PCM*, XVI: 7 (November 1892), 267-272.

[11] Jennings MS Report, PPM.

[12] *Ibid.*

[13] Haller, *Dismissal*, 68-69.

[14] *Ibid.*

[15] *Ibid.*, 65.

[16] Jennings MS Report, PPM.

[17] "In Memoriam: William Wesley Jennings," Rare Collections Library, State Library of Pennsylvania.

[18] *O.R.*, 27:2, 213.

[19] Pennypacker, "Six Weeks in Uniform," 355; *ML*, "Keystone Guards," July 14, 1863.

[20] Edward S. McCormick to SWP, July 11, 1892, PPM; Richards, *Pennsylvania's Emergency Men at Gettysburg*, 12; Richards to Roth, July 24, 1863, GNMP; *ML*, "Keystone Guards," July 14, 1863; McCormick's letter serves as the original testimony to Dailey's wounding—all other sources, such as Henry M. M. Richard's, *Pennsylvania's Emergency Men at Gettysburg* report his account second hand, from Samuel Pennypacker's September 1892 address at the dedication of the 26th's monument at Gettysburg. Pennypacker cites McCormick's letter as his source. McCormick, second lieutenant of Company C, was in command of the company at Marsh Creek and Witmer's Farm. Captain Walker was in the town of Gettysburg commanding a group of men from various companies, while the company's first lieutenant was absent.

[21] William Few to SWP, July 6, 1892, George B. Lessig to SWP, July 18, 1892, Hiram J. Dunbar to SWP, August 20, 1892, Frank Muhlenberg to SWP, August 27, 1892, A Stanley Ulrich to SWP, July 6, 1892, William G. George and Joseph Dunnel to SWP, August 10, 1892, PPM; Nye, "The First Battle of Gettysburg," 17; Pennypacker, "Six Weeks in Uniform," 356. Ulrich also left another account of his service in the 26th in an article entitled, "The Wandering Johnny; or, the 26th Militia on their Muscle," in the *Lebanon Advertiser*, June 14, 1865.

[22] Charles Macdonald to SWP, July 11, 1892, Samuel S. Henry to SWP, July 8, 1892, A.W. Schick to SWP, August 17, 1892, PPM; Jacobs Memoir, GNMP; *Savannah Daily Republican*, August 6, 1863, as quoted in, Mingus, *Flames Beyond Gettysburg*, 124; Philadelphia *Press*, "York and Gettysburg," June 30, 1863.

[23] Nye, "The First Battle of Gettysburg," 16-17; Mingus, *Flames Beyond Gettysburg*, 137.

[24] Jubal A. Early order and roster of captured soldiers, June 27, 1863, copy at PPM.

[25] *The Compiler*, "The Rebels in Gettysburg," June 29, 1863; Mingus, *Flames Beyond Gettysburg*, 154.

[26] Consolidated Morning Report Book, 26th PVM, June 30, 1863-July 28, 1863, RG 19, PASA.

[27] HWS to Frederick Augustus Shriver and Mary Winebrenner, June 29, 1863, SFP, MDHS.

[28] William Few to SWP, July 6, 1892, PPM.

[29] Jubal A. Early order, June 27, 1863, copy at PPM.

[30] William G. George and Joseph Dunnel to SWP, "Statement of Twenty-Sixth Emergency Regiment," August 10, 1892; Both George and Dunnel enrolled with Captain Morgan of Company H in West Fairview, where George and Dunnel also penned their "Statement" 29 years later.

[31] *OR* 27:2, 465-466; Jubal A. Early order, June 27, 1863, copy at PPM; William Few to SWP, July 6, 1892, PPM.

Chapter 5: Such an Awful Time I Never Had: The March Back to Harrisburg

[1] HWS to Mary Winebrenner and Frederick Augustus Shriver, June 29, 1863, SFP, MDHS.

[2] *The Compiler*, "The Rebels in Gettysburg," June 29, 1863; Klinefelter, "An Historical Sketch," GNMP.

[3] Pennypacker, "Six Weeks in Uniform," 344; Richards, *Pennsylvania's Emergency Men at Gettysburg*, 13; Klinefelter, "An Historical Sketch," GNMP; Two of these farmers who served as guides and stayed with the regiment the entire night were later identified as J. W. Diehl and A. F. Gitt. See, Pennypacker, "Six Weeks in Uniform," 355.

[4] Pennypacker, "Six Weeks in Uniform," 344-347; Breidenbaugh, *The Pennsylvania College Book*, 424; Klinefelter, "An Historical Sketch," GNMP.

[5] Richards, *Pennsylvania's Emergency Men at Gettysburg*, 13; Pennypacker, "Six Weeks in Uniform," 349.

[6] Pennypacker, "Six Weeks in Uniform," 347.

[7] HWS Diary, June 27, 1863, SFP, MDHS.

[8] Pennypacker, "Six Weeks in Uniform," 347-349, 355; Klinefelter, "An Historical Sketch," GNMP; Breidenbaugh, *The Pennsylvania College Book*, 424.

[9] Richards, *Pennsylvania's Emergency Men at Gettysburg*, 13-14.

[10] *Ibid.* 14; Pennypacker, "Six Weeks in Uniform," 349-350; Breidenbaugh, *The Pennsylvania College Book*, 424.

[11] Richards, *Pennsylvania's Emergency Men at Gettysburg*, 14.

[12] Pennypacker, "Six Weeks in Uniform," 350.

[13] *Ibid.*; Klinefelter, "An Historical Sketch," GNMP; Breidenbaugh, *The Pennsylvania College Book*, 424; Richards, *Pennsylvania's Emergency Men at Gettysburg*, 14; Samuel Pennypacker, who heard Greenawalt make the quoted remark, wrote that because he did not rush to the roadside fence like nearly all his comrades, he "felt somewhat gratified to know I was not included." See, Pennypacker, "Six Weeks in Uniform," 350.

[14] Pennypacker, "Six Weeks in Uniform," 348.

[15] HWS to Mary Winebrenner and Frederick Augustus Shriver, June 29, 1863, HWS Diary, June 27, 1863, SFP, MDHS.

[16] Pennypacker, "Six Weeks in Uniform," 349.

[17] Breidenbaugh, *The Pennsylvania College Book*, 425; Rupp Diary, June 26, 1863, GC; HWS Diary, June 26, 1863, HWS to Mary Winebrenner and Frederick Augustus Shriver, June 29, 1863, SFP, MDHS.

[18] Klinefelter, "An Historical Sketch," GNMP; HWS to Mary Winebrenner and Frederick Augustus Shriver, June 29, 1863, HWS Diary, June 27, 1863, SFP, MDHS.

[19] Richards, *Pennsylvania's Emergency Men at Gettysburg*, 14.

[20] Pennypacker, "Six Weeks in Uniform," 350; Richards to Roth, July 24, 1863, GNMP.

[21] Richards, *Pennsylvania's Emergency Men at Gettysburg*, 14-15.

[22] Pennypacker, "Six Weeks in Uniform," 350-351; HWS Diary, June 27, 1863, SFP, MDHS; Rupp Diary, June 27, 1863, GC; Klinefelter, "An Historical Sketch," GNMP; Breidenbaugh, *The Pennsylvania College Book*, 425; *ML*, "Keystone Guards," July 14, 1863; Richards, *Pennsylvania's Emergency Men at Gettysburg*, 15; Richards to Roth, July 24, 1863, GNMP.

[23] Pennypacker, "Six Weeks in Uniform," 350-351; Breidenbaugh, *The Pennsylvania College Book*, 425; *ML*, "Keystone Guards," July 14, 1863; *Richards*, *Pennsylvania's Emergency Men at Gettysburg*, 15.

[24] Pennypacker, "Six Weeks in Uniform," 351.

[25] HWS to Mary Winebrenner and Frederick Augustus Shriver, June 29, 1863, SFP, MDHS.

[26] Pennypacker, "Six Weeks in Uniform," 351; HWS Diary, June 28, 1863, SFP, MDHS; *ML*, "Keystone Guards," July 14, 1863.

[27] Klinefelter, "An Historical Sketch," GNMP; Pennypacker, "Six Weeks in Uniform," 351.

[28] For a more detailed account of the operations of Confederate cavalry in York County, See, Scott L. Mingus, Sr., "Jenkins' Cavalry Raid Through Northwestern York County, Pennsylvania," *The Gettysburg Magazine*, 44 (January 2011), 41-52.

[29] Klinefelter, "An Historical Sketch," GNMP; Pennypacker, "Six Weeks in Uniform," 351-352; HWS Diary, June 28, 1863, SFP, MDHS.

[30] Charles Macdonald to SWP, July 11, 1892, PPM.

[31] Pennypacker, "Six Weeks in Uniform," 352; HWS Diary, June 28, 1863, SFP, MDHS; Klinefelter, "An Historical Sketch," GNMP.

[32] Rupp Diary, June 27, 1863, GC; *ML*, "Keystone Guards," July 14, 1863; Klinefelter, "An Historical Sketch," GNMP; Pennypacker, "Six Weeks in Uniform," 352-353; Breidenbaugh, *The Pennsylvania College Book*, 425.

[33] HWS to Mary Winebrenner and Frederick Augustus Shriver, June 29, 1863, SFP, MDHS.

[34] *Ibid.*

[35] Breidenbaugh, *The Pennsylvania College Book*, 425; Rupp Diary, June 28, 1863, GC; Pennypacker, "Six Weeks in Uniform," 353.

[36] Pennypacker, "Six Weeks in Uniform," 353-354; HWS Diary, June 28, 1863, SFP, MDHS; Rupp Diary, June 28, 1863, GC; Breidenbaugh, *The Pennsylvania College Book*, 425.

[37] Wingert, *The Confederate Approach on Harrisburg*, 95; For a more detailed account of the skirmishes in front of Harrisburg, see, Wingert, *The Confederate Approach on Harrisburg*, 85-107; For a more detailed account of the capture of York and Battle of Wrightsville, see, Mingus, *Flames Beyond Gettysburg*, 151-281; For more information on Nounnan's raid through the Dillsburg vicinity, see, Mingus, "Jenkins' Cavalry Raid Through Northwestern York County, Pennsylvania," 41-52.

[38] Pennypacker, "Six Weeks in Uniform," 353-354; HWS Diary, June 28, 1863, SFP, MDHS; Rupp Diary, June 28, 1863, GC; Breidenbaugh, *The Pennsylvania College Book*, 425; *ML*, "Keystone Guards," July 14, 1863; HWS to Mary Winebrenner and Frederick Augustus Shriver, June 29, 1863, SFP, MDHS.

[39] Pennypacker, "Six Weeks in Uniform," 354; Klinefelter, "An Historical Sketch," GNMP.

[40] Pennypacker, "Six Weeks in Uniform," 354; Klinefelter, "An Historical Sketch," GNMP; *ML*, "Keystone Guards," July 14, 1863; HWS to Mary Winebrenner and Frederick Augustus Shriver, June 29, 1863, HWS Diary, June 28, 1863, SFP, MDHS; Shriver reported that the citizens of New Cumberland supplied them with "coffee[,] bread &c." See, HWS Diary, June 28, 1863, SFP, MDHS.

[41] Pennypacker, "Six Weeks in Uniform," 354-355; Klinefelter, "An Historical Sketch," GNMP; *ML*, "Keystone Guards," July 14, 1863; Rupp Diary, June 28, 1863, GC; HWS Diary, June 28, 1863, HWS to Mary Winebrenner and Frederick Augustus Shriver, June 29, 1863, SFP, MDHS.

[42] Pennypacker, "Six Weeks in Uniform," 354-355.

[43] HWS to Mary Winebrenner and Frederick Augustus Shriver, June 29, 1863, SFP, MDHS; Pennypacker, "Six Weeks in Uniform," 355-356; Jacobs, *Notes*, 15.

[44] HWS to Mary Winebrenner and Frederick Augustus Shriver, June 29, 1863, SFP, MDHS; Rupp Diary, June 28, 1863, GC; Pennypacker, "Six Weeks in Uniform," 355; For a more detailed account of Fort Washington and the other fortifications which adorned Bridgeport Heights during the summer of 1863, see Wingert, *The Confederate Approach on Harrisburg*, 26-47.

[45] Pennypacker, "Six Weeks in Uniform," 355-356; HWS to Mary Winebrenner and Frederick Augustus Shriver, June 29, 1863, HWS Diary, June 28, 1863, SFP, MDHS.

[46] HWS to Mary Winebrenner and Frederick Augustus Shriver, June 29, 1863, HWS Diary, June 28, 1863, SFP, MDHS; Pennypacker, "Six Weeks in Uniform," 356-358.

[47] Pennypacker, "Six Weeks in Uniform," 358.

[48] Breidenbaugh, *The Pennsylvania College Book*, 425.

[49] Henry M. M. Richards to SWP, July 5, 1892, PPM.

[50] Mathias H. Richards Letters, HCWRT, USAMHI.

[51] *ML*, "Keystone Guards," July 14, 1863.

[52] HWS to Mary Winebrenner and Frederick Augustus Shriver, June 29, 1863, SFP, MDHS.

Chapter 6: *We Are Treated Very Meanly Here*: Camp Life in Fort Washington

[1] HWS to Mary Winebrenner and Frederick Augustus Shriver, June 29, 1863, SFP, MDHS.

[2] Klinefelter, "An Historical Sketch," GNMP.

[3] Pennypacker, "Six Weeks in Uniform," 356-359; HWS to Mary Winebrenner and Frederick Augustus Shriver, June 29, 1863, HWS Diary, June 29, 1863, SFP, MDHS; Rupp Diary, June 29, 1863, GC.

[4] HWS to Mary Winebrenner and Frederick Augustus Shriver, June 29, 1863, SFP, MDHS.

[5] For a more detailed account on this June 29 action at Oyster's Point, see, Wingert, *The Confederate Approach on Harrisburg*, 111-117.

[6] HWS Diary, June 29, 1863, SFP, MDHS.

[7] Pennypacker, "Six Weeks in Uniform," 359.

[8] HWS to Mary Winebrenner and Frederick Augustus Shriver, June 29, 1863, SFP, MDHS.

[9] *Ibid.*; Pennypacker reported that his company did not receive "shelter tents, blankets and other necessary articles," until the morning of June 30. See, Pennypacker, "Six Weeks in Uniform," 359-360.

[10] HWS to Mary Winebrenner and Frederick Augustus Shriver, June 29, 1863, HWS Diary, June 29-30, 1863, SFP, MDHS; Breidenbaugh, *The Pennsylvania College Book*, 425.

[11] HWS to Mary Winebrenner and Frederick Augustus Shriver, June 29, 1863, HWS Diary, June 29-30, 1863, SFP, MDHS.

[12] Pennypacker, "Six Weeks in Uniform," 359.

[13] *Ibid.*, 328.

[14] Consolidated Morning Report Book, 26th PVM, June 30, 1863-July 28, 1863, RG 19, PASA.

[15] While only four captains were present with the regiment on June 30, Second Lieutenant Edward S. McCormick had been acting as Company C's commanding officer since a short time before the Witmer's farm affair, when

Captain Walker had been detached in command of troops in the town of Gettysburg. McKnight's report concurs with McCormick's reminisce. See, Edward S. McCormick to SWP, July 11, 1892, PPM.

[16] Consolidated Morning Report Book, 26th PVM, June 30, 1863-July 28, 1863, RG 19, PASA.

[17] HWS to Frederick Augustus Shriver, July 4, 1863, SFP, MDHS.

[18] Pennypacker, "Six Weeks in Uniform," 360; Negro servants were not that uncommon within the 26th itself—Captain George Rice of Company F had with him a negro cook named Tom. See, Pennypacker, "Six Weeks in Uniform," 364.

[19] HWS to Frederick Augustus Shriver, July 4, 1863, HWS Diary, June 30, 1863, SFP, MDHS; Pennypacker, "Six Weeks in Uniform," 360; Rupp Diary, June 30, 1863, GC.

[20] HWS to Frederick Augustus Shriver, July 4, 1863, HWS Diary, June 30, 1863, SFP, MDHS; Pennypacker, "Six Weeks in Uniform," 360-361.

[21] HWS to Frederick Augustus Shriver, July 4, 1863, SFP, MDHS.

[22] Pennypacker, "Six Weeks in Uniform," 360-361.

[23] HWS to Frederick Augustus Shriver, July 4, 1863, HWS Diary, June 30, 1863, SFP, MDHS; Pennypacker, "Six Weeks in Uniform," 360-361; Rupp Diary, June 30, 1863, GC; During this time, Samuel Pennypacker was suffering from a bad case of dysentery. "Toward evening ... I went to the Surgeon who had then arrived," he wrote, "and asked for some medicine for my dysentery. He gave me some castor oil in a small quantity of whiskey which I swallowed." Samuel recorded that he "lay about not fit for much of anything." See, Pennypacker, "Six Weeks in Uniform," 361.

[24] HWS to Frederick Augustus Shriver, July 4, 1863, HWS Diary, June 30, 1863, SFP, MDHS; Pennypacker, "Six Weeks in Uniform," 360-361; Rupp Diary, June 30, 1863, GC.

[25] HWS to Mary Winebrenner and Frederick Augustus Shriver, June 29, 1863, HWS to Frederick Augustus Shriver, July 4, 1863, HWS Diary, June 30, 1863, SFP, MDHS; Pennypacker, "Six Weeks in Uniform," 360-361; Rupp Diary, June 30, 1863, GC.

[26] HWS to Frederick Augustus Shriver, July 8, 1863, SFP, MDHS.

[27] HWS to Frederick Augustus Shriver, July 4, 1863, SFP, MDHS; Pennypacker, "Six Weeks in Uniform," 362; Rupp Diary July 2-4, 1863, GC.

[28] HWS to Frederick Augustus Shriver, July 4, 1863, SFP, MDHS.

[29] *Ibid.*; Pennypacker, "Six Weeks in Uniform," 365; Rupp Diary July 2-4, 1863, GC.

[30] HWS to Frederick Augustus Shriver, July 4, 1863, SFP, MDHS

[31] *Ibid.*; Pennypacker, "Six Weeks in Uniform," 365-366; Rupp Diary, July 4, 1863, GC; In relation to the crude lumber cars which finally arrived to house the men, Pennypacker mused, "how fine they were[.]" See, Pennypacker, "Six Weeks in Uniform," 366; For an account of the New York State National Guard brigade of Philip Schuyler Crooke and their departure

by rail around the same time as the 26th PVM, see, *OR* 27:2, 232-233, 241-242; Rupp, initially First Corporal, was promoted to Fourth Sergeant on June 29.

[32] HWS to Frederick Augustus Shriver, July 4, 1863, SFP, MDHS; Rupp Diary, July 4, 1863, GC; Rupp recorded that there were 34 guns in the salute.

[33] Pennypacker, "Six Weeks in Uniform," 362-363.

[34] *Ibid.*

[35] *Ibid.*

[36] Samuel W. Pennypacker, "Fort Washington in 1863," *Transactions of The Historical Society of Dauphin County, Pennsylvania*, 1:1, (1903), 243-244.

[37] Pennypacker, "Six Weeks in Uniform," 362-363; HWS to Frederick Augustus Shriver, July 4, 1863, SFP, MDHS.

[38] Pennypacker, "Six Weeks in Uniform," 363-364; HWS to Frederick Augustus Shriver, July 4, 1863, SFP, MDHS.

[39] Adjutant General's Papers on 26th PVM, RG 19, PASA; Pennypacker, "Six Weeks in Uniform," 364-365; HWS to Frederick Augustus Shriver, July 4, 1863, SFP, MDHS.

[40] Pennypacker, "Six Weeks in Uniform," 357, 359.

[41] Rupp Diary, July 5-7, 1863, GC.

[42] HWS to Frederick Augustus Shriver, July 8, 1863, SFP, MDHS.

[43] Rupp Diary, July 7, 1863, GC.

[44] Richards Letters, HCWRT, USAMHI.

[45] Pennypacker, "Six Weeks in Uniform," 366.

[46] HWS to Frederick Augustus Shriver, July 8, 1863, HWS to Mary Winebrenner, July 9, 1863, SFP, MDHS; Richards to Roth, July 24, 1863, GNMP.

[47] Pennypacker, "Six Weeks in Uniform," 366.

[48] Rupp Diary, July 8-9, 1863, GC.

Chapter 7: Another Trip Down the Valley
[1] Pennypacker, "Six Weeks in Uniform," 369-370; HWS Diary, July 11, 1863, SFP, MDHS.

[2] Pennypacker, "Six Weeks in Uniform," 371; Rupp Diary, July 11-12, 1863, GC; HWS to Frederick Augustus Shriver, July 13, 1863, HWS Diary, July 12, 1863, SFP, MDHS.

[3] Pennypacker, "Six Weeks in Uniform," 371-372; HWS to Frederick Augustus Shriver, July 13, 1863, SFP, MDHS.

[4] HWS to Frederick Augustus Shriver, July 13, 1863, SFP, MDHS; Pennypacker reported that at Mechanicsburg, "the people told us of some of the rebel operations in that vicinity." Additionally, "[o]n approaching Carlisle we saw the ruins of the barracks which had been destroyed[.]" See, Pennypacker, "Six Weeks in Uniform," 372.

[5] *Ibid.*; Pennypacker, "Six Weeks in Uniform," 372-373.

[6] HWS to Frederick Augustus Shriver, July 13, 1863, SFP, MDHS.

[7] *Ibid.*; Pennypacker, "Six Weeks in Uniform," 374-375; Rupp Diary, July 14, 1863, GC; Pennypacker related a touching incident which occurred while at Green Village; "Here, while sitting by the roadside, two little boys, scarcely old enough to wear breeches, came along asking the men for their canteens in order to fill them. I was pleased with the idea of children coming on such an errand, and when one of then [sic] approached me, wishing to hear him talk, I inquired whether he had seen the rebels. 'Yes,' he said, 'they were naughty men; they took my little dog,' and in sorrowful accents he told me further that his dog was black and had a white spot on his tail." See, Pennypacker, "Six Weeks in Uniform," 374.

[8] Pennypacker, "Six Weeks in Uniform," 374-377; Richards Autobiography, LCHS; HWS to Frederick Augustus Shriver, July 13, 1863, SFP, MDHS.

[9] Pennypacker, "Six Weeks in Uniform," 375-377; HWS to Frederick Augustus Shriver, July 13, 1863, HWS Diary July 14, 1863, SFP, MDHS.

[10] Pennypacker, "Six Weeks in Uniform," 377-378; HWS to Frederick Augustus Shriver, July 13, 1863, HWS Diary July 14, 1863, SFP, MDHS.

[11] Pennypacker, "Six Weeks in Uniform," 378-380; HWS to Frederick Augustus Shriver, July 13, 1863, SFP, MDHS; Rupp Diary, July 14, 1863, GC; Pennypacker wrote; "The pike was so cut up by the passage of two armies and their wagons during the heavy rains, that the water in some places stood knee deep, and rendered travelling upon it almost impracticable." See, Pennypacker, "Six Weeks in Uniform," 378-379.

[12] *O.R.*, 27:2, 230-231.

[13] Rupp Diary, July 14, 1863, GC.

[14] Ezra Warner, *Generals in Blue: Lives of the Union Commanders*, (Baton Rouge: Louisiana State University, 1964), 111.

[15] *O.R.* 27:3, 347.

[16] *Ibid.* 27:2, 213.

[17] *Ibid.*, 27:3, 678-679.

[18] Rupp Diary, July 14, 1863, GC; Pennypacker, "Six Weeks in Uniform," 378-380; HWS to Frederick Augustus Shriver, July 13, 1863, SFP, MDHS.

[19] HWS to Frederick Augustus Shriver, July 13, 1863, SFP, MDHS.

[20] Pennypacker, "Six Weeks in Uniform," 379-384; Rupp Diary, July 15-16, 1863, GC.

[21] HWS Diary, July 16, 1863, SFP, MDHS.

[22] Pennypacker, "Six Weeks in Uniform," 384-385; Rupp Diary, July 17, 1863, GC; William S. Bordlemay to Respected Friend, July 18, 1863, Civil War Document Collection, USAMHI; William Shuey Bordlemay was a relative of Dennis Bashore Shuey of Company A. Born on December 20, 1841, according to the Shuey family history (written by Dennis Shuey), Bordlemay "taught school a number of terms and during the summer worked in his uncle John H. Shuey's woolen mill, where he and the author [Dennis B. Shuey] worked together one summer and thus became intimate friends. He was superintendent to Walmer's Sunday School for several years... He took interest in politics as a republican. He is an attorney at law in Lebanon.

He was elected to the office of Recorder of Deeds and Clerk of the criminal courts, and after his term expired, he was appointed deputy, and has thus been in that office continuously for forty-five years, and in Jan. 1916, was appointed for another term of four years. He married Anna M. Dressler of East Hanover. They have one daughter, Carrie Bordlemay, who is an accomplished musician, and taught music a number of years in Lebanon." See, Shuey, *History of the Shuey Family*, 134-135.

[23] Pennypacker, "Six Weeks in Uniform," 387.

[24] *Ibid.*, 387-388; HWS Diary, July 21, 1863, SFP, MDHS; Rupp Diary, July 21, 1863, GC.

[25] Pennypacker, "Six Weeks in Uniform," 388; Rupp Diary, July 22, 1863, GC.

[26] Pennypacker, "Six Weeks in Uniform," 388.

[27] Rupp Diary, July 23-25, 1863, GC.

[28] Pennypacker, "Six Weeks in Uniform," 390-392; Rupp Diary, July 25, 1863, GC.

[29] Rupp Diary, July 25, 1863, GC.

[30] Pennypacker, "Six Weeks in Uniform," 390-392; HWS Diary, July 26, 1863; Rupp Diary, July 25-26, 1863, GC.

[31] Pennypacker, "Six Weeks in Uniform," 392-393; HWS Diary, July 26, 1863; Rupp Diary, July 26, 1863, GC.

[32] Pennypacker, "Six Weeks in Uniform," 393-394; HWS to Frederick Augustus Shriver, July 27, 1863, SFP, MDHS.

[33] Harrisburg *Evening Telegraph*, "Reported Rebel Raid," July 28, 1863; Pennypacker, "Six Weeks in Uniform," 394-395; HWS Diary, July 28, 1863, SFP, MDHS; The *Telegraph* reported its' belief that "the rumor doubtless originating by the appearance of a force of Union cavalry operating under the orders of General Couch.... We can assure our readers that the disposition of the forces under the command of General Couch, are of such a nature as to afford a sure guarantee that the soil of Pennsylvania will not again be polluted by the tread of an armed rebel force."

[34] Pennypacker, "Six Weeks in Uniform," 395-396; HWS Diary, July 30, 1863, SFP, MDHS; Rupp Diary, July 30, 1863, GC; Shriver noted the farmhouse where Bush mustered the men out as "the white house[.]" See, HWS Diary, July 30, 1863, SFP, MDHS.

[35] HWS Diary, July 31, 1863, SFP, MDHS.

[36] Pennypacker, "Six Weeks in Uniform," 395-396; HWS Diary, August 1, 1863, SFP, MDHS; Rupp Diary, August 1-2, 1863, GC.

Chapter 8: Return Home
[1] Pennypacker, "Six Weeks in Uniform," 319, 388, 396.

[2] *Ibid.*, 396.

[3] *Ibid.*

[4] Lorenzo L. Greenawalt Record, Historical Register of National Homes for Disabled Volunteer Soldiers, 1866-1938, Records of the Department of Veteran Affairs, RG 15, National Archives.

[5] J. H. Beers & Co., *Biographical Annals of Lebanon County, Pennsylvania*, (Chicago: J. H. Beers, 1904), 120-122; Gerhart married Catherine Ritter in 1864.

[6] Pennypacker, "Six Weeks in Uniform," 396-397.

[7] *Ibid.*, 397.

[8] 26th PVM File, GNMP.

[9] Biographical Sketch courtesy of Carl Klase, Assistant-Administrator, Pennypacker Mills County Historic Site, Schwenksville, Pa.

[10] Pennypacker, *Autobiography*, 95.

[11] HWS Diary, August 1-2, 1863, SFP, MDHS.

[12] Gettysburg *Times,* February 28, 1910; Shriver was born on December 9, 1837, to Andrew and Catherine Shriver in "the old Shriver homestead at Union Mills, in which his father was born, and died, and where he lived continuously until his death."

[13] Francis A. Walker, *History of the Second Army Corps in the Army of the Potomac*, (New York: Charles Scribner's Sons, 1891), 708; Information courtesy of Scott L. Mingus Sr., York, PA.

[14] Richards, "Lebanon County's Emergency Volunteers at Gettysburg," 175.

[15] Rupp Diary, August 1-2, 1863, GC.

[16] "William H. Rupp Taken By Death," Gettysburg *Times*, February 25, 1913; Rupp was born on March 6, 1839, the son of Henry and Catharine Rupp, who owned a tannery at the corner of York and Stratton streets. For "a number of years," Rupp operated the tannery with his father.

[17] *The Alumni Record of Gettysburg College, 1832-1932*. (Gettysburg, PA: Gettysburg College, 1932), 62; Richards to Roth, July 24, 1863, GNMP; Richards was born on April 21, 1840, in New Middleton, Ohio.

[18] Richards Autobiography, LCHS.

[19] Beers & Co., *Biographical Annals of Lebanon County, Pennsylvania*, 10-17; Henry M. M. Richards was married on Dec. 26, 1871 to Ella VanLeer. The two had four children.

[20] *The Alumni Record of Gettysburg College*, 58.

[21] *The Morning Call*, "Col. Jennings Dies Suddenly," March 1, 1894.

[22] *Ibid.*; "In Memoriam: William Wesley Jennings," Rare Collections Library, State Library of Pennsylvania.

[23] *The Morning Call*, "Col. Jennings Dies Suddenly," March 1, 1894; "In Memoriam: William Wesley Jennings," Rare Collections Library, State Library of Pennsylvania; Buoy, "Address by C.W. Buoy," Rare Collections Library, State Library of Pennsylvania; Kelker, *History of Dauphin County*, 10-11.

[24] Buoy, "Address by C.W. Buoy," Rare Collections Library, State Library of Pennsylvania.

[25] Kelker, *History of Dauphin County*, 10; *The Morning Call*, "Col. Jennings Dies Suddenly," March 1, 1894.

[26] Kelker, *History of Dauphin County*, 10-11; *The Morning Call*, "Col. Jennings Dies Suddenly," March 1, 1894.

[27] *The Morning Call*, "Col. Jennings Dies Suddenly," March 1, 1894.

Chapter 9: Reunion At Gettysburg

[1] Resolution of the Board of Commissioners of Gettysburg Monuments, 1889, SWP to Board of Commissioners, January 10, 1890, 26th PVM Monument File, GNMP.

[2] SWP to Board of Commissioners, January 10, 1890, 26th PVM Monument File, GNMP

[3] Samuel Pennypacker, "Before the Pennsylvania Commission on Gettysburg Monuments: In reright of the 26th Pennsylvania Emergency Regiment to a Monument at Gettysburg," pamphlet at PPM.

[4] 26th PVM Monument File, GNMP.

[5] Board of Commissioners of Gettysburg Monuments, undated resolution, 26th PVM Monument File, GNMP.

[6] Board of Commissioners of Gettysburg Monuments Journal, January 16, 1891, 26th PVM Monument File, GNMP.

[7] "26th Emergency Infantry," Articles of Agreement, 26th PVM Monument File, GNMP.

[8] Harvey W. McKnight, "Twenty-Sixth Regiment P.V.M.," *PCM*, XVI:7 (November 1892), 267-272.

[9] Pennypacker, *Autobiography*, 97.

[10] "26th Pennsylvania Emergency Regiment Monument," Photograph, W. B. Van Amringe, No. 3 Bromfield Street, Boston Massachusetts, handwritten text on the back of the photograph by SWP, PPM.

[11] Printed Circular, June 8, 1892, PPM.

[12] These letters are in the archives of Pennypacker Mills Historic Site.

[13] Frank Muhlenberg to SWP, August 27, 1892, PPM.

[14] Monument Dedication Materials, PPM.

[15] Photograph of the 26th Pennsylvania Volunteer Militia Reunion, LCHS.

Appendices

[1] Newspaper Scrapbook, PPM

[2] Jennings MS Report, PPM

[3] Pennypacker, *Autobiography*, 96-97.

[4] Dedication Materials, PPM; Harvey W. McKnight, "Twenty-Sixth Regiment P.V.M.," *PCM*, XVI:7 (November 1892), 267-272.

[5] Harvey W. McKnight, "Twenty-Sixth Regiment P.V.M.," *PCM*, XVI:7 (November 1892), 267-272.

[6] *Ibid.*

Bibliographic Note

[1] Pennypacker, "Six Weeks in Uniform,"307.

[2] Samuel Pennypacker to John Bachelder, August 26, 1881, Bachelder Papers, New Hampshire Historical Society.

[3] Pennypacker, "Six Weeks in Uniform," 307-308.

[4] *Ibid.*, 308.

[5] William Few to SWP, July 6, 1892, PPM.

Index

Reynolds, John, 119
Rice, George, 24, 44, 52, 59-60, 65, 84, 111, 117, 127, 135, 139, 141
Richards, Frank, 18, 42, 70, 79, 105, 125, 143
Richards, Henry Melchior Muhlenberg , 37, 42, 49, 60, 71, 76-77, 81-82, 89, 101-04, 111, 128, 143-44
Richards, Mathias H., 28, 30-31, 37, 111
Rise, George D., 51
Rishel, Elias C., 25, 44, 52, 117
Roherer, Jeremiah, 39-40, 52
Rupp, William Henry, 31, 35, 71, 108, 119-20, 122, 124-26, 130, 135-37, 143

Schick, Rudolph M., 70, 79-80
Schuykill County, PA, 20
Schuykill County Company, 39
Schuykill River, 141
Shenandoah Valley, VA, 47
Shick, Augustine W., 85
Siddonburg Road, 107
Siddonsburg, PA, 108
Smith, William "Extra Billy", 73
Shriver, Henry Wirt, 19-20, 27-28, 33-35, 59-60, 64, 66, 71, 77-79, 101-02, 104-08, 110-11, 113-15, 117-19, 121-25, 127-29, 132, 136-138, 142-43
State Capitol, 24, 32
Stuart, J.E.B., 75, 96
Susquehanna Rangers, 39
Suquehanna River, 11, 27, 33, 54, 68, 85, 88, 109-10, 124, 126, 137-38, 159, 161
Swift Run Hill, PA, 58-60

Table Rock Road, 71, 75

Union Mills, MD, 19, 111, 113
United States Artillery
   5th Battery E, 131
United States Infantry
   4th, 56
   7th, 57
   13th, 137
United States Military Academy, 131
United States Naval Academy, 144

Virginia Cavalry
   17th (French's), 72-75, 77, 81, 83-85, 91, 96-98
   35th, 68-69, 72

Walker, Christopher Wilson, 44, 52, 85-88, 96, 117, 205, 209
War of 1812, 11, 37
Washington, DC, 40
Washington Light Infantry, 22
West Virginia, 9
White, Elijah V., 68-69, 72, 97-98
Witmer's Farm, skirmish of, 76-79, 81, 83-85, 89-92, 95-98, 102, 104-05, 111, 113, 117-19, 186
Wrightsville, PA, 68, 87-88, 102, 109, 117, 170-71, 203, 208

Yellow Breeches Creek, PA, 107
York County, PA, 24, 45, 47, 56-57, 61, 68, 86, 109, 165
York, PA, 55-56, 68, 88, 94, 98, 102, 106, 113, 118, 159, 170-71
York Road, 62
York Springs, PA, 101

Zion Lutheran Church, 35

For a complete book and price list contact:

SCHROEDER PUBLICATIONS
131 Tanglewood Drive
Lynchburg, VA 24502
www.civilwar-books.com
E-mail: civilwarbooks@yahoo.com
434-525-4431

Titles Available:
* **Thirty Myths About Lee's Surrender** by Patrick A. Schroeder
  ISBN 1-889246-05-0

* **More Myths About Lee's Surrender** by Patrick A. Schroeder
  ISBN 1-889246-01-8

* **The Confederate Cemetery at Appomattox** by Patrick A. Schroeder
  ISBN 1-889246-11-5

* **Recollections & Reminiscences of Old Appomattox and Its People**
  by George T. Peers ISBN 1-889246-12-3

* **Tar Heels: Five Points in the Record of North Carolina in the Great War
  of 1861-5** by the Committee appointed by the North Carolina Literary and
  Historical Society ISBN 1-889246-02-6 (Soft cover) ISBN 1-889246-15-8
  (Hard cover)

* **The Fighting Quakers** by A. J. H. Duganne ISBN 1-889246-03-4

* **A Duryée Zouave** by Thomas P. Southwick   ISBN 1-561900-86-9 (Soft
  cover) ISBN 1-889246-24-7 (Hard cover)

* **Civil War Soldier Life: In Camp and Battle** by George F. Williams
  ISBN 1-889246-04-2

* **We Came To Fight: The History of the 5th New York Veteran Volunteer
  Infantry, Duryée's Zouaves, (1863-1865)** by Patrick A. Schroeder ISBN 1-
  889246-07-7

* **Campaigns of the 146th Regiment New York State Volunteers** by Mary
  Genevie Green Brainard ISBN 1-889246-08-5

* **The Bloody 85th: The Letters of Milton McJunkin, A Western
  Pennsylvania Soldier in the Civil War** Edited by Richard A. Sauers, Ronn
  Palm, and Patrick A. Schroeder ISBN 1-889246-13-1 (Soft cover)
  ISBN 1-889246-16-6 (Hard cover)

* **The Highest Praise of Gallantry: Memorials of David T. Jenkins & James
  E. Jenkins of the 146th New York Infantry & Oneida Cavalry** by A.
  Pierson Case (1889) with New Material by Patrick A. Schroeder
  ISBN 1-889246-17-4

* **Where Duty Called Them: The Story of the Samuel Babcock Family of
  Homer, New York in the Civil War** by Edmund Raus
  ISBN 1-889246-49-2

* The Opportunity Is At Hand: Oneida County, New York, Colored Soldiers in the Civil War by Donald M. Wisnoski ISBN 1-880246-20-4 (Soft cover) ISBN 1-889246-18-2 (Hard cover)

* So You Want to Be a Soldier: How to Get Started in Civil War Re-enacting by Shaun C. Grenan ISBN 1-889246-19-0

* The Pennsylvania Bucktails: A Photographic Album of the 42nd, 149th, 150th Pennsylvania Regiments by Patrick A. Schroeder ISBN 1-889246-14-X

* A Summer on the Plains with Custer's 7th Cavalry: The 1870 Diary of Annie Gibson Roberts Edited by Brian C. Pohanka ISBN 1-889246-21-2

* The Life of Ely S. Parker: The Last Grand Sachem of the Iroquois and General Grant's Military Secretary by Arthur C. Parker ISBN 1-889246-50-6 (Hard cover) ISBN 1-889246-52-2 (Leather bound limited edition)

* "We Are Coming Father Abra'am": The History of the 9th Vermont Volunteer Infantry, 1862-1865 by Don Wickman ISBN 1-889246-23-9

* A Vermont Cavalryman in War and Love: The Civil War Letters of Brevet Major General William Wells and Anna Richardson Edited by Elliott W. Hoffman ISBN 1-889246-51-4

* While My Country is in Danger: The Life and Letters of Lt. Col. Richard S. Thompson, 12th New Jersey Volunteers by Gerry Harder Poriss & Ralph G. Poriss ISBN 0-9622393-6-4

* No Middle Ground: Thomas Ward Osborn's Letters from Field (1862-1864) Edited by H. S. Crumb & K. Dhalle ISBN 0-9622393-4-8

* Unfurl the Flags: Remembrances of the American Civil War Edited by W. E. Edmonston ISBN 0-9622393-0-5

* Out of the Wilderness: The Civil War Memoir of Corporal Norton C. Shepard Edited by Raymond W. Smith ISBN 1-892059-00-2

* The Telegraph Goes to War: The Personal Diary of David Homer Bates, Lincoln's Telegraph Operator Edited by Donald E. Markle

* Shepherdstown: Last Clash of the Antietam Campaign September 19–20, 1862 by Thomas McGrath ISBN 1-889246-39-5

* The Appomattox Campaign, March 29–April 9, 1865 by Chris M. Calkins ISBN 1-889246-55-7

* Charlie's Civil War: A Private's Trial by Fire in the 5th New York Volunteers, Duryée Zouaves, and the 146th New York Volunteer Infantry Edited by Charles Brandegee Livingstone ISBN 1-889246-42-5

* **Sailor's Creek: Major General G. W. Custis Lee, captured with controversy** by Frank Everett White, Jr. ISBN 1-889246-56-6

* **Four Years in the First New York Light Artillery: The Papers of David F. Ritchie** by David F. Ritchie ISBN 1-889246-61-1

* **Loyal Hearts: Histories of American Civil War Canines** by Michael Zucchero ISBN 1-889246-57-3

* **From the Bowery to Bull Run and Beyond: The History of the 11th New York Fire Zouaves, 1861-1862** by Brian C. Pohanka and Patrick A. Schroeder ISBN 1-889246-44-1

* **Civil War Animal Heroes: Mascots, Pets and War Horses** by Charles G. Worman ISBN 1-889246-45-X

* **Aurthur O. Alcock: With the 11th New York Fire Zouaves in camp, battle, and prison.** Edited by Brian C. Pohanka and Patrick A. Schroeder ISBN 1-889246-46-8

* **Like Leaves in a Storm: The Sacrifice of Iverson's Brigade at Gettysburg** by Jason Amico ISBN 1-889246-41-7

* **A History of the 117th Regiment, New York Volunteers (Fourth Oneida)** by James A. Mowris ISBN 0-9622393-8-0

* **"My Country Needs Me": The Story of Corporal Johnston Hastings Skelly Jr., 87th Pennsylvania Infantry—A Son of Gettysburg and Confidant of Jennie Wade** by Enrica D'Alessandro ISBN 1-889246-59-X

* **117 Facts Everyone Should Know About African Americans in the Civil War** by John Gourdin ISBN 1-889246-47-6

* **A History and Guide to Civil War Shepherdstown: Victory and Defeat in West Virginia's Oldest Town** by Nicholas A. Redding ISBN 1-889246-60-3

* **The Beau Ideal of a Soldier and a Gentleman: The Life of Col. Patrick Henry O'Rorke From Ireland to Gettysburg** by Brian A. Bennett ISBN 1-889246-48-4

* **Vortex of Hell: History of the 5th New York Volunteer Infantry, Duryée's Zouaves, 1861-63** by Brian C. Pohanka ISBN 1-889246-73-5

Have your Revolutionary or Civil War ancestors researched
at the
National Archives.

by

Schroeder Publications

Union or Confederate.

Military Service Records and Pension Records